The Prize

CW01082703

Sydney C. Grier

Alpha Editions

This edition published in 2024

ISBN 9789362512093

Design and Setting By
Alpha Editions
www.alphaedis.com
Email - info@alphaedis.com

As per information held with us this book is in Public Domain.
This book is a reproduction of an important historical work.
Alpha Editions uses the best technology to reproduce historical work
in the same manner it was first published to preserve its original nature.
Any marks or number seen are left intentionally to preserve.

Contents

CHAPTER I.
DANAË PLAYS THE EAVESDROPPER.

THE scene was a picture in itself. Sea and sky vied with one another in the depth of their unruffled blue, and in the glorious sunshine and clear air the cliffs were vividly, even startlingly, white. All round the island they presented an inhospitable front to the voyager save at one point, where advantage had been taken of a steep ravine running down to the sea to find room for a number of white-walled, red-roofed houses, which seemed to cling precariously to successive steps in the rock, from the primitive harbour at its foot to the rude fortress at the summit. On the land side, grey olive-trees came so close to the fortress walls that either of the girls lounging in a shady spot on the ramparts and lazily nibbling sunflower seeds could have touched the upper branches with her hand by leaning over the parapet. In the palmy days of Strio, when her pirates were the terror of the surrounding waters, the rulers of the isle would have seen in the olive-grove so near their walls merely a cover for probable enemies, and would have swept it ruthlessly away. But these were peaceful times, and the head of the Christodoridi was more concerned to wring the last drachma from his rocky acres than from the reluctant hands of seafarers.

The Despot of Strio (both Prince Christodoridi and his subjects clung proudly to the ancient title) was a very great person—in Strio—and was wont to talk familiarly of his sovereign, the King of Morea, as of an equal whose state was bound to his by ancestral treaties. On the mainland, however, and still more in what both Striotes and Moreans called respectfully "Europe," people were apt to laugh at the pretensions of the island potentate, when they were not irritated by them. Very wisely, therefore, Prince Christodoridi preferred to remain where his authority was undisputed, and bestrode his rock, glorying in the fact that not a woman within its confines could read or write. Five years ago, his elder daughter Danaë, visiting her mother's relatives in a neighbouring island, had been swept with her cousins into the "vacation school," established in her holidays by an energetic American lady teacher from the mainland, aghast at the ignorance which surrounded her. But before the school had been a week in session, Prince Christodoridi stalked grimly into the awed circle and carried off his daughter, favouring the foreigner with his opinion of her proceedings in language so exceedingly plain that it was well she did not understand it. In that week Danaë had earned the reputation of a terror with her schoolmistress, and a cause of awful joy to her schoolfellows, but she resented bitterly the dramatic close of her education. In a day or two more she would have possessed a Frank dress—she was learning to make it—which she could have flaunted proudly before the eyes of her mother and the other Striote ladies, who still wore the embroidered skirt and apron and voluminous girdle, the long coat and loose vest, of the days before Independence, the poorer women replacing the skirt by wide trousers. Prince Christodoridi was, supreme in sumptuary matters, as in all else, and "Frank clothes" were anathema in his eyes.

Stretched upon the sun-warmed stones of the rampart, the parapet just shielding them from the rays of the declining sun, Danaë and her sister Angeliké squabbled noisily over the heap of sunflower seeds between them. Danaë ate fair, taking one seed at a time, but Angeliké had a greedy habit of selecting four or five of the plumpest at once, and keeping them in her hand till they were wanted. She always did it, and it always led to bickering, but this never occurred to her as a reason for leaving it off. The handsome childish faces of both girls were flushed with resentment, for as usual on these occasions, grudges in no way connected with the matter in hand had been brought up on either side. Their household tasks were finished, and what had they to do but quarrel, until the happy hour should come when Prince Christodoridi, having duly locked his family in, would swagger down to the coffee-house to ruffle it among his subjects, and his daughters would slip out, by ways best known to themselves, to join the other girls of the place, who, shrouded in their dark shawls, flitted ghostlike down back alleys and over roofs, to visit one another and exchange the gossip of the day?

The heap of sunflower seeds was finished, though a remnant was still left within the shelter of Angeliké's fingers, when footsteps below caused Danaë to look down into the courtyard. She withdrew her head hurriedly. "It is our father and Petros!" she whispered, with repressed excitement.

"There is nothing interesting about Petros," said Angeliké, yawning with disappointing indifference.

"Owl! does he not come from Therma?" demanded Danaë. "If our brother has sent any message, he will give it now."

"Owl yourself! There will be no message. My lord Romanos cares nothing about us. When he was made Prince, you said he would send for us to his court and give us kings for husbands, but he has never taken the slightest notice. He cares no more about establishing us than he did about our fighting for him." Angeliké sneered unpleasantly.

Danaë flushed. "You never wanted to fight for him," she said.

"I should think not! What good is it to us that he was chosen Prince? And even if he had sent for us to Therma," with a sudden change of ground, "would there have been any pleasure in it? We don't know

European ways, we can't even speak French. People would have laughed at us. If I can once get a husband and escape from Strio, that is all I want, and you may be quite sure our father would never let us marry Europeans."

"I suppose a husband like Narkissos Smaragdopoulos would satisfy you?" sneered Danaë in her turn.

"Of course he would. You can be nasty about him if you like. Everyone knows that he never speaks to you since you upset the coffee over his kilt in handing it to him."

"And do they know who told him that I did it on purpose?"

"If they don't, they probably think you told him yourself. It would be just like you. What are you going to do?" as Danaë began to crawl along the rampart in the direction taken by her father and the handsome ruffianly fellow, half guard, half servant, who swaggered after him.

"Hush!" said Danaë angrily. "I am going to hear what they are saying, of course."

"Then I shall tell our father that you listened." The offensive and defensive alliance against those in authority on the part of the two girls was always liable to an interruption of this sort, when one of the malcontents deserted temporarily to the side of power and brought punishment upon the other.

"Then I shall tell our mother of the sweets that made you ill on the vigil of Hagios Jakōbos, when she thought the fasting had been too much for you," Danaë flung back, and saw, as she expected, that Angeliké had no answer ready. Satisfied with having thus protected herself, she crawled on, until she found herself exactly above the two men as they sat on one of the rude flights of steps that ran up to the ramparts. Just here there was no parapet in whose shadow she might shelter herself, but they had their backs to her, and were far enough below not to see her, even if they turned round, when she was lying flat on the wall. Listening anxiously to discover whether any interesting topics had already been discussed, she was relieved to find that her father was apparently still leading up to some important point on which Petros seemed to be in no hurry to afford him information.

"My son is too young to know his own best interests," said Prince Christodoridi, with dignity.

"His Highness is not exactly a boy," growled Petros.

"And therefore his elders must do their best to save him from the consequences of his youthful mistakes," went on the Prince, as though his sentence had not been interrupted.

"Then let his elders do their own work themselves, so that his Highness may know to whom his gratitude is due," was the surly response.

"Miserable dog!" cried Prince Christodoridi in a fury. "Is it for this I have maintained you close to my son's person, charging you to keep me acquainted with all that touches one so dear to me, from whose side I am kept by my responsibilities here?"

"Some folks say it is his Highness's own wish that keeps you here, O my Prince—that since you refused to aid him with a single drachma in gaining his position, he does not see why you should expect to derive any benefit from it."

"Thickhead! why should I spend money in championing the cause of God and the saints? Is their power not sufficient? Has the cause not triumphed? Yet my son, who derives from me the rights which are now fully recognised, expresses no desire for my presence at his side."

"Perhaps his Highness thinks less of his rights than you do, my Prince." Petros was keenly enjoying the inconsistency of his lord's last two utterances. "I have heard him say that he owed his success to the intrigues of the Powers, and that right was altogether on the side of the Englishman, him of Klaustra."

"And after that you still think my son is able to take care of himself?" asked the Prince pathetically. "I tell you, Petraki, he will be his own ruin. Come, earn your wages, and let us save the misguided one from the destruction that threatens him."

"I take his Highness's wages too, and I don't know what he will think about my earning them," grumbled Petros. "If the Lady had not distrusted me and tried to turn the Lord Romanos against me——"

Danaë raised her head a little, and bent forward, so as to make sure of not missing a word. There was nothing revolting to her in the idea that her father should employ her brother's confidential servant as a spy upon him, for it was of a piece with the methods which she saw in operation around her every day, and it was only natural that he should wish to participate in the good fortune of the son he had banished and wished to disinherit. Romanos Christodoridi, elected Prince of Emathia by the free vote of the inhabitants, under the auspices of the Powers of Europe, ought to have been a gold mine to his relatives, and Danaë felt no reluctance to subject the brother whose indifference had so deeply disappointed her to a little interference with his plans. Besides, "the Lady" sounded interesting.

"I did not ask for your reasons, friend Petros," said Prince Christodoridi, disposing, with a snap of his fingers, of the belated scruples of conscience which were troubling his instrument. "I ask for obedience and truth. What of this woman, then? Who is she?"

"They call her 'the Lady' in Therma, O my Prince," Petros spoke doggedly. "She lives in a retired house outside the city, and never goes out, and receives no one but his Highness."

"She is perhaps old enough to be his mother?" asked the Prince sarcastically.

"Nay, my Prince, she is young and very beautiful. Also she is a Latin, and she calls his Highness her husband."

Prince Christodoridi laughed ferociously. "Husband, indeed! and she a Latin! How do you know these things, Petros?"

"His Highness takes me to guard him when he visits the house, my Prince, and I alone have been permitted to pass within the gates."

"Then if you are able to enter, you must do what has to be done." The words came with lightning swiftness.

"Nay, my Prince, the gate can only be opened from within. His Highness says some word which I have not heard to the old woman who keeps the door."

"And you are too feeble to climb a wall, my poor Petraki?"

"O my Prince, the wall is guarded on the outside. It is through the sentries that the common people have learnt to laugh and jest about the Lady."

"Then this disgrace is a matter of common talk—at a moment when the Emperor of Scythia is offering his daughter as a bride to my son?"

"I think it is his cousin, my Prince. The Emperor's daughters are all very young, they say."

"His daughter," repeated Prince Christodoridi firmly. "Anything else would be an insult only to be washed out in blood. And is this fair prospect for Emathia and our ancient house to be destroyed for the sake of a Latin woman?"

"That is for you to say, my Prince. I have no love for the Lady. Why should I, when the Lord Romanos desired to leave me to guard her, and she refused, saying that she disliked my looks and did not trust me? Had she accepted my services, I must have defended her to the death, but now I should not be sorry to see her dealt with as she deserves."

"Then who was left to guard her in your place?"

"No one, my Prince. The Lady refused to have anyone with her but her women-servants, saying that the guards outside were sufficient."

"I think the Lady has consulted our convenience rather than her own," smiled Prince Christodoridi. "Come, friend Petros, will you venture to tell me now that it is impossible to reach her?"

"Impossible unless one had a confederate inside the gates, my Prince. The door must be opened, as you see."

"Then introduce a confederate, by all means. Holy Michael! does this fellow call himself a Striote?"

"And who is the confederate to be, my Prince? For I have no wish to put my neck in jeopardy over this—removal, nor do I think that you have. *Kyrie Eleëson!* look at that, lord!"

Crossing himself hastily, he clutched at the Prince's wrist with a trembling hand, and pointed to the shadow of the rampart on the ground in front of them. Fully evident in the treacherous beams of the sinking sun was the outline of a human figure on the summit of the wall, with head raised to listen greedily to what was said.

"Thickhead! why speak of it?" Prince Christodoridi was up the stairs in a moment, with an agility highly creditable to his sixty years, and had Danaë's wrists in an iron grasp and a hand over her mouth, before she could even move. "Take her feet, fool! and bring her here." They were inside one of the deserted towers in an instant, and before Danaë realised fully what had happened, she was bound hand and foot with the sash which Petros stripped off at his lord's sharp command. Prince Christodoridi chose out deliberately a long thin dagger from the armoury in his belt, and dangled it before his daughter's horrified eyes.

"How much have you heard, wicked one?" he demanded.

"Everything, lord." The words would hardly make themselves audible.

"What were we talking about?"

"About my brother Romanos—how he has given himself over to an evil witch of a Latin woman, who has made him forget his own house and his duty to it."

"But what affair is it of yours?" Prince Christodoridi was puzzled by the warmth of personal feeling in the answer.

"Is it not the affair of all when one of us disgraces himself, lord?" Danaë was regaining her courage now that discovery had not been followed by instant death.

"No, insolent one! Has your mother not taught you yet that it is no affair of a woman what any of her men choose to do? Then you will have time to learn it in solitude here while Petros returns to his master."

Danaë grew pale, for there were dreadful tales of the dungeons under the tower, but she answered undauntedly, "So be it, lord. If the guilty one is punished, I shall but rejoice."

"And what would you do to the guilty one?" asked her father curiously.

Her eyes flashed. "Lord, I would tear her from that fair house whither she draws my brother to his destruction, and she should never see it again."

"So the woman is the guilty one!" said Prince Christodoridi with grim amusement. "And what then, my lady?"

"I would bring her here, lord, and cast her into a dungeon from which she should never escape. But when her beauty was gone, and her face as evil and ugly as herself, I would summon my brother and bid him behold her, that he might laugh at his own foolishness, and go his way."

"And that you would account sufficient punishment?"

"Surely, lord, for her it would be worse than death, and she deserves it. But my brother has been led away."

"Worse than death?" said Prince Christodoridi meditatively. "But not so safe, daughter—not so safe. Still," he stopped and cut the knots in the sash with his dagger, and allowed Danaë to rise from her cramped position on the floor, "you are a worthy child of the Christodoridi, I believe. Would you help in carrying out this vengeance, little one?"

"Try me, lord! This fellow needs a confederate, does he? Let me go. I will enter the woman's household as the meanest of her servants, and wait patiently until I can deliver her bound into his hands to be brought hither. Then I will dance for joy above her dungeon."

"But what has she done to you?" asked Prince Christodoridi, still moved entirely by curiosity, and not by any disapproval of his daughter's sentiments.

"She has bewitched my brother, lord. Is it not enough for you that she has bewitched your son?"

"Lady Danaë knows nothing of the matter. She is too young to do what has to be done, and I will not risk discovery by taking her with me," growled Petros.

"Friend Petros, the women of the Christodoridi are never too young to do what the head of their house commands," said the Prince.

"And you know, lord, whether any weakness of mine would lead to discovery," cried Danaë eagerly. "I have risked much for my brother already—even your displeasure."

This reminder was a bold stroke, for Danaë had suffered severely at her father's hands when, warned secretly by Angeliké, he had instituted a search of the fishing-boat in which a band of volunteers from Strio were going to the help of Prince Romanos and his insurgent companions in Hagiamavra, and had discovered among them his elder daughter dressed in boy's clothes. She had been brought back with ignominy, and cruelly beaten, but the incident had given Prince Christodoridi a certain reluctant respect for her. Moreover, she had promptly repaid the faithless Angeliké by revealing her gratified acceptance of the serenades addressed to her by a young Striote who had travelled as far as Alexandria, and in so doing had rubbed off some of the awe with which his lord and his lord's family should properly be regarded. Prince Christodoridi was nothing if not impartial, and Angeliké's shoulders vied with Danaë's in the bruises they exhibited for many weeks, while she had the added sting of knowing that her father considered Danaë had far the best of the fray.

"There is no question of displeasure here," said Prince Christodoridi pointedly. "Successful, you may return. Unsuccessful, no one must know that you belonged to the Christodoridi."

"Be it so, lord. I go under a false name to deliver my brother from his enchantment. If I succeed, the girls will sing of me in the dance; if I fail, I disappear. What is a woman more or less when the hope of the house is concerned?"

"All-Holy Mother of God! I could wish you had been my son, Danaë," cried the Prince, with unwonted enthusiasm, "instead of that popinjay Romanos! But make no mistake," he added repressively, "I send you merely because I would not reveal to any other the disgrace that threatens us. You will swear to obey the worthy Petros as if he were myself, since he will answer to me for your failure or success."

"I am putting my neck in a noose," grumbled Petros.

"Promise me first, lord, that you will wait to see if I succeed, and not suffer my sister to be married before me," said Danaë, greatly daring. Her father frowned heavily.

"Would you make conditions with me, insolent one? Is a younger sister ever married before her elder? You will obey Petros in everything, and he has my authority to take any steps that may be necessary with regard to you."

"The old woman at the Lady's house said they wanted a girl to look after the child," said Petros, with a slow grin. "I said I might be able to bring a niece of mine back from the islands. If Lady Danaë will be my niece, and obey me in all things, I will take her, but not otherwise. Holy Antony! if the Lord Romanos knew what was plotting against his love"—Prince Christodoridi glanced at him sharply—"perpetual imprisonment, no less—my life would not be worth a drachma, and I desire to continue in his service until he enters Czarigrad in triumph as Emperor."

"Peace! you talk too much. Lady Danaë will obey you, and you will be responsible for her," said Prince Christodoridi sharply. "Come, girl!" and with a hand on Danaë's shoulder he marched her down the steps, across the courtyard, and into the room where her mother, roused by his approach from an unlicensed nap, looked up with eyes not unlike those of a comfortable but apprehensive cow.

"What has Danaë been doing now?" she asked feebly.

"She is ill brought up. I have often asked you why you did not train her better," replied Prince Christodoridi, mindful of discipline. "I am going to send her to be educated where she will learn obedience."

Princess Christodoridi had never defied her husband, nor even disappointed him, save in failing to provide the son who was to have supplanted Romanos, but at this extraordinary betrayal of past convictions she ventured a mild protest.

"But, lord, you have always said——"

"May I not do what I will with my own daughter?" cried the Prince furiously. "The girl goes to-morrow."

Princess Christodoridi collapsed, and Angeliké, from a sheltered corner, made signs of derision. But Danaë had provided beforehand against any undue elation on Angeliké's part, and was content.

CHAPTER II.
THE LADY.

IT was a very woe-begone and dishevelled Danaë, not at all like an inspired deliverer, who stumbled ashore on the quay at Therma at the rough bidding of Petros. The passage had been a stormy one, and the island girl, who could have faced a gale without serious discomfort in a fishing-boat, had succumbed hopelessly to the vile odours and eccentric motion of the wretched little steamer that carried her from the neighbouring island of Tortolana, Strio's nearest link with civilisation, to the capital of her brother's principality. Either his qualms of conscience, or the possession of uncontrolled authority, had transformed the stolid Petros into a very truculent ruffian—or perhaps it was merely that he had determined to subject his "niece" to a severe test at the outset of their relationship. However this might be, he reviled her with much choice of language whenever he came across her prostrate and suffering form, threatening her with his stick when she roused herself to protest, and when they entered the harbour, locked her up for some hours in an empty cabin while he went on shore to arrange for getting her to "the Lady's" house. Returning, he summoned her forth with curses—which she divined were drawn from him by some fresh proof of confidence from the master he was plotting to betray—and she followed him meekly through the streets, carrying her modest bundle, while he swaggered ahead, never deigning to cast a glance at her. The new Therma, rebuilt on European methods after its bombardment by the Powers, was a city of enchantment to the little barbarian from Strio, but she durst not let her eyes wander to the tall white houses or the astonishing shops. The swarming crowd of all nationalities that jostled her as she stumbled along, ill and miserable, in the wake of Petros, was simply a collection of moving obstacles, blocking the way to the attainment of her aim, the deliverance of the brother who represented all the romance that had ever touched her life from the spells of the witch-woman. Danaë knew very little about the Powers of Europe, but she was a great authority on witches, like all the women of her island.

Her weary feet had carried her through many wide streets, past the ruined fortifications, now fast becoming overgrown with bushes, and out into a region of villas, set in lofty gardens, all enclosed with high walls, when the sudden apparition of a soldier on guard reminded her of what she had heard on the rampart. The sentry winked at Petros as he pointed with his thumb over his shoulder at a gateway in the wall.

"He's there," he said. "Told me you'd be coming."

Petros grunted, and went on to the door, which opened as if by magic. Danaë followed him in, and the door was closed instantly by an old woman behind it. Inside was one of Petros's fellow-guardsmen, in full Greek costume, in charge of three horses, and Petros joined him immediately, after a perfunctory gesture, suggestive of washing his hands of Danaë, in the direction of the old woman, who sniffed significantly.

"Well, I can't say very much for your island girls," she observed, eying the newcomer. "I expected a fine strapping lass who would be some good at work. But it's not your fault, child," she added more kindly, "and I daresay you won't look so bad when you have some decent clothes on. Come and have something to eat before you go before the Lady."

"Couldn't I see the Lady first?" asked Danaë meekly, anxious to get the first interview over.

"Certainly not," was the decisive reply. "Come this way, and do as you're told." Danaë was whirled along a path between the bushes, and into a large disorderly kitchen, where another old woman was arranging afternoon tea on a tray with the utmost nicety, in the midst of onions, wine-jars, oil-flasks, raw meat and other unusual accompaniments. "This young person thinks she can give orders here, Despina," remarked the guide.

Despina looked up from her tray. "Then the sooner she learns to the contrary the better," she observed succinctly, carrying it off.

"Yes, indeed," said the other old woman, setting food before Danaë. "Everyone that comes inside these walls may as well know that whatever the Lady says, that has to be done, whether it's having English tea in the middle of the afternoon, or dressing the blessed child like a grown-up person, without any swathings. They may call her Princess outside or not, as they like, but she is Princess here."

"But why should she be called Princess?" ventured Danaë, looking up from her bread and cheese.

"What else should the Prince's wife be called, girl?"

"Petros—my uncle—always calls her the Lady."

"And so she is the Lady, but she's the Princess too. Didn't I myself see her married to him at Bashi Konak, with the Princesses of Dardania looking on?"

"But I thought she was a Latin?" said Danaë, aghast.

"So she is, I suppose, and that's why the wedding was kept private. But Latin or not, a marriage is a marriage, and when it's acknowledged, the Princess will remember those who have been faithful to her. Not that I would tell you all this if there was any chance of your going and talking about it outside, girl," she added hastily, as Despina returned, "but there isn't. Once you're here, you stay here."

"But will the marriage always be kept private?"

"Of course not," said Despina, with considerable irritation. "How could it, with the young Prince growing up, and all? And the sooner his Highness acknowledges it the better, say I."

"And so anyone would say," agreed the other old woman. "But how it's to be done now, Despina, is more than you or I can tell, wise as you may think yourself. It seems to me that the Lady has missed her chance."

"Missed her chance?" cried Despina angrily. "She's missed three chances, and you know it as well as I do, Mariora. She missed one when she let him marry her privately, instead of standing out for her rights, and she missed the second that night she came to me all trembling to say he swore he could not live without her, and would she not come to Therma secretly until he could safely acknowledge the marriage? That was her worst mistake, but she might have redeemed it when the child was born, and she refused, even when I begged of her to do it. 'I will not stoop to extort recognition from my husband, if my entreaties cannot avail, my Despina,' she said, and stuck to it. And entreaties! you can see she tries them every time he comes, and what's the good? She's tiring him out, she is."

Danaë's eyes were aflame with indignation, not against her brother, but the Lady. The enchantress was not satisfied with ensnaring her victim, then; she wished to keep him for ever, to ruin his future without hope of remedy. It never occurred to Danaë for a moment to regard the marriage at Bashi Konak as binding—she was far too strongly Orthodox to admit that a Greek could marry a Latin by Latin rites—but she feared that Prince Romanos might be induced to go through a second ceremony, prior to which the bride would renounce her schismatic creed. Then woe to all hopes of an alliance with Scythian royalty, to the great aggrandisement of the Christodoridi. Danaë's courage rose again, and she felt that the trials of her journey were well worth enduring if they enabled her to defeat the Lady's plans.

"If you have finished, my girl, you can go to the Lady now," said Mariora. "The Prince will be with her, but you need not be afraid of him. He comes from the islands himself, though I'm glad to say he doesn't talk the island talk."

This slur on the purity of her Greek sent Danaë haughtily out of the kitchen, and guided by the loud directions of the two old women, she passed through a stone-paved hall, and across a wide shady verandah.

Under a tree on the sloping lawn in front a lady and gentleman were at tea. Danaë advanced boldly, with no fear of being recognised, since her half-brother and she had never met. The lady heard the sound of her slippers on the gravel and looked round, then turned back to the gentleman and spoke rapidly in French.

"Such a tiresome thing!" she said. "It seems that foolish Despina asked Petros to find me a nurse-girl in the islands, and he has brought back some niece of his own. And I dislike Petros so much that I don't want any of his family here."

"Put the blame on me," said Prince Romanos softly. "I was glad to think that my son would know the lullabies his father used to hear as a child."

"Poet!" said the lady, half fondly, half in scorn.

"But if the idea displeases you, by all means send the girl back at once, my beloved. What are my fancies compared with your wishes?"

"We will see what she is like. Come here, child."

Danaë approached, continuing to scan the pair with sharp suspicious glances. Even her prejudiced mind could not deny that the Lady was very beautiful, and she fastened greedily on a slight droop at the corners of the finely formed mouth, a lift of the delicate eyebrows, as signs of ill-temper counterbalancing good looks. But the discontented expression was far more evident in her companion. He was a handsome man, a good deal older than his wife, and his sallow face bore abundant marks of anxiety and worry. These Danaë set down promptly to the Lady's account. She was worse than a witch, she was a vampire, drawing forth the Prince's vitality and feeding upon it for the enhancement of her own youth and beauty.

"Such a terribly rough-looking girl! so uncouth!" said the Lady in dismay. The tone was intelligible, if not the words.

"Not so bad for Strio, where we think more of strength than refinement. I suppose my sisters must be somewhere about her age now."

"I hope they are differently dressed, then. With those looped-up trousers and bare legs she might be a boy."

"This is a fisher-girl," said Prince Romanos, with some coldness. "They always have their clothes short for scrambling over the rocks. My sisters wear the proper national dress, of course."

"Well, there is no fishing for her to do here," said the Lady sharply. "Tell Despina to see that you are properly dressed before you come into my presence again, child," she added in Greek, spoken with a foreign accent.

"At your pleasure, my Lady," muttered Danaë, with a wrathful glance which the Prince took for one of reproach.

"Fear not, little one," he said pleasantly. "The Lady is not angry with thee, but she does not know the island of the blue sea and the white rock and the grey olive as thou and I do. What do they call thee?"

"Eurynomé of the Andropouloi, lord."

"The Andropouloi! Is the island as full of them as ever? Why, thou art surely the daughter of Petros's sister Theano? I remember she was to marry an Andropoulos soon after I left Strio."

"Stephanos is her husband's name, lord—sword-bearer to the Despot."

"Why doesn't she call you *Despoti mou*, instead of *Kyrie?*" asked the Lady sharply.

"Probably because to her there is only one Despot in the world. Tell the Lady whom you mean when you speak of the Despot, child."

"He of Strio, lord," with evident surprise.

"Just so. But here there are two other Despots, he of Therma, which is myself, and he of Klaustra, who is——"

"My dear Romanos! She will think you are in earnest."

"And am I not, my most beautiful? But come, child, tell me whether the girls run about over the roofs in the spring evenings in Strio as they used to do?"

Danaë was horrified. "But no one knows about it, lord—especially no man."

"Not even the lad who hides in a doorway to get speech with one particular girl? If not, how do I know?"

The memory of certain experiences of Angelikë's made Danaë hesitate to repeat her negative. She hung her head miserably, and the Prince laughed.

"Aha, little one! There was a certain pretty Praxinoë twenty years ago——" The Lady withdrew herself slightly, with a little motion of disgust, and his laugh became embarrassed. "Well, she drove me from Strio and cost me my father's favour, so perhaps the less said about her the better. Go back to the old women, little one, but grow not into a Fate or a Grey Sister like them, and take good care of the little lord. Sing him the island songs, that he may grow up with the sound of the sea in his ears."

"Your foot is on my head, lord," responded Danaë, in a choking voice, as she turned away. Her whole heart went out to this handsome, tired-looking brother of hers, who had loved the stones of Strio throughout twenty years of exile. How gladly would she have fought and died to win him his principality, and how willingly now would she submit to contumely and harshness to save him from the clutches of the beautiful, cold-hearted, discontented woman at his side, who was living on his very life-blood!

"That girl won't be bad-looking, when you have brushed her up a little, Olimpia," said the Prince, in French again, when she was gone. The same little shudder of repulsion as before answered him, and he turned round quickly. "Alas, my beautiful one! you should not have married Apolis the poet if you did not expect him to discern beauty wherever it was to be found."

"You are right. I should never have married Apolis the poet—nor Romanos the Prince either," she answered, in a strangled voice. "Nor would I have done it if I had dreamt how it was to turn out."

"I thought, we had agreed it was useless to enter upon this subject again for the present," said the Prince, with polite weariness.

She fired up at once. "Agreed? I never agreed. You said it was useless, but how can it do any good to leave things as they are? The longer you delay to acknowledge me publicly as your wife, the more difficult it will be. Even now, how will you account for the two years that I have lived concealed here?"

"It is more than difficult. It is impossible," he said through his teeth.

She glanced at him with mingled terror and indignation in her eyes, and he raised his hand soothingly.

"Do not mistake me, my most beautiful. It is quite possible for you to leave this house, force your way into the Palace—the guards shall have orders not to stop you—and lay the proofs of our marriage before the Council, calling in those good, kind-hearted meddlers"—the sneer was terrific—"Princess Emilia and her mother-in-law, to vouch to your words. The result is simple. Exit Romanos, Prince of Emathia, and enter the Englishman, Prince Maurice Theophanis, with his wife and his sister and his sister's husband, to succeed to all the honours your husband lays down."

"You know I don't want you to lose your kingdom. For what other reason have I submitted to this two years' concealment? But how can things ever be better? What hope is there that you will ever find it safe to acknowledge me as your wife?"

"Ah, now my beloved is becoming more reasonable! Listen, then, my little dove. I have a hope—a great hope—that I may be able to accomplish your wish—and my own—very shortly. This railway imbroglio must be settled first. At present Scythia and Pannonia are bidding against one another for the privilege of traversing your husband's state, while he merely intimates that the price offered is not high enough. They are raising their offers. I have already had a shadowy hint of the bare possibility that my position may be made permanent instead of merely renewable after five years—even that it may become hereditary."

"Who offers that?" she asked, with a gasp.

"Ah, that I can hardly tell you at present. But you see, my Olimpia, the frightful delicacy of the situation. The merest breath of suspicion would blast irretrievably this charming prospect—and incidentally your husband's whole career. Wait until the proposal is made definitely, until the bargain is completed, and instead of the mere temporary nominee of Europe, Romanos the First is acknowledged ruler of Emathia in his own right. Then is the moment for him proudly to present his Princess to an admiring world, and to announce that the succession is already secured in the person of a remarkably vigorous infant heir."

The Lady's troubled features relaxed into an involuntary smile. "Ah, that would be magnificent!" she said. "You swear it, Romanos? that there shall be no more delay, no more of this vain entreaty on my part, but that the moment your position is assured you will justify me to the world?"

"I swear it! by all the natural objects to which poets have ever appealed to ratify their vows."

His lightness jarred upon her. "Do you think it is any pleasure to me to lower myself by these continual appeals to you?" she demanded.

"I hope so, my soul, for you can hardly imagine it is any pleasure to me. Ah, beautiful one, not more tragedy, I beseech you! Smile and look lovingly upon your poet. The Prince has enough of seriousness outside."

She repressed with an effort the words thronging to her lips. "Very well, I will say no more. But I must tell you this, that my father is more than ever dissatisfied with my position here. He writes that he proposes to visit Therma, and hopes to induce you to acknowledge me publicly. If you refuse, I know he will wish to take me away with him."

"He may wish, but you will not go. When you vowed yourself to me, Olimpia, you put it out of the power of your father or mine to part us."

"But, dearest, his patience is sorely tried. You know he only consented to keep the secret of our marriage on condition that it was announced as soon as you were established in power, and the announcement has been put off so long and so often. His honour is his dearest possession, and he fears a stain upon it."

"Then let him remain at home until he is summoned to his daughter's entry into Therma as Princess. No, Olimpia, I am not joking. Make your father understand that if he even shows himself in Emathia while this negociation is proceeding, he will set tongues wagging, and the mischief will be done. He must not come."

"He hints that he has something to communicate which would make it easier for you to acknowledge the marriage," she faltered, cowed by his tone. "He meant to tell us about it after the acknowledgment, but now——
"

"Holy Spiridion! let him write it, then. Anything to make the announcement easier will be welcome enough to me, the saints know. But no visit at present. I see what it is, Kyria Olimpia, you are dull! Shall I bring Theophanis and his brother-in-law here to tea when they come?"

"And their wives?" she asked pointedly.

He flushed with annoyance. "The ladies, with unusual discretion, have not proposed to accompany their husbands on this visit. It is purely on business—this railway business. Nothing less would drag our two virtuous Englishmen from their herculean labours at Klaustra to this frivolous place."

"You may bring them to call on me if they know the truth—not otherwise."

Prince Romanos swore under his breath. "Some demon of obstinacy seems to possess you to-day, Olimpia. I thought you were satisfied."

"Forgive me, my husband. Surely it seems a good thought, to bring the Englishmen here and tell them the truth under a promise of secrecy? They are honourable men, and would watch over Janni's rights if anything happens to you and me."

"You are incorrigible, Olimpia. Don't you see that those two men are the very last to whom the secret must be revealed? Theophanis is my rival, and bound for his own sake to take advantage of any slip on my part."

"But he is so honourable, Romanos—punctiliously, quixotically honourable, as you have often said yourself."

He moved restlessly. "That's all very well, but he may be secretly plotting against me all the time. And to give him a hold upon me now—it would be sheer insanity. I told you it was the railway business they were coming to discuss. Doesn't it occur to you that these good simple fools would never willingly consent to allow either Scythia or Pannonia to gain the power over us that the concession would give them?"

"But what do they propose you should do?"

"They have some idea of an international guarantee, which would merely mean that we should have ten nations claiming control over our affairs instead of one. No, if they like to construct the line entirely from their own resources, and so keep it all in the family, as one may say, I am quite willing. It will leave Emathia independent, and keep them from intriguing against me by using up their money. But they won't. So they are coming to argue about it, and I shall have to ply them with fair words and try to hustle them back to Klaustra before the negociations come to a head."

"But do you think it safe to give Scythia or Pannonia the control of the line?"

"I should not, if they had not something supremely desirable to offer in exchange. You know what that is, and you should be the last person to have scruples about it."

"Yes, let me see," she said meditatively. "You are confirmed in the absolute possession of Emathia, and it is secured to your heirs. "And—" she paused—"you marry the third cousin twice removed of the Emperor of Scythia. You intend to murder me, I suppose? For I warn you, Prince Romanos Christodoridi, that I will not accept a divorce, nor will I go tamely away disgraced. I am your wife," her voice broke, "and for my child's sake, I mean to be acknowledged as your Princess." She burst away from him in a passion of tears, and ran into the house.

"Now how in the world did she manage to hear of that little point?" demanded Prince Romanos of himself, as he rose reluctantly to follow her. "The most delicate matter of all—to reap the benefit without paying the price. She will ruin everything in this mood. Olimpia! Olimpia!" he raised his voice, "you are cruelly unjust to me. I insist upon your hearing what I have to say."

CHAPTER III.
THE LITTLE LORD.

EVEN when the first strangeness had worn off, Danaë remained an incongruous element in the Lady's secluded household. As a Striote, speaking the island *patois*, she was a predestined adherent of the Prince in the eyes of the two old women, and therefore an enemy of their mistress, and to make things worse, she was ignorant of the standard of "European" culture to which they had painfully attained. Life within the bounds of the garden, mitigated only by a saint's-day visit to the nearest church, was miserably confined after the active existence to which Danaë had been accustomed, and she scandalised her custodians by her exploits in climbing trees and scrambling up walls. Old Despina went out every day to do the household shopping, in the course of which she managed to pick up and bring home to her mistress an extraordinary variety of gossip reflecting on the Prince, but she would never take the girl with her. Danaë's longings to make closer acquaintance with the crowded streets and the enticing shops were in no way satisfied by the short walks to church in the company of Mariora, both of them so closely swathed in their shawls that nothing of their faces could be seen. But Despina assured her mistress that the girl was such a savage that if she was allowed into the town she was sure to make a scene of some kind, or at least to attract attention by her staring and her uncouth remarks, and as the Lady was above all things desirous to escape notice until the moment of her vindication arrived, Danaë was sentenced to remain within the grounds.

Even the thought of the punishment in store for the Lady would not have enabled the girl to endure the confinement but for the society of the baby. He was a notably joyous child, the brooding sorrow of his unhappy mother leaving him untouched. Danaë and he took to one another at first sight, and she became his devoted slave. With sublime inconsistency, she saw in him the heir of the Christodoridi. He was named Joannes, after the patriot Emperor who had fallen on the walls of Czarigrad in the vain attempt to repel the final onslaught of the conquering Roumis, and from whom the Christodoridi were descended in the female line, and Danaë told herself proudly that he should yet sit upon his ancestor's throne. His preparation for this exalted future should be her task, and hers alone. Released from the baleful influence of the Lady, Prince Romanos might be trusted to make his Imperial marriage and safeguard his own career, but Danaë would carry off Janni to Strio, and bring him up a fearless climber and a daring seaman, as became a son of the sea. Whether the Prince allowed her quietly to take possession of his son, or whether she was obliged to act without consulting him, she hugged herself daily in the thought that the Lady would have no voice in the matter. Nay, from her prison the unfortunate mother should be permitted to see her child in the distance, growing up without knowledge of her and happy in his ignorance.

It was impossible for the Lady to be unaware of the feelings with which Danaë regarded her, though she found the girl's island Greek almost unintelligible. Sullen looks, deepening into positive hostility when Janni was taken to his mother, could not be mistaken, but the Lady set them down to an excessive loyalty to the house of Christodoridi, and jealousy of the foreigner who had married into it. Eurynomé suffered from home-sickness, no doubt, and that was why she was always so cross. Kindness was wasted on her, since one could not import her native rock bodily into Therma harbour, and after one or two careless attempts to break down the nurse-girl's enmity, her mistress shrugged her shoulders and left her to herself, secure in her devotion to Janni. Danaë breathed more freely when the Lady ceased her efforts, for was she not a witch? and kindness from her could only be looked upon with suspicion. But it was possible that her indifference was merely a ruse, and therefore Danaë exhausted all her store of charms to protect herself and the baby. Mariora caught her one day stealing into the kitchen to rub her finger on the sooty side of a saucepan, for did not everyone—save foreigners and atheists—know that a dab of soot behind a child's ear was the surest means of averting the evil eye? But Despina and Mariora laid aside their differences to drag the culprit into their mistress's presence, and accuse her with one voice of laying spells on the illustrious little lord—a charge which Danaë found particularly galling from those who ought to have shared her Orthodox beliefs had they not been corrupted by European incredulity. The Lady would have been merely amused, had not the remedy been such a dirty one, but as it was, Danaë received so severe a scolding that Despina ventured hopefully to ask leave to give her a good beating. The Lady looked annoyed.

"No," she said; "if Eurynomé cannot do what she is told, she must go back to her island. I am not going to take the responsibility of teaching her common sense. Her uncle is the person to do that. You may go, Eurynomé."

"Alas, Lady mine!" lamented Despina, "you have lost a chance. There is great evil in this wicked girl's heart towards you, and I would have beaten it out before it grows into deeds."

"My good Despina, what harm can a wretched nurse-girl, who could not even make herself understood outside, do to me? It is the Prince's fancy that she should attend on the little lord, and I should be sorry if he thought

I had a prejudice against her. If he sees for himself that she is troublesome, he will tell Petros to take her away."

Danaë, lingering shamelessly to listen at the door, stamped her foot as she hurried away, boiling over with rage.

"So be it, Lady! so be it!" she muttered. "I can do you no harm, can I? And I can't talk your mincing foreign Greek? You will find before very long that I can! I make my bow to you, my Lady. You will know me better when I bring my Jannaki to the window of your dungeon, and teach him to spit upon you!"

Danaë could not have explained why her mistress's indifference wounded her more than active dislike would have done, but so it was. The company of the two old women, with their taunts and nods of triumph, was equally intolerable, and she never rested until she had found a hiding-place for herself and Janni where they could be by themselves. It was close to the house, so that she could hear at once if she was called, in the grove of ilex-trees which masked the approach to the kitchen premises. The branches of one of the trees grew close to the ground, and to Danaë it was child's play to clamber into them with Janni girt closely to her with a shawl. Once well above the ground, she climbed higher and higher until they were quite concealed by the foliage from anyone below, reaching a convenient forked branch where she could sit in comfort, and where she broke away the twigs cautiously to give herself a view over the garden. In spite of all her care, it was not long before her two enemies divined that she had some hidden refuge, and began to hunt for it. Shaking with laughter, and holding up a warning finger in front of Janni's rosy face, she would hear them shuffling among the stiff dead leaves below her, peering round the tree-trunks and scanning the lower branches keenly. They knew that she must be in the wood, unfortunately, for the first time that she took Janni up the tree the climb made him fractious, and she was obliged to sing to quiet him, so that it was no use denying the fact when Mariora demanded where she had been, making that noise so close to the house, but when they required further particulars, she assumed an expression of idiocy that was absolutely impenetrable. The old women were equal to her, however, and one unfortunate day, descending her tree hastily in answer to Mariora's loud summons from the kitchen door, Danaë almost fell into the arms of Despina, crouching among the dead leaves. Then indeed there was a moment of triumph for the Lady's two faithful attendants. Gleefully they haled Danaë by main force before their mistress, and charged her with endangering the little lord's life and limbs by taking him to the top of the tallest tree in the gardens. She was voluble in her denials, but the tell-tale leaves and pieces of bark, traces of her hurried descent, which decorated her hair and clothes and the shawl in which Janni was wrapped, belied her words, and her mistress was the more disturbed because of her former confidence.

"I knew you were disobedient to the servants and disrespectful to me, Eurynomé, but I thought I could trust you to take care of the little lord," she said. "This is too much. Your uncle must deal with you. I can stand no more."

With huge delight Despina and Mariora dragged their prisoner away and shut her up in the wood-shed until Petros should arrive with the Prince. Janni's piteous wailings for "Nono," which could only be calmed by undivided attention from his mother, troubled them not a whit, but they added fuel to the fire which burned in the rebellious heart of the girl who crouched exhausted on the ground after a wild and futile attack on the door. If Danaë had felt before that she did well to be angry with the Lady and her household, she would now gladly have seen them all lying dead before her. Her wrath was still hot when the two old women reappeared, and with various kicks and pinches, which were returned with interest, pulled and pushed her into the presence of her judges. Her cap, with its rows of silver coins, was half torn off, the many little plaits of her hair ragged and dishevelled, as she stood with sullen face and heaving breast before the Prince; but Janni, seated on his father's knee, held out his arms to her with a delighted "Ah, Nono!" The girl's face changed as if by magic as she started forward to take him, but Despina and Mariora held her forcibly back, and the Lady took instant possession of her son—a precaution which he resented by a violent howl.

"Give him your watch to play with," she said hastily to her husband, "or we shall not be able to hear ourselves speak. Eurynomé is the only person who can manage him when he gets into these passions."

Obediently Prince Romanos dangled his watch by the chain before his son's face, held it close to his ear that he might hear it tick, and finally relinquished it to him to suck—as is the wont of inexperienced fathers confronted with a crisis of the kind, until the howls subsided sufficiently to allow his wife to make herself heard.

"You understand," she said to Petros, who stood deprecatingly by, "that this is not the first time your niece has behaved badly. I have borne with her as long as I could, but we have had no peace since she entered the household. She is a most extraordinary girl. Why can't she do what she is told? Is it your island independence?"

"If it please the Lady, I think some demon must have taken up his dwelling in her," said Petros helplessly, and Despina and Mariora exchanged triumphant glances.

"She had better go home at once. The little lord's life is not safe while she is here," said the Lady decisively.

"Will it be safe when she is gone?" asked the Prince, with a desperate effort to rescue the watch, which Janni, now growing black in the face, was attempting to swallow.

"All-Holy Mother! you will kill the child, lord!" shrieked Danaë, tearing herself from her warders and rushing forward. A moment's struggle and the watch was once more in its owner's possession, and Janni in his nurse's arms, crowing with delight as he grabbed at the coins in her cap.

"See how fond the child is of her!" said the Prince to his wife. "Is it true, Eurynomé, that thou wouldst have killed the little lord?"

"Lord, I would die for him," replied Danaë fervently.

"You see, Olimpia. There must be some mistake."

"I can never have her about him again."

"My most beloved, you don't understand our island-people. The women make the most devoted nurses in the world, and have died for their charges, as she says. She is a wild creature who does not understand civilised ways, but I would trust her with the child through anything. Let Petros speak to her seriously, and I'll be bound you will see a great change in her."

"If Petros can make her understand that she is to do what she is told, and that Janni is to be brought up in my way, not hers, I might think of it."

"Surely, my Lady, there is a way of making women understand, and I have never known it fail," said Petros unctuously, with a glance at his master's riding-whip. The Prince laughed uncomfortably.

"No, no, friend Petraki, we are not in the islands now. Give the girl a good talking-to, that's enough."

Petros looked at the Lady, whose delicate brows were drawn into a slight frown. "Leave it to me, lord. Does not the girl come from my place? Is she to bring disgrace on me by angering the mistress I brought her to serve? In five minutes she shall kiss the Lady's foot and ask pardon—yes, and promise amendment. Follow me, wretched one."

"Well, don't be too hard upon her. Follow thine uncle, little one, and fear not. The Lady and I will come to thy help if he beats thee."

"He will not, lord." The words were uttered with such concentrated fury that Prince Romanos turned rather uneasily to his wife as Danaë, with head held high, followed the retreating form of Petros.

"That is really a very remarkable girl, Olimpia. Our women are usually kept in better order."

"Then I wish Petros had not chosen the exception to bring here. If you knew the trouble Eurynomé has made in the house, you would not be so horrified by the thought of her getting a beating. She thoroughly deserves it, and no doubt, as her uncle says, it is the only argument that people of that type understand. I have stood endless unpleasantness, but when it comes to risking Janni's life——"

"My beautiful one, you are agitating yourself needlessly. Rather than bring a tear into the eyes of my Princess—" he stole a glance at her to see how the word was received—"the girl shall go back to her place to-morrow. But if she is really penitent, and promises to do better, is it not well to have one about the child who is truly devoted to him?"

"And who recalls to you, lord, those happy days of your youth in Strio?" said the Lady, imitating sarcastically Danaë's island-speech. "Well, as it seems quite certain that Petros is not beating her, do you think we might venture to have tea?"

Behind the screen of trees, Danaë was facing Petros with blazing eyes. "If you dare to lay a finger upon me, I will tell everything to the Lord Romanos," she said hoarsely.

"I am not such a fool, my lady. I will leave my lord your father to do the beating when you are packed back to Strio with the work undone that you came for."

"And why is the work undone?" Danaë recovered herself after a momentary pause of consternation. "Because you were not ready! I have been waiting eagerly to do my part, but you have never called upon me. You may be sure, insolent one, that the Despot shall hear the truth, whatever he may be pleased to do to me."

The hereditary tendency to obedience in Petros responded immediately to the hectoring tone. "Indeed, my lady, I am to blame, but it has not been my fault. This is the first time that I have seen you alone, to make the final arrangements."

"Is everything arranged on your side?" demanded Danaë, unappeased.

"Everything, lady mine. The helpers are secured—and indeed it was not difficult to find them. There are those in Therma as well as in Strio who hate the Lady. And it will be well to do it soon—this week—while the English lords are here. The Lord Romanos will have less time for coming here, nor will he so easily remark my absence. Moreover, he will have less opportunity for inquiring into the matter afterwards."

"That does not concern me," said Danaë loftily. "It is your part to leave no traces. You have a boat ready at a suitable place, able to sail at any moment?"

"A boat, my lady?" Petros was taken aback. "Why a boat?"

Danaë stamped her foot. "Fool! to carry off the Lady to Strio to her prison, of course. And how are the little lord and I to return thither, pray? Did you think the Lord Romanos would willingly part with his son?"

"My lady"—Petros looked at her with cunning eyes—"you are wiser than I. I have indeed been remiss, but the boat shall be ready. How could my lord your father be other than delighted to receive the beloved wife and child of his illustrious son?"

"She is not his wife!" cried Danaë. "His wife must be Orthodox and of royal blood. She is neither."

"Yet the little lord will be welcomed and honoured as the heir of the Christodoridi?" insinuated Petros humbly.

Danaë felt as though a pitfall had opened before her feet, but she faced him undauntedly. "That does not concern you, friend Petros. The Despot will do as he pleases. I have not felt obliged to share with you the secret instructions he gave me."

"And I did not expect it, my lady. Only—there are some who would willingly make everything secure by killing the Lady instead of merely carrying her off."

The chronicles of the Christodoridi included a not inconsiderable variety of cold-blooded murders, but Danaë blenched. Nevertheless, she endeavoured vigorously to justify herself, realising that Petros was gloating over her horror.

"What is that to us? You have the Despot's orders to bring her to Strio, not to kill her. To remove her evil influence from the Lord Romanos is a good deed, but to shed blood would be to bring sin upon our souls. Moreover, I, at least, would sooner have the witch in captivity, where I knew her to be secure, than set her malicious ghost free to haunt me."

"Great is the wisdom of Kyria Danaë!" said Petros, with extreme respect, "and her words shall be obeyed. Take this, my lady," he handed her a minute wedge of iron, "and hide it safely. The time we choose must be when Despina has gone to do her shopping, for the fewer witnesses the better, and therefore you must find means to let me know if she has not been out yet any day when I attend the Lord Romanos hither. Then I will keep her in talk while she lets us out, and you must slip the wedge into the hole of the lock, so that the bolt cannot shoot home. The rest you can leave to me."

Danaë considered her instructions. "It will be difficult to get near the gate, but I will manage it somehow. You have made arrangements for getting the Lady unperceived to the boat?"

"Is it for me to share with you the secret instructions I have received from my lord your father, lady?" asked Petros sulkily—then, with a spasm of geniality, "But all the Despot's thoughts are yours, as we know. Does the idea of a mock funeral procession, with yourself and the little lord among the mourners, please you, my lady?"

"Excellent!" cried Danaë. "Nothing could be better."

"Then all is well, and all is ready. Therefore return now, Eurynomé, and kiss the Lady's hand, and promise her to behave better in future."

"I will not do it!" cried Danaë, her anger reviving.

"Then you return at once to Strio, my lady, and the plan falls through. No vengeance on the Lady!"

"Even for that I would not do it," she said wrathfully. "But to save my brother and Janni from her evil arts—" she pushed past Petros, and marched doggedly to the tea-table. "Grant me pardon, Lady mine. I will not risk the little lord's life again," she forced herself to say.

"On your knees, Eurynomé!" said Prince Romanos sharply, conscious of his wife's raised eyebrows, and the girl obeyed sullenly. The Lady held out a delicate hand with obvious lack of eagerness, and Danaë kissed it and dropped it as if it had been a hot coal, retiring awkwardly enough at an imperative sign from her brother.

"I can't congratulate you on your *protégée's* manners," said the Lady lightly.

"No one is better fitted to improve them than yourself, my beloved Olimpia. And at least she is staunch, and would give her heart's blood for Janni."

"What is the danger at which you are always hinting? Is there something new?"

"There is always a certain amount of unpleasantness," he replied evasively. "And this visit of Theophanis and his brother-in-law will stir up their supporters. My beautiful one, it is my particular wish that you have a proper guard for the present—inside the garden."

"To guard the Princess—or the Lady?" she asked coldly.

He uttered a furious exclamation. "Olimpia, you are enough to drive a man mad! Do you think I have invited Theophanis here to hand over the crown to him? It will task all my powers to hoodwink him and Glafko as to the promising negociation which is to end by seating you beside me on the throne, and would you have me ruin everything by making him aware of your existence now?"

"Perhaps you are also hoodwinking me on the same subject? No, I will have no guards within these walls. Here, at any rate, I need not see the pointing finger, or hear the things your people say of me. Any danger that may threaten Janni or me is entirely due to your refusing, in defiance of all your promises, to acknowledge us, and I will not accept further protection at your hands while the concealment lasts."

"Olimpia!" Prince Romanos had thrown himself on his knees, in an attitude that would have been impossibly theatrical in any other man. "You wrong me deeply; I call all the saints to witness to it. Believe me, you should not remain in concealment another hour, if the necessity were not urgent. It is your throne and mine—Janni's throne, our son's throne—that is in danger. Trust your husband," he leaned forward and enfolded her hands in his—"or if not your husband, trust the poet to whom you plighted your troth on the marble terrace among the orange-trees."

"I do trust you," she said wearily, allowing her hands to rest in his— "because I must. I remain here because I have nowhere else to go. I have wounded my father grievously for your sake by begging him not to come. You may send your guards here if you will tell them the truth about me. But within these walls everyone must know that I am the Princess and your wife."

"It is impossible," he murmured gloomily.

"So I thought. So it will always be when I urge you to make the truth known. You have no intention whatever of acknowledging it."

"My most beautiful and best beloved, you are cruelly wrong, and I will prove it to you. If I place in your keeping the most sacred treasure of our house, handed down for hundreds of years before the birth of John Theophanis himself, will you believe me then? If anything should happen to me, you have only to produce that jewel to show that I acknowledged you as my honoured wife, and as rightful Empress of the East. Ah, my beloved, you are yielding! I will not ask you to see me again until I can put the treasure into your hands, and you will own how much you have misjudged your Apolis."

CHAPTER IV.
THE GIRDLE OF ISIDORA.

IT was about ten o'clock in the morning, and Despina was clattering things furiously in the kitchen as she collected baskets and other aids to shopping, for she was late in starting. The Lady sat in the morning-room opening on the verandah, writing a letter which seemed, from her frequent pauses, to be difficult to frame, and Danaë was playing bo-peep with Janni in and out of the window. Above the child's shouts of laughter came the imperative sound of the door-bell, and Danaë caught him up in her arms, and followed at a discreet distance in Despina's wake as she went to open the door.

"Aha, old mother, you won't be able to start just yet!" she cried mockingly, as the Prince rode in, followed by Petros, for Despina would never delegate even to Mariora the duty of keeping the door in her absence.

"May he that is without and afar [*i.e.*, the devil] fly away with that girl! If I catch her, I'll teach her saucy tongue a lesson!" muttered the old woman furiously.

"I should recommend a red-hot skewer," was the soothing suggestion of Petros, as he flashed a glance towards Danaë to show that he had understood her intimation. "A monk at the Holy Mountain told me that the worst of scolds could be cured by marking a cross on her tongue with it, if the proper prayers were said at the same time."

Despina requited his sympathy with another curse, and Danaë laughed as she followed the Prince, who had taken Janni in his arms. He gave the child back to her as they reached the house, and she sat down again on the verandah while he greeted his wife. Reading in her eyes the question she was too proud to ask, he unbuttoned his tunic, and took out something wrapped in linen which had been concealed there. Danaë, her curiosity aroused, watched him with eager eyes while he unrolled it, but she sang mechanically to Janni the while, lest her interest should be observed. One by one he released from the protecting folds a series of circular plaques of gold, gleaming with jewels and translucent enamel, while the Lady looked on, puzzled and a little disappointed, and Danaë's breath came quick and fast.

"Byzantine, I suppose?" said the Lady, fingering one of the plaques; "and not intentionally comic?"

"Wait!" said Prince Romanos sharply. He was fitting the plaques together by means of the little gold hooks and chains attached to each, until they formed a small portrait-gallery of severe-featured saints, with jewelled halos and dresses. He held it up. "If the people in the streets as I passed had known that I was bringing this to you, Olimpia, they would have torn me limb from limb. It is the girdle of the Empress Isidora."

Danaë gasped, in spite of herself, at the sound of the name, which was the only word she understood, but she had already guessed what the jewel was. Handed down in the Christodoridi family was a metrical version of the exploits of the famous, and infamous, Empress, in which the girdle figured largely, and Danaë could have named each ill-favoured saint from memory. And this treasure, the badge of Orthodox sovereignty, her infatuated brother was now handing over to the schismatic woman who had bewitched him! Even the Lady, who knew nothing of its legendary fame, was impressed as she took it into her hands.

"It is a magnificent thing!" she said. "Why have you never shown it to me before?"

"Because I have never had it in my possession, or even set eyes upon it, till now. In fact, I did not know that it was still in existence. For your possession of it, my most beautiful, you may thank Prince Theophanis, or rather Lady Eirene, his wife."

"You will hardly ask me to believe that Princess Theophanis has acknowledged the justice of your claims so far as to send you this by her husband?"

"Very far from it, my dearest. She has no knowledge of its present whereabouts, and if you are to keep it, she had better not know."

"But to whom does it really belong?"

"To the head of the descendants of John Theophanis. That, my Olimpia, is your husband, as the inhabitants of Emathia testified by their free vote. But the girdle has been preserved since the fall of Czarigrad in the family of the Princess Eirene, and I have reason to believe that she regards it as her own property."

"And you have contrived to rob her jewel-case during her husband's absence here?" asked the Lady lightly.

"Your poet does not go to work quite so crudely, Olimpia. No, it seems that it is ten years or more since anyone saw the girdle. Before her marriage the Princess was detained in a sort of honourable captivity at the old Scythian Consulate here, from which she escaped to join Theophanis. Unfortunately for her, knowing that the Scythian Imperial family were most anxious to possess the jewel, in order to support their claims to the heritage of the Cæsars, she contrived a hiding-place for it, from which she had not time to rescue it when the opportunity of escape came. There it must have remained ever since, for even when the Consulate was burnt by the Roumi mob before the bombardment, the walls in great part remained standing. But just lately she saw in the papers that we were clearing away the ruins to make the new boulevard, and immediately hurried her husband off to make inquiries. Knowing Maurice Theophanis, you won't be surprised to hear that he chose me, in strictest secrecy, as the recipient of his inquiries—for which I should imagine his wife will have a word or two to say to him when he gets home. It seems that Princess Eirene managed to pick a large stone out of the wall with her scissors, and hide the girdle in the rubble behind it. As she had fitted the stone in again neatly enough to escape the observation of the spies who surrounded her, I thought it was very likely the treasure was there still, but I said a good deal to Theophanis about fire and plunderers. We visited the ruins, and Glafko—who has a plaguy exact mind—located as nearly as he could the spot where the Princess's room had been. In their presence I promised the workmen a large reward if they found anything, and fearful penalties unless they gave it up, and then I carried our friends off to a review. The walls were duly knocked down, and nothing was found. But Daniloff, the chief of police, used himself to be employed at the Scythian Consulate in the old days, and he had visited the spot the night before. He found the girdle and brought it to me, wrapped up in odds and ends of paper, and he and I cleaned it and polished it ourselves. No one else on earth dreams where it is."

"That girl outside will know," said the Lady, without looking towards Danaë.

"Nonsense! she doesn't understand French. All she knows is that I have brought you a present of jewellery to-day—surely a very natural thing to do. It is not as if she had ever heard of the girdle and its history."

"And the obvious thing, to her, would be that I should put it on at once." She passed the glittering links round her waist, confining the folds of the loose flowing gown of rich wine-colour she was wearing. Before she could snap the clasp into place the Prince's hand stopped her.

"Wait, Olimpia. I must tell you that they say the girdle brings ill-luck with it."

The Lady laughed, and fastened the clasp. "I will risk the ill-luck if it makes me Empress," she said.

Prince Romanos gazed at her in unfeigned admiration. "Olimpia, you are magnificent! You look the Empress to the life. May I yet see you wear the girdle at our coronation in Hagion Pneuma!" He knelt and lifted the edge of the wine-coloured robe to his lips. "Hail to the Orthodox Empress!" he said fervently in Greek, and Danaë thrilled with horror at the sacrilege. Were there no bounds to her brother's infatuation?

The Lady blushed slightly at the fervour of her husband's tone. Perhaps she also saw, as she looked dreamily far beyond him, the dim splendours of the great cathedral of Czarigrad, rescued from the Moslem and restored to Christian uses, and crowded with rejoicing people assembled to welcome back the descendant of John Theophanis to the throne of his ancestors— saw herself in imperial robes beside him, and Janni, grown a goodly youth, acclaimed as the heir of the Eastern Empire. Then she shivered a little, and unfastened the clasp again.

"Don't speak Greek; it is not safe with the girl about. You have made me almost afraid of letting even Despina know that I have the girdle, yet she has my keys. I will put it here," she opened a drawer of her bureau by a spring, and laid the jewel inside it, Danaë watching her every movement, "until I can make an excuse to get them and hide it in the safe. And now tell me what it is you want me to do for you in return for it."

"Most beautiful and beloved, will you not believe that your poet brought you a gift solely that he might feast his eyes upon your beauty adorned with it, and enjoy your pleasure?"

"Not for a moment," said the Lady decisively.

"Ah, hard-hearted one! will nothing move you? Well, then, dearest, I claim your promise made the other day. You will allow me to quarter a guard for you within these walls?"

"I made no promise!" she said quickly.

"Not in words, I own, but it was implied, in return for the gift I hoped to bring you, and have now brought. Listen, Olimpia; I am in a very difficult position. Theophanis and his brother-in-law have made this week a perfect hell to me. The shifts and excuses to which I have been driven to baulk their curiosity are really humiliating to look back upon. I am compelled—simply for the sake of averting the suspicions I saw beginning to spring up in their minds—to appear to fall in with their scheme for the railway route. Of course it is exactly opposite to the one on which your hopes—our hopes—depend, but I must throw them off the scent for a week or two, or until I can get things definitely settled. Theophanis and Glafko are returning home fairly satisfied, but to make things quite smooth I was obliged to volunteer to go part of the way with them, to see a place where there would be difficulty in getting the line through. It is a Moslem colony—*evkaf* [or *wakf*, land set apart for religious uses] land, a mosque and a cemetery—and any sensible person would have seen at once that it was an insuperable obstacle to their pet route, but they want to negociate about it, relying on Glafko's influence with the Roumis, I suppose, and—in a moment of thoughtlessness, I confess—I proposed enthusiastically to go with them and see what could be done."

"Which means that you will be away from Therma—how long?"

"Four days, not more; three, if I am lucky."

"And you have never gone away before without sending Janni and me into safety at Thamnos first!"

"My dear Olimpia, this is such a short time. And the notice was so brief; I start with them to-day, and there was no time to arrange anything. Then consider what is to be gained—the fulfilment of our dearest hopes. You on the throne beside me, Janni acknowledged heir of Emathia—safety and recognition, in short, if I can only keep those two meddlesome Englishmen in the dark till my great *coup* is made."

"And your police are not capable of protecting this house against the mob, even with the help of the soldiers outside?"

"It is not the mob I am afraid of, but those who are your—our— enemies for political, dynastic reasons."

She raised her eyebrows. "The Theophanis family?"

"Let me beg you not to consider me altogether a fool, Olimpia. No, not the Theophanis family. But you are aware that your existence is not entirely unknown in the city; you have often complained to me of the fact. I have reason to believe that it has reached the knowledge of the very people with whom I am carrying on my secret negociations. They may not know your real position, but they are quite capable of seeing in you and Janni a possible obstacle to the realisation of their aims, and in that case you and Janni would be sentenced to disappear. Now do you see what I mean? I may have been brutal, but you have forced me to speak plainly."

The Lady frowned, paying little attention to his excuses. "In plain words, then, you think that opportunity will be taken of your absence to murder your wife and son?"

"I don't think it will be so, or I should not go, but I think it is possible that such an attempt might be made. Consider Janni, Olimpia, if you will not consider yourself."

"I am considering myself," she said quickly; "or rather, I am considering the dignity of your wife. The Princess of Emathia may be pardoned a little pride, Romanos—may she not? But Janni is in danger, you say? Well, then,

I well yield as far as this. You may post your guards round the house at night. Arrange matters with Despina, and let me hear nothing of them. They must be gone before I come out of doors in the morning, and they must only arrive after dark—I will not walk in the garden late. I will not see or be seen by any more of your subjects till you acknowledge me; that piece of pride I keep. But we shall be protected, according to your wish; for I suppose even you do not expect a murderous attack to be made upon us in the daytime?"

"No, I think that ought to be enough," he said reluctantly. "I shall be a little happier in my mind, knowing that the garden is thoroughly patrolled. Accept your poet's gratitude, my Princess, and vouchsafe him a gracious farewell. I have innumerable things to do before I join Theophanis and Glafko this afternoon. They start this morning, with a patriarchal paraphernalia of tents and baggage-mules, for the fancy for exploring their proposed new route forbids their making use of the railway, and I catch them up, travelling light. But I dare not stay longer."

"And poor Despina will be distracted by the delay in her marketing," said the Lady lightly. She took her husband's arm, and walked with him into the garden, Danaë following with Janni in her arms, and the little iron wedge which Petros had given her clasped tightly in her hand. The Lady remained out of sight of the gate, but while his father was speaking to Despina, Janni clamoured to see the horses, and Danaë carried him to watch the riders mount. She hardly knew how she could contrive to slip the wedge into the lock, for Despina, fuming with impatience, was clearly in a desperate hurry. To add to her irritation, the horse which Petros rode began to dance hither and thither, apparently desiring to go anywhere rather than through the gate, and in his efforts to control it, Petros caught his spur in the old woman's embroidered apron, and the stuff only yielded with a jagged tear. Then the horse went through the gateway with a bound, and Petros was left sitting on the ground with an expression of such intense astonishment that even Despina, while reviling him loudly, could hardly help laughing.

"Come on, Petraki! What's the matter?" cried his master, turning round.

"I knew something would happen when we met that priest just as we were starting, my Prince," moaned Petros lugubriously, noting with the tail of his eye that Danaë, venturing as far as the doorpost in sympathetic curiosity, had slipped the wedge into the hole.

"If you hadn't been so clumsy, nothing would have happened, fellow," snapped Despina, contemplating her ruined apron. "I didn't meet a priest, so why should I be unlucky?"

"And I did meet him, and nothing has happened to me," said Prince Romanos gaily. "Get yourself a new apron with that, old mother, and don't croak. Make haste, friend Petros," as the sentry brought up the horse, which he had captured; "or shall I send the police for you with an ambulance?"

"O my Prince, I think I can get to the Palace," said Petros, rising with many groans, "but after that——"

"You will have to go on the sick-list instead of coming into the country with me. That's where my ill-luck comes in," said the Prince, as his retainer hoisted himself with tremendous difficulty into the saddle.

"Take the little lord in, Eurynomé," cried Despina wrathfully. "How often have I not told you that no modest girl goes peeping out of gates, and there you are, absolutely outside! You're a bad one, and I always said so."

Danaë obeyed, too much excited even to give Despina as good as she gave, so near and clear to her mind was the culmination of the plot. Her brother was going away somewhere, and Petros had contrived to avoid going with him, and the door could be opened by anyone who knew the secret of the obstructed lock. Moreover, the saints—so she gratefully phrased it—had put in her way the means of escape from the fears of Janni's future in Strio which had been suggested by the words of Petros when last they met. With the Girdle of Isidora in her possession, she could bargain for his safety with her father. Prince Christodoridi was an unsatisfactory person to bargain with—she recognised it quite dispassionately and not without admiration—since he never kept any promises that were not strictly in accordance with his own interests, but with the treasure of the family in her hands, it would be hard if Danaë could not manage to bind him down to tolerance of Janni's presence, if not to actual recognition of his rights. To leave the girdle where it was, for her brother to bestow on some other schismatic woman, was a thought which only suggested itself to be scouted.

The morning passed quietly. Despina went out with her baskets, shutting the gate with a tremendous bang, since the lock was difficult to manipulate. The Lady compassionated her on having to start so late on such a hot day, and called Mariora to carry her chair and table out of doors. The favourite spot on the lawn in front of the house was not sufficiently shady to-day, and only the thick foliage of the ilexes afforded tolerable shelter. The Lady sat down to finish her letter, with Danaë and Janni playing on the ground beside her, and Mariora returned to her work. As the day grew hotter and the air and the hum of insects more drowsy, the child became sleepy and fretful.

"Carry him indoors, Eurynomé," said the Lady, looking up from her writing. "It is early for his sleep, but the excitement this morning must have tired him. I will come and sit beside him while you have your dinner."

"It is done as you command, my Lady," responded Danaë, with unusual meekness, and she lifted the child to carry him into the house. On the verandah she paused. There were sounds at the gate. The Lady had heard them too, and risen from her chair, just as Mariora rushed through the hall from the kitchen.

"Fly, my Lady, hide yourself! Murderers!" shrieked the old woman. "I will keep them back!" and she pushed her mistress violently inside the house and ran towards the gate, brandishing a chopper. The Lady turned to snatch Janni out of Danaë's arms, but drew back suddenly.

"Hide him, my Eurynomé, save him! You love him, I know."

"They will do you no harm, Lady," responded Danaë confidently, "nor the little lord either."

"What do you know about it, girl? Listen!" as the clash of weapons and a terrible sobbing shriek reached their ears. "Ah, my poor Mariora! Take him, hide him—you have some place. I will go and meet them and give you time." She pressed a passionate kiss on Janni's sleepy eyes. "Save him, I charge you, Eurynomé. Go, go quickly!"

Overmastered by sheer force of will, Danaë fled through the hall and kitchen and out into the ilex-grove, seeing nothing but the tall red figure stepping out with uncovered head into the blinding sunshine. A clamour of words followed her, menaces and evil names, then the Lady's voice, very clear and distinct in her foreign Greek.

"I am the wife of the Lord Romanos. If you kill me, you kill your Princess."

Again that clash of steel, and Danaë's stubborn heart misgave her. Pausing only to wind her shawl firmly round Janni and herself, she began to climb, hurriedly and furiously, and never ceased until she had reached her eyrie, where no one could see her from below. She found a cradle among the branches for Janni, and tied him there safely before she ventured to look out of the window she had made for herself. On the lawn lay a prostrate figure in a red gown, dreadfully still, with a deeper red spreading from it to the grass, and men in the uniform of the Prince's guard were searching eagerly among the trees. Others came rushing out of the house as she watched.

"Not a soul there! Where are they?" was the cry. "What is the use of killing the she-wolf if the cub is left alive?"

Then Petros was false! More than that, it came upon Danaë like a blow that her father had planned this murder all along, and deliberately made use of her to further his plot. In the sudden revulsion of feeling she forgot her own hatred of the Lady, and the ignoble part it had led her to play. Janni was alive, left to her charge by his murdered mother, and she would save him if she died for it. Sick and shaking, she crawled back to where she had left him, and found him peacefully asleep. Seating herself in a fork of the branches beside him, she loosened her dagger in its sheath. If they were tracked to the tree, no one should touch him while she remained alive.

CHAPTER V.
THE BRAND OF CAIN.

DANAË woke from the sleep or stupor that had overcome her to find Janni patting her face.

"Wake up, Nono, wake up!" he was saying, as he was wont to do in the early morning. "Breakfast!"

With a horrible spasm of fear, she covered his mouth quickly with the shawl, fearing his voice might have been heard, then listened apprehensively. But no sound came from below, and Janni was struggling to get rid of the shawl, and insisting, in his own language, which only Danaë understood, that he was very hungry, and would shortly roar if breakfast was not forthcoming. Judging by her own sensations that some hours must have passed since she had climbed the tree, she ventured to crawl back to her point of vantage and peer cautiously forth. The dreadful red form still lay where it had fallen, marring the peaceful beauty of the garden with its rigid lines and clenched hands, but of the murderers there was no sign. Could they have guessed that she and Janni were hidden in the grounds, and be lying in wait in the house, ready to pounce upon them when hunger should drive them forth? Danaë shook from head to foot as the thought occurred to her, but a howl from Janni brought her back to him in a panic, and made action inevitable. Quieting him with promises and entreaties, she let herself down from the tree, and starting at every sound, crept through the bushes and reconnoitred the kitchen door. There was no one to be seen, and she ventured inside. Everything was thrown about and broken, but no one was there. Kicking off her slippers, she crept through the hall to the front of the house. Curtains had been roughly pulled down, pieces of furniture dragged from their places, evidently to make sure that no one was hiding behind them, and all receptacles ransacked. The sight of the bureau standing open gave her a shock, but she saw at once that the secret drawer had not been discovered. Approaching noiselessly, she touched the spring, and the Girdle of Isidora, in all its antique and sacred beauty, lay before her worshipping eyes. With a sudden impulse she snatched it up, and fastened it with trembling fingers round her waist, hidden by her long coat and apron, leaving the drawer open.

A distant wail reminded her of her charge, and she returned hastily into the kitchen to look for food. Some milk she was able to rescue from a broken crock, but there was none of the white bread which was always bought for Janni. Surely Despina ought to have returned with her purchases by this time? Danaë ran out towards the gate, avoiding with a shudder the tumbled heap which showed where Mariora had made her gallant and ineffectual stand on behalf of her mistress, but recoiled hastily. Almost at her very feet lay Despina, dead among her baskets. She had been attacked from behind and cut down as soon as she was inside the gate. With iron resolution the girl crushed down the desire that seized her to run away screaming—anywhere, anywhere, away from those three corpses. Janni remained alive and dependent on her, and she must take care of him. Setting her teeth, she stepped forward gingerly until she was able to seize one of the baskets. Happily, it was the one containing the bread, and she hurried back to Janni, and brought him down from the tree and fed him. She found a hiding-place in the bushes, close to the spot where the Lady had sat writing that morning, and tried to get the child to sleep again while she thought things out. How she was to place him in safety she could not tell. She did not even know the way to the Palace, and besides, her brother might even now have started on his expedition. Moreover, there was the disquieting fact that the murderers had all worn the uniform of the guard, which seemed to ring her round with fresh perils. The guard were then in the plot to destroy the Lady and her son, and to go to the Palace would be to walk straight into their clutches. Worse still, they were to provide a detachment to garrison the garden that night, so the Prince had told Despina when he announced his approaching journey before he rode out, and they would no doubt use the opportunity to place the three dead bodies inside the house, and remove all traces of the tragedy from the outside. They were not to come near the house itself, nor to see anything of the inmates, so their orders ran, and therefore the horrible business would in the most natural way remain undiscovered until Prince Romanos returned to Therma and came to see his wife.

And in the meantime? Danaë's heart sank. Her brother would be away three or four days, as he had told Despina, and it would fall to her to keep Janni safely concealed and fed for that time. The slightest sign of their presence, the faintest wail from the child, and the murderous crew who had killed his mother would be upon them. There would be no more milk, even if she could make the bread last which she had found in the basket, and Janni was not accustomed to bear privation silently. Nor was a tree an ideal sleeping-place for three or four nights, especially when any movement in the branches might betray your presence to bloodthirsty enemies below. Slowly a plan grew up in Danaë's mind. She and Janni would escape from the garden while there was time, before the guard arrived that evening. The gate was out of the question owing to the presence of the sentry, but the wall was easy to climb, especially where trees grew close to it. Danaë had no mind to trust herself in Therma, but she knew, by longing observation from her treetops, which way lay the open country, and there it must be possible to find villages where she and Janni might be sheltered until she could manage to communicate with her brother. Crawling out of her concealment, she picked up the letter which the Lady had been writing, and which had fallen to the ground, folded it and hid it in her dress. It would be a credential should she be forced to approach Prince Romanos through a third person, less likely by far to arouse suspicion or to provoke danger than the famous girdle. Then she ventured back into the house to collect a few clothes for herself and Janni, which she made into a bundle with the rest of the bread, and hid among the trees at the point she thought best for crossing the wall. Returning to fetch the child, she was horrified to hear violent blows upon the gate. The guard had arrived early—the mob of the city were attacking the house—the conjectures, both equally alarming, chased one another through her brain as she caught up Janni, and rushed with him once more to the tree of refuge. But before she could mount it she heard her brother's voice.

"Open the door, Despina! it is I. The lock will not work. Unfasten the bolt. Are you all asleep?"

Saved as by a miracle! Danaë left Janni on the ground, and ran joyfully to the gate, where she struggled vainly with the lock, while the Prince demanded impatiently why the door was not opened.

"It is I, lord—Eurynomé; and the bolts are not fastened, but the key will not turn."

"The key? What are you doing with the key? Where is Despina? She knows how to open it."

"Alas, lord! I found it in the door. An evil fate has overtaken Despina."

"Holy Basil! what do you mean, girl? Call Mariora, then. What has happened? Will you fumble to all eternity?"

"Lord, there is no one to call." In spite of herself, tears were very near Danaë's voice. "There came men——"

"Men? what men? What did they do? Open the door, girl! What of my wife—of the Lady?"

"The little lord is safe, lord."

The words were spoken very low, and they were downed by the noise of a vigorous assault on the door. Evidently Prince Romanos had called the sentry to his help, for the stout planks gave way with a crash, and he burst in. "Where is your mistress?" he cried fiercely, seizing Danaë by the shoulder.

"She lies there, lord. She has not moved," she faltered.

"A doctor! fetch a doctor!" cried Prince Romanos to the sentry, "and, Christos," to the guard who was holding his horse, "the police—no, the chief of police. He is to come alone. Show me where your mistress is, Eurynomé. You say she has fainted?"

He passed the bodies of the two old women without heeding them, dragging Danaë with him at a pace which almost whirled her off her feet, until he released her with a suddenness that sent her staggering among the bushes. He had seen the rigid red figure on the grass. For the moment Danaë thought he would have fled, unable to face it, but he pulled himself together and went on, treading with fearful, uncertain steps. He was kneeling beside his dead wife, laying a hand on heart and brow, assuring himself of the awful truth, and then he broke into a wild lamentation which thrilled Danaë to the core, for its rough island Greek showed her the primitive Striote under the mask of the denationalised European.

"Alas, Olimpia, my fairest! Dear love of my heart, whom I wooed under the orange-trees in the twilight, who shouldst have sat beside me on the throne! Beloved, thou hast left me too soon; thou, who didst lay a healing hand upon my tortured brow, shouldst have worn with me the diadem of New Rome. Like a shy proud fawn wast thou when I first beheld thee, fearing to hear of the love to which thine own heart leaped out in response; like the stricken deer wounded by the huntsman do I see thee now. In thy glory did I behold thee last, beautiful exceedingly, worthily apparelled—not Helen's self could have excelled thee. But now thou liest low; cruel Charon has snatched thee from me, who wast my eyes, my soul, my life, my all——"

Danaë could bear no more. Her brother was unconscious of her presence, and she burst through the bushes and ran across the lawn to the spot where she had left Janni. Catching him up, she hastened back and tried to put him into his father's arms.

"See, lord, you are not left wholly desolate. There is yet one to love and that loves you."

"Take the child away!" said Prince Romanos angrily.

"But, lord, your little son!"

"Take him away. What do I care for him? It is his mother I want—not a baby that cannot speak." He turned again to the Lady's body. "Sweet, hast thou no word for thy lover? How has he sinned that those lips are closed and silent which have so often overflowed with words of love? But no, it is neither his sin nor thine, but the iniquity of those who sought to strike him through thee——"

A howl from Janni, whom the indignant and perplexed Danaë had been vainly endeavouring to console for his father's repulse, broke into the lament.

"Will you take that child away, girl? Is this a scene for his young eyes? Take him to the nursery, and keep him there until I send for you."

"You bid me go, lord, and take with me the little lord?" demanded Danaë, thrilling with outraged pride and affection on behalf of her little charge.

"Yes, go, in the name of the All-Holy Mother of God, and leave me alone with my dead!"

"I go, lord!" said Danaë impressively, but she doubted whether he even heard her. He was bending over his wife again.

"Most beloved, open those lips but for an instant, and tell me to whose cursed treachery I owe this blow. Let thy spirit visit me at night, my beautiful one, and keep vengeance ever in my mind. If there be one left alive of those who slew thee——"

The familiar voice, raised in a half chant, grew faint in Danaë's ears. She was stalking majestically across the grass, hushing the protesting Janni in her arms, and listening greedily for some word of recall. No one should say she had stolen away secretly, but if she was driven out she would go. His son, his heir, was nothing to Prince Romanos in comparison with the dead body of the schismatic woman! He would leave him without protection in the house, till the conspirators returned and finished their deadly work! Very well, then; he should see no more of Janni until he had learnt to value him properly. Danaë would at once save the child and punish the father. Mingled with her lofty resolves was perhaps a vague idea of averting retribution. The death of the Lady was without doubt in some measure due to her; she would blot out her guilt by saving the Lady's son.

Prince Romanos did not call her back, and when she looked round from the edge of the wood he was still kneeling over his wife's body. Her heart hardened against him, and she picked up the bundle she had left under the trees and went on as far as the wall. She climbed up easily enough, and dropped the bundle over, then returned for Janni, and wound him closely in her shawl. The ground outside was happily soft, for on this side the garden adjoined a large piece of land belonging to the Prince which he had planted with trees, with the intention of making it into a park in future, and she was able to let herself down safely by her hands. She had often longed to explore this piece of woodland, and when it was once crossed she would be well away from the city. She started very happily, beguiling the way by conversation with Janni, though after a time it occurred to her that there was nothing very interesting in the rows of young trees and the growing shrubs. Janni was heavy to carry, too, when it was not a question of merely rambling about the garden, but she held on stoutly, sustained by her very mingled motives.

Sitting down at last to rest at the top of a hill up which she had laboured with considerable difficulty, she looked back over the way she had come. The sea in the distance gave her a moment's wild longing for Strio, but there would be no safety there for Janni, she saw that now. Rather must she look nearer, to the new Therma, with its streets of tall white houses crossing and recrossing with mathematical regularity, and the Emathian flag flying over the Palace, the position of which she could easily distinguish now, dominating the broad road leading from the great square called the Place de l'Europe Unie. But between the Palace and herself was the villa among its woods, with her brother mourning over the tragedy she had helped to bring upon him, and she wondered hopelessly how the tangle was ever to be unravelled, how she could keep Janni in her own charge, and yet see him restored to his proper position. But her desultory musings were suddenly focussed into a keen and pressing anxiety. Among the young trees between her and the wall of the garden something was moving. At first it looked like a bright bird flying low, but as she watched it she realised that it was the gay fez and golden tassel of a man of the Prince's guard. There was no need to ask herself who it could be. Petros had guessed that she had fled with the child, had tracked her path, and was following hard on her heels, that he might finish his evil work, and make sure of the victim who had been snatched from him in the morning.

Terror lent wings to Danaë's tired feet, and catching up Janni, she hurried on down the hill. There was no time to look for villages, and what village would shelter her against the demand of a servant of the Prince? She stumbled along wildly, looking hopelessly round for some hiding-place that might enable her to evade the pursuer. But he had reached the top of the hill while she was still full in view, and his shouts of "Eurynomé! stop, girl!" his adjurations and threats of vengeance, came to her faintly on the wind, though she strove to shut her ears to them. Tired as she was, and burdened with the child, she had no hope of outdistancing him, but she struggled on, though it seemed to her that he was now so close that she could hear his heavy footsteps. Then, as she reached the foot of the hill, and an artfully contrived glade opened before her, she saw one single chance of safety, for there were the figures of men and horses under the trees. Two men wearing "European" clothes, and evidently not Emathians, were walking up and down impatiently, as though waiting for somebody, and behind them were four horses under the charge of two armed guards. There was no doubt in Danaë's mind as to the identity of the strangers. They must be the

Englishmen whom Prince Romanos had told Despina he was to meet and accompany on their journey—and therefore they were an additional danger. The single subject on which Danaë and the two old women were in agreement was that of the preposterous baselessness of the claims of the schismatic Englishman who dared to put himself forward as heir of the Eastern Empire by right of direct descent from the Emperor John Theophanis. When the Orthodox position was triumphantly vindicated by the election of Prince Romanos, who could trace his lineage only in the female line, to the throne of Emathia, he had relegated the rival claimant, so Danaë firmly believed, to a species of honourable imprisonment in a remote part of the principality. Here he could amuse himself by playing the ruler under strict supervision, and was even allowed to visit Therma on asking permission. Judging him by herself, however, Danaë had no faith in his gratitude for this considerate treatment, and saw in him merely another menace to Janni's safety if he discovered who he was. But the danger of Petros hot on her heels was more pressing, since she had always understood that Englishmen were easily to be deceived. Yet how, in any case, was Petros to be kept from publishing the perilous truth? Her quick scheming brain worked at tremendous pressure during the last agitated minutes of her stumbling run.

"Come back, girl! Will you ruin everything?" she heard Petros cry, as he made a final attempt to head her off, and only found himself at the top of a slope too steep to descend. He was obliged to go round, and she reached the two Englishmen, who had paused, astonished, in their walk, and threw herself panting at the feet of one of them, a keen hard-faced man with noticeably blue eyes.

"Mercy, lord! justice! protection!" she sobbed.

"This is Prince Theophanis, if you want to speak to him." The blue-eyed man indicated his companion, and Danaë transferred her plea to him almost mechanically, her tired arms loosing their hold of Janni, who slid to the ground and began to investigate the strangers' boots with much interest.

"Save us, lord, this poor child and me, from the evildoer who pursues us! He will tell you that he is my uncle, but it is not true. I have nothing to do with him, nothing whatever."

"Why, it is Petros!" said Prince Theophanis in surprise, as the guardsman made his appearance, hot and angry. "Do you say that this girl is your niece, friend Petros?"

"Why should I say it, lord, when it is not true? Thank the saints, she is no kin of mine!"

He stopped abruptly, and Danaë could have cried aloud with joy. She had Petros in her power; he was afraid of her, or he would have contradicted her words. He was waiting for her to tell her story; obviously, then, he did not wish these strangers to know of his treachery to his master, and she might use her hold over him to save Janni. With an admirable transport of gratitude, she flung herself down and kissed the ground before the Prince's feet.

"Ah, lord, what power is yours since even this wicked wretch must tell the truth in your presence! You will permit your suppliant to lay her woes before you?"

"Tell me your trouble, by all means, if I can help you, but don't kneel there. What is your name?"

"Lord, it is meet for me to kneel at your gracious feet, and this child with me." She captured Janni's hands, and made him embrace the Prince's boots, then sat up and poured forth her tale. "Lord, my name is Kalliopé Vlasso, and I dwell in Therma with my sister and her husband, who is in the Prince's guard—a comrade of that ruffian there. He it was who led my brother-in-law into the love of strong drink—not *mastika*, lord, but *raki* and such horrible things—so that he would come home and frighten and grievously abuse my sister and me. But last night he was like one possessed of a demon, and after beating us both, he dragged my unhappy sister out of the house by the hair of her head, and beat and kicked her till she died—the neighbours all looking on and fearing to interfere. Then, terrified lest he should kill us also, I snatched up the child, my nephew, and fled away, out of the street and the city, seeking only safety. But why this evil wretch should have pursued us I know not, save that it can be for no good reason."

"You come from the islands, as he does, and he meant to take care of you, perhaps?" suggested the blue-eyed man. Danaë repudiated the suggestion with terrified vigour.

"Nay, lord, I have never been out of Therma in my life. I speak but as the people in our street speak."

"Well, friend Petros, what have you to say?" asked Prince Theophanis. "Why were you chasing the girl?"

"For no pleasure of my own, I assure you, lord," responded Petros, with excellent indignation. "The ungrateful minx may say what she likes, but I came merely because I was sworn by the holy cross to do it, and I wish I had never promised. All the morning I was busy helping—busy, I mean—" he paused, embarrassed.

"Helping the murderer to escape, I suppose?" said the blue-eyed man, and he brightened up.

"There is no deceiving the Lord Glafko, I know that of old. Well, lord, my unhappy comrade found means to entreat me to seek out this girl and the child, his son, and see that they did not starve, so I tracked them as far as this. Your excellencies can see that compassion alone made me do it. The girl has the tongue of a demon, and the brat is too young to work. I have nowhere to put them, but I came, and you see my reward."

"The girl will be wanted as a witness, surely?" said the Prince.

Petros shrugged his shoulders. "Oh, as to that, there will be witnesses enough," he said. "But it will relieve me of her. The police will clap her into prison and keep her safe."

"My Prince!" cried Danaë frantically, "you will not let them throw me into prison, and rob me of the child entrusted to me with her last breath by my dying sister?"

She stopped abruptly, for the dramatic instinct was leading her into possible pitfalls, but the two Englishmen were consulting apart for a moment, and had not noticed the slip. An Emathian prison, though better than in Roumi days, was not an ideal training-school for a respectable girl.

"The place is overrun with servants already," said the blue-eyed man.

"One more would not make much difference. Zoe might find work for her in the nursery, and the child is about your boy's age. Make a good playfellow for him."

"H'm! we had better leave that to Zoe," remarked the blue-eyed man, with distinct hesitation. "A child from the slums of Therma———"

"Lord," interposed Danaë tearfully, aware that her case was being discussed, "you will not give me up to him?"

"See, lord," said Petros, with the air of one conferring a vast benefit, "why not take the girl to serve in your house? She has been taught to work, and a good beating now and then will keep her up to it. If her witness should be needed, I will get a letter written to say so, but I should be glad to let my poor comrade know that she and the child were safely away from the city, and not getting into mischief."

"We will see," said Prince Theophanis. "Will you come to Klaustra, Kalliopé, to serve my wife, or my sister, the Lord Glafko's wife, as they shall decide? You can bring the child with you, of course."

Danaë bowed her head again at his feet. "Your handmaid could ask no better, lord," she said.

CHAPTER VI.
THE SPY.

"YOU understand, then," said Prince Theophanis to Petros, "that I will take the girl into my service for the present, but that if she is required as a witness, the police have only to let me know, and the Princess will see that she is sent down under proper escort to Therma?"

"The Lady Eirene will hardly thank you for burdening her with such trash, lord," said Petros, with the familiarity of old acquaintance; "but my poor comrade will kiss the *icons* for you night and morning, in gratitude for your protection granted to his son. When the matter has been forgotten, he will obtain pardon from the Lord Romanos, and come and claim the child."

"Ah, by the bye, what has happened to Prince Romanos?" asked the man called Glafko quickly. "He was to join us here at three, and we have waited nearly two hours."

"Truly, lord, I know not. I have not seen my master since the early morning, when I was thrown from my horse while in attendance upon him, and he graciously excused me from duty for the rest of the day."

Danaë listened with delight. Petros was a worthy fellow-conspirator, after all. He was taking pains to round off her story neatly, and provide against any chance allusion to the fact of his having been seen out in this direction.

"You pursued the girl all the way from Therma after getting a bad fall?" said the blue-eyed man. "Truly, you are a stout-hearted fellow, friend Petros!"

Petros looked down, with admirably simulated confusion. "Perhaps I may have been glad to get the day to myself, lord," he admitted. "There was the promise to my poor comrade—and I could not broach the matter to my master, lest he should feel compelled to hand over to the police one whom he would much prefer to protect."

"Exactly. Prince Romanos knows nothing." But Danaë detected a mocking undercurrent in the blue-eyed man's speech. He was suspicious about something, she saw, and she wished she had not told that purposeless lie about the islands. However, since it was told, it must be maintained.

"If I might venture to offer counsel, it would be that the Lord Theophanis and the Lord Glafko should ride on to the end of to-day's short stage, and wait for the Lord Romanos at the inn," said Petros respectfully. "Since he is late, he will doubtless ride fast thither by the road, but if not, I shall meet him in my return to Therma, and can tell him where they are."

"I suppose we can't do better," said Prince Theophanis, beckoning to the guards to bring up the horses.

"Many be your years, friend Petraki!" said Danaë triumphantly, prudence forgotten for the moment.

"Wait, my lady, only wait!" he responded, with heartfelt warmth. The blue-eyed man called Glafko was watching them closely, so that no more was possible.

"Logofet," said the Prince, as the guards came up, "you had better walk, and let the girl ride your horse as far as the inn. To-morrow we can find her a place on one of the mules."

The man called Logofet obeyed without demur, much to Danaë's astonishment, for she had expected nothing better than to trudge alongside holding a stirrup. The guards were Thracian Emathians, she knew by their dress and equipment, and she was prepared to regard them, as Exarchists, as rather worse than ordinary schismatics, but they seemed to treat women better than the staunch Patriarchists to whom she was accustomed. She was just making up her prejudiced little mind that this was due to poorness of spirit, when she was forcibly undeceived. She had never mounted a horse before—there were none in Strio—and when Logofet swung her into the saddle, it was with such unnecessary force that she went over on the other side. Happily his comrade was there, and caught her.

"Fool!" he growled, as he restored her to her place. "If the Prince had seen thee——!"

"The devil fly away with the Prince and the girl too!" snarled Logofet. "If I had known we were to be ruled by women, I would never have joined thee, Gavril."

"Peace! thou art a wild savage from the hills," said Gavril contemptuously, "and both the Prince and I can do very well without thee, if the honour of serving him and Glafko is not enough for thee. There! Glafko looks round. Thou hast delayed us both with thy foolishness, and we shall not again be chosen to attend the Prince."

"So much the better!" muttered Logofet, inciting the horse to a disquieting prance as he led it. "Hold tight, girl! Is it not enough for thee to be taken to Klaustra, where kitchen-wenches must be treated like queens, that thou shouldst try to dismount every step of the way?"

Horribly frightened, and much encumbered by the necessity of holding Janni firmly on her knee, Danaë did her best to obey, but the horse's movements under Logofet's leading made her perfectly sick with terror, until she cried out a despairing appeal to be allowed to walk. The Prince and his brother-in-law turned instantly, and Logofet received a sharp rebuke, while Gavril was ordered to lead both horses. Thus relieved, Danaë succeeded in maintaining her position for an hour or more, until, as dusk was falling, they reached a wayside inn, the inner courtyard of which was full of horses and mules and guards and servants. Those of the latter who wore the livery of Prince Romanos were separating themselves and their beasts from the rest, so that there was much confusion.

"No sign of him yet, Wylie," said the Prince to his companion.

"No, but here is a messenger, I imagine," as one of the Therma guardsmen swaggered up with a note.

"He says he can't come—sudden severe personal bereavement," said the Prince, after reading it.

"Ah, he's playing us false, as I expected. Well, let us get rid of his fellows, and then I will commend Miss Kalliopé Vlasso to the special care of the landlord's wife. I mean to keep an eye on that young lady."

* * * * * * * *

"What maggot have you got in your head about this luckless girl?" asked the Prince, when he and his brother-in-law met at supper. They spoke English, as was usual when they were alone together.

"I presume that even you can see there's something remarkably fishy about her. Why did she and friend Petros, after breathing such violent mutual hostility, fall like lambs into the same story, and back each other up?"

"Because it was true, I suppose. But I see. You think they were both in the plot, and that the hostility was only a blind?"

"And very badly carried out. What makes me certain is the girl's denying that she comes from the islands. If ever I heard an island voice, it's hers."

"But her ancestors may have come from there."

"But she has the type of face. Look here, we'll ask Armitage when he comes. If he doesn't say it is an island type——"

"Yes, but if he does, what does it prove?"

"That she and Petros are acquainted, and probably related, in spite of her strenuous denials."

"I suppose you mean me to understand that she was an accomplice in the sister's murder, and that we are helping her to fly from justice?"

"By Jove! I shouldn't wonder," cried Wylie. "No, I hadn't thought of that, though it did cross my mind that the philanthropic Petros was in all probability the murderous husband of the story. We are certainly introducing a novel element into our home circle."

"But that's absurd. We won't take her with us."

"What are we to do—leave her here? That's exactly what I don't want to do. You don't see my point. What will you take that there has been no murder at all?"

"I don't see what you mean."

"Well, listen. I will send a man back to Therma to-night to bring out the earliest issues of the papers in the morning. If the girl was concerned in the affair the fact will have come out by this time. By her account, the thing was public enough. But if there is no murder in the papers at all?"

"Because it has been hushed up?"

"No, because it never happened. Because the story was ingeniously contrived to furnish a reason for the girl's foisting herself on us, and going with us to Klaustra."

"But why burden herself with the child?"

"To make it look more natural, I suppose. How can I tell what's at the back of their minds? But you can see that Romanos has contrived to make us introduce of our own accord the spy who is to keep an eye on us."

"We send her back with compliments, I suppose?"

"Not a bit of it. We take her home—the little serpent!—and cherish her in our collective bosom, keeping a sharp look-out as to her possibilities of stinging. In other words, we'll put her where she can see everything—in the nursery, if I can get Zoe to agree—and take good care that she tells nothing but the truth. The more she lives in our very midst, the easier it will be to supervise her correspondence and her comings and goings."

"I don't see making things easy for her, Wylie."

"Why, what harm can she do, provided she tells the truth? We have nothing to be ashamed of. And surely it's better to have our spy labelled, than not to know who could be trusted and who not?"

"Wylie, I don't like it. The child—it occurs to me—what if there is some design against your boy?"

Colonel Wylie's face showed signs of wavering for a moment, then regained its decisive lines. "Can't help that, Maurice. If Zoe and I and Linton can't look after the child, why, we deserve to lose him. At any rate, there's no plan of substitution, for this baby would be a puny creature beside him. But I'll warn Zoe, of course, and get her help in keeping a watch on the girl. We must sift this thing to the bottom, for it's all part and parcel of the disloyalty which I am convinced Romanos is plotting, and which you won't believe in."

"And if the papers confirm the girl's story in the morning?"

"Why shouldn't he have had the whole thing made up and inserted? No, perhaps that's a little too much. I will beg the young woman's pardon if it is so."

But the papers were entirely on Wylie's side in the morning, containing not a word of any such tragedy as Danaë had described. On the other hand, the landlord's wife beckoned him mysteriously aside, and expressed it as her opinion that there was something very queer about that girl who said she was going to Klaustra to wait on the Princesses. She had cried out in the night so loud as to wake the servant-girls who slept with her, and one of them who understood Greek said that her cries were all of knives and blood, and her own share in some dreadful deed. The others had teased her to tell them about it, but she refused to say a word, and they were now sending her to Coventry in consequence. The news was perplexing, for Wylie could scarcely believe the girl to be such a practised plotter as even to support her story by the simulation of nightly terrors. In the faint hope of clearing up the mystery, he tried to take her by surprise.

"Why did you call out in the night that your sister's death was your fault, Kalliopé?" he asked her.

The questioning of the girls had prepared Danaë for further curiosity, and she answered demurely, "Alas, lord! it is true. I stirred up my sister to scold her husband when he came home drunk, or she would have received him meekly, and he would not have killed her."

He was not prepared with further questions, and she retired in mild triumph, to take her place with Janni on one of the mules. Wylie's obvious suspicions put her on her mettle. She was far too clever to make palpable efforts to disarm them, but set herself to learn all she could of her new surroundings, that she might provide against further attempts to take her by surprise. From some of the guards who could speak Greek she discovered, much to her astonishment, that the position of the Theophanis family was by no means that of dependants upon Prince Romanos. They were the recognised rulers of the northern or Slav portion of the principality, raising troops and administering justice, though in subjection to the Therma Government. Danaë's assertion of their inferior lot was laughed to scorn, and she was informed, to her great indignation, that the brunt of the struggle for freedom in the Hagiamavra peninsula, the glory of which she had always believed to be her brother's peculiar possession, had been borne by them. Why they had allowed themselves to be defeated in the *plébiscite* that followed, when their followers would gladly have manipulated the voting in their favour, no one quite knew, but it was understood that they had weighty and cunning reasons for accepting temporarily a subordinate place, from which they would emerge as undisputed masters of the whole of Emathia. Danaë's heart leaped when she heard this. To the glory of saving Janni should be added that of unmasking the plot which threatened her brother's rule, and she would return to Therma doubly a deliverer.

Information regarding the family life of her hereditary foes was equally easy to obtain. Prince Theophanis and the Lord Glafko were inseparable friends, neither taking any action without consulting the other. It was shrewdly suspected that this complete unity was not altogether to the taste of the Lady Eirene, the Prince's wife. Her title to represent the Imperial line was equal, if not superior, to his, and she was believed to advocate a much more energetic policy than that pursued by her husband and his friend. But much less had been heard of her views and wishes since the death of her little son at the time of the apparent collapse of the family fortunes, and the guards considered that she had learnt to accept the inferior place proper to a childless woman. Her sister-in-law, the Lady Zoe, ranked far higher in the estimation of the Emathians, since in the veins of her son ran the blood not only of the Theophanis Emperors but of their adored Glafko, whom they handsomely credited with having led them to victory in Hagiamavra. To Danaë's ears this feeling supplied only the crowning proof of the impiety and heresy of the Slavs among the Emathians. They could welcome a mere ordinary Englishman, schismatic to the backbone, without one drop of royal blood, as the ancestor of their future Emperors! Little did they know that the child she held in her arms could trace his descent through a succession of Despots of Strio and Venetian Patricians of unbroken Orthodoxy, until—— A chill seized her as she remembered Janni's schismatic mother, but after all, that mother was dead, and the obvious course was to declare that she had been Orthodox from her youth up.

A new idea for Janni's future suggested itself to Danaë's active mind on the journey. The child had taken a great fancy to Prince Theophanis, and held out his arms whenever he came near—an invitation which the bereaved father could never neglect. The jealous pang which seized Danaë at first soon gave place to approval. If Prince Theophanis should wish to adopt Janni! The ironical prospect of his bringing up his rival's son to supplant himself, and unconsciously destroying the prospects of his own nephew, gave her the keenest delight. She spared no pains to deepen the fondness of the man and the child for each other, but it was impossible to find out whether the Prince had any such thought as she desired in his mind.

"Ah, lord, take care of him!" she said impulsively one day, as he bent to lift Janni before him on his horse. "He is greater than he seems."

A whimsical smile crossed the Prince's face. "And are you also greater than you seem, Kalliopé?" he asked her.

"I am only a poor servant-girl, lord. Do not mock me!" she entreated, covering her very real confusion by a hasty retreat.

"There's something mighty queer about her, whatever she is," said Wylie, looking after her. "If she has been coached in all she says, the plot is too deep for my poor brain."

"It was awfully good of the plotters to send us this little chap, at any rate," said the Prince. "I wonder whether Eirene could bring herself to take to him?"

"I don't know whether she could, but she certainly won't. No, I beg your pardon, Maurice; I had no right to say that. When she sees how fond you are of him——"

"That would make no difference," said Maurice sharply.

"Well, we can't tell. Don't force the idea on her. She may think of it for herself. I'll take the little chap and Kalliopé straight to Zoe when we get in, so that your wife can just come in and see them casually."

"Thanks, Wylie. You and Zoe are really frightfully good——"

"Oh, shut up, old man! I thought we agreed long ago that there was to be no more of that sort of thing. It's little enough we can do to make things easier for you—and your wife, and we're heartily glad to do it."

Danaë, unaware of these arrangements, was rather taken aback on her arrival at the Konak at Klaustra. The place had been the abode of the Roumi Governor in the days before liberation, and had been adapted to European use by the erection of a second storey on three sides of the hollow square of buildings surrounding the paved court. The central portion, facing the gateway, was evidently the residence of the Prince, and a lady in black stood at the top of the steps, with a background of gaily dressed servants. She came forward to welcome her husband, and bestowed also a greeting—not a specially cordial one—on Wylie, who saluted in return, and reined his horse round as soon as Prince and Princess

Theophanis had gone indoors. Danaë was preparing to dismount and follow them, but he told her hastily to stay where she was, and turned the mule. The buildings on the left-hand side of the square formed another dwelling, of less pretensions, and here also a lady was waiting on the steps. Before Wylie could dismount she ran down to him, and Danaë watched their greeting with curiosity and interest. The Lady Zoe was not beautiful, nor particularly young, but she was unaccountably reminded of another couple she would fain have forgotten—Janni's mother and Prince Romanos, now sundered for ever through her instrumentality.

"And where is the autocrat?" inquired Wylie gaily of his wife.

"Just inside. I would not let Linton bring him out here, lest Maurice should see—and be reminded——"

"Of course. Let's go in and pay our respects. Oh, by the bye, Zoe, what do you say to starting an understudy for him? We have picked up rather a jolly little waif of about his age, and brought him along with his nurse."

"Graham! what an extraordinary thing to do! A child that you know nothing of? Show him to me at once. He looks clean, at any rate," she admitted reluctantly, "and he has rather a dear little face. Are you sure he hasn't been anywhere where there's infection?"

"I can only say that he hasn't come out with anything between Therma and here. The girl is tremendously careful of him, too, but I don't know anything about his surroundings before we got him. It is a queer business altogether."

"Lady, my little lord is tired and hungry," said Danaë piteously, as Janni's eyes began to wrinkle up, and his mouth to open, while the lady addressed as Zoe stood undecided.

"Poor little man! so he is." She took him into her arms, and the impending yell collapsed as if by magic. "He shall share Harold's supper, at any rate. Come in, nurse. What is your name? Kalliopé? Have you had charge of him long?"

"Since he was born, my lady," lied Danaë with her usual hardihood, resisting the impulse to snatch her darling from the stranger's arms, and following meekly up the steps. At the top stood an elderly English maid holding a child of about Janni's age, and dark-haired like him, but more strongly built, and with his father's deep blue eyes.

"Hasn't he grown?" demanded the mother ecstatically, as Wylie took the child, with a kind word to the maid. "He gets more like you every day. You must see it."

"Never was such a likeness, sir," corroborated the nurse dutifully. "And so knowing, bless his little heart!"

"Here's a companion for him. Let's see what they think of one another," said Wylie, waiving judiciously the question of likeness. "Put yours down here, Zoe. Nonsense! why shouldn't they like it?"

His wife had demurred, and as it proved, with reason, for when the two children were set face to face upon the divan, their first acknowledgment of each other's presence, after one horrified stare, was a simultaneous yell. Danaë flew to the rescue of her charge, and the English nurse of hers, and Wylie stood astonished, while his wife laughed.

"They will make friends over their bread and milk," she said. "Come, Kalliopé."

Mounting the steps to the roof of the original buildings, they reached the modern rooms, fitted up in English style, which formed the home of the Wylies. Danaë glanced round with something like awe at the appointments of the nursery. She had thought Janni's nursery at the villa "European" in the extreme, but it had been nothing like this. Wylie brought in a second high chair from another room, and the two nurses were speedily engaged in feeding their respective charges with bread and milk. Very quickly Danaë observed, to her confusion, that Janni's table manners were not producing a favourable impression. He grabbed at the spoon, filled his mouth too full, and choked, to the great scandal of his neighbour opposite, who commented on his behaviour obviously, though unintelligibly, in the nurse's ear.

"There, there, Master Harold! he don't know no better," she said reprovingly, turning to the parents to add admiringly, "Did you ever see anybody so quick to notice things, ma'am?"

CHAPTER VII.
THE EDUCATION OF KALLIOPÉ.

BEFORE the meal was over, Danaë became aware that the number of the spectators was increased. Prince and Princess Theophanis had come in quietly, and were watching the children as they ate.

"Not a bad little chap, is he?" said Maurice at last.

His wife shrugged her shoulders. "Not a bad-looking child, certainly. But no look of race about him."

Danaë understood the tone, if not the words, and bristled angrily in Janni's defence. But the Prince was speaking again. "You wouldn't like us to take charge of him, I suppose, Eirene, as Zoe and Wylie have their own?"

"Maurice!" She turned upon him with poignant reproach. "To take Constantine's place?"

"No, nonsense! No one could ever take Con's place. But I thought it might be an interest for you, to have a child about the house."

"What interest could there be for me in any ordinary child like that? He would not be a descendant of John Theophanis."

The name caught Danaë's attention, and she looked up so sharply that Wylie noticed it. "What do you know of John Theophanis, Kalliopé?" he asked her in Greek.

"He was the great Roman Emperor, lord, the blessed martyr from whom the Lord Romanos is descended," she replied. Princess Theophanis turned quickly.

"The Lord Romanos!" she cried. "Girl, that upstart can only trace his descent from the Emperor's daughter. Here in this room are the true descendants of John Theophanis, my husband and his sister descended from his elder son, I from the younger. And this child—" her voice grew harsh—"is the sole representative of the line in his generation. Do you understand? Tell me what I have said."

"That you are all descended from John Theophanis, lady," said Danaë sullenly, "and that this child is his rightful heir." But her hands were on Janni's shoulders, though her defiant eyes wandered from little Harold's face to that of the Princess.

"My dear Eirene!" said Zoe, laughing uncomfortably, for there was a sense of something electric in the atmosphere. "Is it really necessary to require a confession of the Theophanis faith from every wretched servant-girl who comes into the house? What does it signify whether she believes in our claims or not?"

"If you are inclined to belittle your child's rights, Zoe, I am not," said the Princess coldly. Evidently her husband felt the moment was not propitious for urging his wishes, for the matter dropped. But when Zoe and her husband were alone together, Wylie showed that he had not forgotten it.

"That girl has some closer association with the name of John Theophanis than merely her Prince's descent, Zoe," he said. "Find out all you can about her—without letting her see that you are cross-questioning her, if possible. I don't know what to make of her."

"But what is there suspicious about her, Graham? She seems devoted to the child."

"Yes, but the whole thing is so queer. I had better tell you exactly what we know of her." He related the story of their first meeting, and mentioned the points which had struck him at various times as suspicious, his wife listening with close attention.

"But I don't see how it fits in," she said at last. "If she is a spy, why hamper herself with the child?"

"That's what Maurice said. And then it struck him afterwards—I don't want to frighten you, Zoe—that there might be some design against Harold. But I don't see it. Still, surely the very purposelessness of bringing a baby with her would tend to make her less likely to be suspected?"

"But what design could there be against Harold? Graham, what have you heard? You must tell me."

"My dear girl, I have heard nothing. It is simply that there were the usual rumours in Therma that Romanos was trying to negociate a royal alliance, and I suppose it is possible that the interested parties might wish to get rid of any other aspirants to the throne."

"By kidnapping Harold?" She paused in sheer horror, then laughed. "You mean that they hope to deceive me by leaving that poor little shrimp in his place? I think that is really rather far-fetched. At any rate, I promise you that Linton and I will keep a very wide-open eye on Janni and his nurse, and if any wiles can get the truth out of her, it shall come to light. Then you still think Prince Romanos is not to be trusted?"

"His whole manner was most unsatisfactory. Putting off and putting off, slipping out of things and drawing red herrings across the trail. Of course, if the story of the projected Scythian marriage is true, one can understand it——"

Zoe interrupted him. "I don't think you need be afraid of that, Graham. Think how long the rumours have been going on. Besides—I can't give you my authority, because it was told me in confidence—but I have every reason to believe that no such marriage can possibly take place."

"Then the mystery is deeper than ever—unless he is coquetting with the idea in the hope of getting some good out of it. But in that case he ought to let us into the secret. What are you to do with a man who won't play fair to his own side?"

"But suppose you disapproved of the secret? It seems to me that he is very wise—from his own point of view. But it is horribly tiresome, of course—not being able to trust him, I mean. Oh, Graham, what about Eirene's girdle? Were you able to get it back?"

"No, unfortunately. Everything seemed all right and above-board. The wall might never have been disturbed since the day she hid the thing, but there was merely an empty hole. And one can't help remembering, you know, that the Scythian Imperial family would do anything to lay their hands on the Girdle of Isidora. But then, according to you, there's nothing in that idea——"

"Nothing at all, I firmly believe. But I think Prince Romanos is capable of a good deal in other ways—which makes me not at all anxious to have a tool of his in the house. So I shall watch pretty keenly to catch Kalliopé tripping."

"Begging your pardon, ma'am, might I speak to you a minute?" said Linton on the threshold, and Zoe joined her. She had a heap of little clothes on her arm. "I'm sorry to disturb you, ma'am, but I thought I should like you just to see these. They are what was just taken off of that little boy Johnny. That nurse of his is singing him to sleep now—a thing I never have allowed in my nursery, nor never will—and he as naughty as possible, a fine contrast to Master Harold; so I've put his bed in her room."

"But the things look very nice, Linton—and very clean," said Zoe, fingering them in some perplexity.

"That's just it, ma'am. Look at the stuff—and the trimmings. And all English-made—leastways European, as they call it. It's my belief, ma'am, that child has been stolen, and from a good home, too."

Zoe gasped. The variety of explanations of which Kalliopé and her proceedings were capable was becoming bewildering. Under Linton's stern eye she recovered herself quickly.

"Well, Linton, we must take great care of him, and make sure that she does not carry him away anywhere else, while we watch the papers and see if any child has been lost. I will talk to Kalliopé, and try to find out something more about her, but we must be careful not to let her see she is suspected."

Unfortunately, Linton was not a person who found it easy to disguise her feelings, when they were of an unflattering character. Her whole demeanour, to Danaë's quick eye, was instinct with suspicion, and the girl improved the opportunity given her by the night to put her defences in order. The next morning, while Linton was busy in the nursery, Zoe came as usual to sit on the wide verandah when her house-keeping duties were done, to look after Harold, and naturally found Danaë there, keeping an eye on both children. After trying in vain to lead up to things gradually, she asked a direct question.

"Why does Janni wear European clothes, Kalliopé?"

The girl turned with a flash of bright eyes and white teeth. "I wondered when you would notice it, my lady. My sister was in the service of a great Frank lady before her marriage, and the lady has always sent Jannaki the clothes that her own little boy has outgrown."

"He must grow very fast. The clothes look nearly new."

"So much the better for Janni, my lady."

"Why do you call Janni 'my little lord'—*kyriaki mou?*" asked Zoe, changing the conversation abruptly.

"But I don't, lady. Why should I?"

"You called him so to me last night." Zoe's voice had hardened, imperceptibly to herself. Danaë gave her one glance out of her black eyes, then laughed confusedly.

"It was only foolishness, lady. Does he not wear the little lord's clothes? And we are proud of a first-born son in—" she had all but said "in Strio," but substituted just in time—"in the islands. He is often called the little lord by the women."

"Then you do come from the islands? Why did you tell my husband you had never been there?"

"Because I never have, my lady. I have always lived in Therma, but my family come from the islands. I suppose that is why that wretch Petros sought us out," she added hardily. "Being island-born himself, doubtless he wished to hear the island-talk again."

Zoe reflected for a moment. The explanation was glib enough, but it did not altogether satisfy her. "Do you always tell the truth, Kalliopé?" she asked boldly.

"O my lady, I never told a lie in my life!" replied the unblushing Danaë, with virtuous indignation. Her hostess abandoned the unpromising field of inquiry, and began to talk about the children.

"They are very much of an age," she said.

"But the Lord Harold is much fatter," said Danaë politely, yet with an air that implied size was by no means everything.

"How well you have caught his name, Kalliopé! Have you ever heard it before?" Danaë's eyes were uncomprehending, but she declined to give herself away by answering, and Zoe went on. "His first name is Maurice, after my brother, but we could not have two Maurices, so we called him Harold, after a dear friend of ours who nearly lost his life in trying to help us in Hagiamavra. Sometimes we call him Childe Harold, to distinguish him. You have heard of Byron's poem?"

Any other Greek girl would have kindled to enthusiasm at the name of Byron, but Danaë remained woefully perplexed, though she muttered, in a hopeless attempt to save appearances, that she knew the poem well. Then, perceiving that she had made a blunder, she dashed into a bold confidence.

"Lady, I will tell you a great secret. I feared at first, but now I know that I can trust you, since you received my Jannaki kindly, and gave him a place with your own child. Once I told the Lord Theophanis that the child was greater than he seemed, which made him laugh, and doubtless the Lord Glafko believed I was speaking falsely. But it is true. Janni is not my sister's child. Her boy died, and this is the son of the great Frank lady in whose house my sister served, as I told you."

Danaë stopped suddenly. In the Lady Zoe's eyes there was a look of dawning comprehension. Was it possible that the scandals agitating Therma had reached her ears, and that she was within an inch of guessing the truth? The girl plunged wildly into further invention. "He was her youngest child, lady, and she had children enough before. She desired to make a long journey with the great lord her husband, and they did not wish to take the child, for they were to be away for two whole years. So she sent for my sister to Czarigrad, and entrusted the little lord to her, with money for his food and clothes, and started with her husband. That was how the little lord came to us."

"And how long ago was this?"

Danaë embarked on elaborate calculations with the aid of her fingers. "Eight—nine weeks, my lady."

"But you told me you had been with him from his birth!"

"Well—almost from his birth, lady," conceded Danaë pleasantly.

"And where is his mother now?"

"I know not, my lady. How can I tell?"

"But were you not to write to her?"

"Nay, my lady. Who of us could write?"

"But she could not leave her child without making some arrangement— What is her name?"

"That also I know not, lady mine. My sister knew."

"But this is absurd! No one could have been so mad. What about the money she paid to your sister?"

"It was hidden somewhere in the house, lady. Perhaps my brother-in-law found it, or Petros."

"Does Petros know anything about the Frank lady?"

"I cannot tell, my lady. Why should he?"

Zoe gave up her questioning for the moment in despair. "Then all that you told me about the clothes was false?"

"Well, it was not quite true, my lady."

"But I thought you never told lies? If you say different things on different days, which am I to believe?"

This seemed a new idea to Danaë, and she pondered it. "Whichever pleases you best, lady," she said at last.

"But what I want is the truth. Can't you understand, Kalliopé, that I prefer an unpleasant truth to a pleasant falsehood?"

"You may think so now, my lady, but you do not know," said Danaë in a tone which clearly promised Zoe immunity from unpleasant truths so far as it lay with her.

"I can't make anything of her!" Zoe told her husband afterwards. "She is very pretty, and she seems to have taken a fancy to me, but I am beginning to think you can't believe a word she says."

"Her flights of fancy are certainly surprising," agreed Wylie.

"Yes; as if any mother could be so unnatural! But meanwhile, who is the child, and what are we to do about him? And another thing, Graham: I don't believe the story of the Frank lady a bit. There is a great likeness between Kalliopé and the child—I have seen it several times. They both remind me of some one else, too, but I can't think who it is. It is most mysterious."

"Well, the likeness—if it is not a mere imagination of yours—makes it probable that the tale of the Frank lady is only invented to add to the child's importance. Otherwise——"

"You think we ought to put the whole thing into the hands of the Therma police?"

"Not while she tells a different story every day. I still think that it's to the secret police we owe her presence here at all. Therefore I should say wait a little, and see if we can arrive at any residuum of truth by the time her invention is exhausted."

"But it's so dreadful to feel that everything one asks her leads her to tell fresh falsehoods!" lamented Zoe. "She doesn't seem to have an idea that it's wrong."

This was quite true. That falsehood should be a sin—as bad as eating meat on a fast-day, or neglecting to salute an icon—was absolutely incomprehensible to Danaë. Moreover, the fact that her new acquaintances so regarded it did not in the least raise them in her estimation. She thought of them, not as occupying a pinnacle of lofty if austere morality, but as fools, and the impression was deepened by a conversation she held with Linton, who laboured faithfully to awaken her to a sense of her lamentable moral condition. They had been watching from the verandah the stream of claimants and suppliants who sought the presence of Prince Theophanis every morning, and Danaë remarked on this accessibility. So far as she could see, his guards let them enter impartially in the order of their coming, and no one obtained first place by means of a bribe.

"Well, I should think not!" cried Linton, in vigorous if colloquial Greek. "Colonel Wylie would have something to say to any man who took a bribe."

"Do the Prince and the Lord Glafko divide the presents that are brought, or does the Prince keep them all?" asked Danaë.

"Presents? what presents?"

"The presents that they will not suffer the guards to take."

Linton snorted. "You don't know what you're talking about, my girl. Neither the Prince nor my master have anything to do with presents. What is needed for the household is honestly bought and paid for, and the people are beginning to understand it."

Danaë laughed. "The great ones take their commission on the taxes, then?"

"You seem to think the Roumis are still here, Kalliopé. The taxes are collected by the Therma Government, and the Prince merely sees that it's done. And little enough gratitude he gets for all his work, and the peace and order the Colonel keeps with his police. This tumble-down old place, and nothing more."

"You would have me believe that this is all kept up upon nothing?" with open incredulity.

"The Prince spends out of his own pocket to do it."

Danaë laughed freely. "That is very fine—to talk about. The money returns to him somehow, of course. He is laying up a great store—or the ladies spend it upon jewels."

"My lady's jewels could be bought with a hundred-pound note any day," said Linton indignantly. "The Princess has a better show, but they came to her from her own family. And the one thing she prizes most of all has been stolen, and she can't get it back—a waistband with pictures of saints all over it."

"These English people are mad," was Danaë's inconsequent rejoinder. "Or else you must think I am, to expect me to believe such things. I am not a child, to be deceived with fairy tales."

She left Linton rather abruptly, and went to play with the children. It was disquieting to remember that she had brought the Girdle of Isidora under the roof of the person who considered herself its rightful owner. On the night of her arrival, she had hidden it cunningly, with the Lady's unfinished letter, inside her mattress, and now as soon as she could steal away, she went to make sure that it was safe. She would have liked to make Zoe an accomplice by entrusting it to her, but something told her that in that case the Princess Eirene would very quickly receive it again, and she pushed it sadly back into its hiding-place.

"I could bear to see my own lady wearing it," she said to herself, "but not the evil-eyed one."

For ever since her first sight of Eirene, Danaë had been convinced that she regarded little Harold with an evil eye. It was quite natural, since he stood in her own son's place, but it was also strongly to be resisted. For several days Linton and her mistress were perplexed by the overpowering smell of garlic which hung about Harold. Garlic was a forbidden delicacy in the nursery, and when Danaë felt an irresistible craving for it, she was obliged to seek the hospitality of the kitchen. But Harold's hair and pinafores were strongly scented, and the smell was obvious in the room itself. It was Wylie who at last discovered a clove of garlic placed on the lintel of the door, and Zoe, watching while Linton was out of the way, caught Danaë rubbing the child's head and shoulders with it. The offender was impenitent.

"It is to avert the evil eye," she said. "Everyone knows it is the best thing—almost infallible."

"You are never to do it in future," said Zoe.

"Then the Lord Harold will pine away and die, my lady."

"Nonsense! I won't have it, do you hear?"

"As you will, lady," reluctantly. "But at least I will say *Skordon! skordon!* [garlic] whenever the Lady Eirene comes in. I will do what I can, though that is not nearly so much good."

It was in the faint hope of breaking Danaë of some of her superstitions that Zoe began to teach her to read. She would not have suspected in the girl any desire for such an accomplishment, if she had not caught her poring diligently over a torn newspaper held upside down. Linton could read, and therefore Danaë owed it to herself to pretend to be able to do so. She received her mistress's offer without enthusiasm.

"Of course I could read as well as anyone when I was a child, but I have forgotten it," she observed airily.

But when the lessons had continued some few days, she astonished Zoe by looking up and remarking, "I told you a lie the other day, my lady. I never got beyond *theta* at school."

"Then you were at school, Kalliopé? Where?"

"Only for a week, lady—in Tortolana."

"Tortolana? But that is one of the islands—near Strio?"

"Yes, my lady." Danaë looked up smiling, and then realised the admission she had made. She grew crimson to the very tips of her ears as she bent over the book again, and Zoe bemoaned herself afterwards to her husband.

"Oh, Graham, I thought she was getting a little more truthful, and now I find she has been deceiving us all this time, and never meant to confess it! But if she does come from the islands, Petros may be her uncle after all, and there may not be a word of truth in any of her stories. What is one to believe?"

"What is one to do, rather?" said Wylie.

"Yes, about Janni. If his poor mother should be looking for him!—and yet there is nothing in any of the papers about a lost child. And if she is away on a journey, it is no good putting a notice in a Therma paper——"

"None whatever. But think, if she gets anxious because of getting no news, she will put the matter into the hands of the Therma police, and a reward will be offered for tidings of the little chap. You must remember that our friend Petros knows where he is, and I think we may be quite sure he won't be backward in claiming that reward if it is offered. So don't worry yourself."

CHAPTER VIII.
ROOTED IN DISHONOUR.

YES, Petros knew where she and Janni were, and the recollection caused grievous anxiety to Danaë. She could not believe that he would sit down meekly under the defeat she had inflicted on him, and his continued silence, as time went on, became ominous. How he could have accounted to Prince Romanos for the complete disappearance of his son and the nurse-girl was a mystery, and so was the Prince's acquiescence in it. Even if Janni was not to be acknowledged as heir, his father would surely wish to have him brought up under his own eye, and in this case Petros would presumably be sent to fetch him away without unnecessary publicity.

"Lady"—desperation drove Danaë at last to appeal to her mistress—"if the thrice accursed Petros came hither and demanded my little lord and me, would you give us up to him?"

Zoe looked at her searchingly. "Why should he, Kalliopé? What right has he over you?"

"None, my lady; none whatever. His fathers were the dirt beneath the feet of ours."

Zoe frowned, but the fear of embarking the girl upon a fresh venture of falsehood kept her from asking further questions. "If he has no authority over you, Kalliopé, and is not sent by anyone who has, the Prince would certainly not give you up to him."

For the present Danaë's anxiety was relieved. Her brother's interest in Janni could not be admitted unless he had decided to acknowledge him publicly, and her own father was the only other person whose authority she owned. But Prince Christodoridi was not in the least likely to leave his island fastnesses for the sake of anything so unimportant as a daughter, and if Petros should have the hardihood to produce a letter from him—well, Danaë would deny its authenticity and everything he alleged, let him assert it as much as he liked. From which it is evident that her views of truth had not yet reached a very high standard.

Confiding in the moral support of her hosts, and in the material protection of the guards who, under Wylie's orders, patrolled the approaches to the Konak night and day, Danaë permitted herself to regard her position as practically a permanency, and to plan how she might best take advantage of it. She looked back with something like contempt on the little savage who had left Strio on a barbaric mission of vengeance, and was inclined to plume herself on having deliberately made use of her father's plottings to overthrow his own schemes with regard to her. How keen had been her insight into human nature when she sought help from Prince Theophanis and Glafko, how shrewd her cunning in hiding her identity and taking a humble place on the outskirts of their circle! For already she was in a fair way to realise the ambitions which her father had crushed down with such a heavy hand, and Strio had no place—or at best a very minor one, in her dreams for the future. She was almost inclined to regret the promise, in strict accordance with local etiquette, which she had obtained from Prince Christodoridi, that in no case should Angeliké be married before her. The regret was not due to any pity for poor Angeliké, who had none of the consolations of change of scene she herself was enjoying, but to the conviction that if Angeliké was permanently sundered, not only from Narkissos Smaragdopoulos but from all possible suitors, she would make things so unpleasant at home that her father would be driven in self-defence to recall his elder daughter and provide both with husbands forthwith. But there would be considerable difficulty in the way of his finding her, and in the meantime things might happen that would prevent her returning to Strio at all—save as a "European" lady with no intention of remaining there.

In Danaë's own opinion, she was now well on the way to becoming "European." Was she not learning to read, and making valiant efforts at reproducing *deltas* and *epsilons* whenever she could find a blank wall and a piece of blackened stick? Then in manners she was conscientiously modelling herself upon Zoe, much assisted by Linton, who had formed the habit, after hearing of her connection with the islands, of alluding to her as a "fisher-girl," and excusing her lapses from strict propriety for that reason. In Danaë's former world, great ladies as well as fisher-girls had stormed when they were angry, over-eaten themselves on feast-days, and spent long hours of leisure in gossiping and eating sweets, but things were different here. Some effort towards self-restraint began to show itself, and was warmly encouraged by Zoe, without any idea of the motives which were actuating the girl, and with a disconcerting blindness towards her "European" aspirations. When Danaë received her first month's wages, and her mistress suggested that a little attention to her wardrobe was advisable, two whole days of sulks followed the prompt thwarting of her desire to buy European clothes. Zoe's horror at the suggestion she could not understand, not realising in the least what a picture she made in her Greek dress, with her splendid hair hanging down almost to her knees in the two thick plaits which now replaced the multitude of tiny braids which had taken hours to do. But Linton, who was a Philistine of the Philistines, and disapproved of national costumes as theatrical, used to allow her to put on one of her gowns when her mistress was out, and Danaë would sweep about in it, admiring the trailing folds over her shoulder, and bitterly resentful of her own short skirts. Otherwise she was submissive enough, embroidering herself an apron in the characteristic Strio pattern, and adding what coins remained over to the store that decorated her cap.

It was not often that the girl's self-complacency over the improvement in herself was disturbed, but however resolutely she might put it behind her, it was not possible entirely to forget the tragedy in which she had borne a part. Assure herself as she might that Janni was perfectly happy, and far healthier than he had been at Therma, she could not escape occasional rude reminders that his present position of dependence on his father's enemies was due to her. On Sunday afternoons it was Zoe's habit to come into the nursery and read aloud to Linton, whose eyes were not as good as they had been, but who did not like to be reminded of the fact. True to her desire for Danaë's moral advancement, the good woman herself suggested that the reading should be in Greek, and Danaë listened with more or less edification. One day, however, she rose suddenly from fanning the children as they slept on the divan, and knelt down beside Zoe.

"Lady, is it true what that book says—that what is done can never be undone?"

"A thing done can never be as though it had not been, Kalliopé. But what sort of thing——?"

"But not if one goes on pilgrimage, my lady—to Jerusalem, even? to bathe in the Jordan? If one gives crowns and jewels to the icons——?"

"Nothing can undo a wrong once committed, Kalliopé. We may repent of it, and it may be forgiven, but not even God Himself can take away the consequences."

"But if it was atoned for, lady mine, and—and forgotten? Can one never say, 'That is done with'? May it rise up at any time to torment one?"

"That is our punishment. But, Kalliopé—" Zoe looked into the girl's face and took the hands which were clasping her knees—"you can have no such terrible thing in your life, my dear child. But if you are planning anything of the kind, then stop. It is as you say, one can never get away from it."

"It is so; it is so." Danaë rose and wrung her hands. "It returns, and one cannot escape it. The Furies pursue even those who had least——" She checked herself hastily, but the tears rolled down her face as she went slowly out of the room. Before her eyes, as vividly as though it lay before her feet, she saw the rigid form of Janni's mother prone upon the grass in her red gown, with the deeper red spreading beneath her.

But when Zoe and Linton saw her again, the fit of remorse had gone by. She was as unconcerned and impenetrable as if she had not a care in the world—as different as possible from the girl whose mental agony had impressed them both with the misgiving that there might after all be a dark shadow in her past. They watched her with lynx-eyes for a time, jealous lest the faintest contamination should approach Harold, and the next time Zoe found that Danaë had told her an untruth—now a less frequent occurrence than at first—she spoke sharply and without reflection.

"Take care, Kalliopé. I cannot keep you in the nursery unless you tell the truth."

"Why, my lady? What will you do with me?" asked Danaë, with much interest.

"Send you to help in the kitchen, I suppose," said Zoe reluctantly, thinking how unsuitable such a fate would be for the brilliant creature before her. The girl's face darkened with passion.

"You would send my little lord to the kitchen?" she cried.

"Of course not. He stays here."

"He stays nowhere without me, my lady. If you try to separate us, I shall take him in my arms and run away again as I did before. I will never give him up."

"This is absurd, Kalliopé. He is no relation of yours, as you have often told me, and you have no rights over him. Until his own parents claim him, we are his guardians, and must do our best for him."

Danaë was trembling with anger. "He is mine," she controlled her lips sufficiently to say. "I saved him when his mother was killed——"

"His mother? Oh, Kalliopé, you said she was abroad!"

"I am mad! I know not what I say!" cried Danaë furiously. "If you take away my little lord, you take away my heart, my soul. But he shall not be taken away!"

"I don't want to take him away. I should be miserable if I had to separate you. But if it was necessary for his good and Harold's? How could I leave them in charge of a person who didn't tell the truth?"

"But I always tell the truth unless I can't help it." In her anxiety Danaë condescended to excuse herself.

"Which means unless it is inconvenient, or dangerous, or humiliating. But that's just it, Kalliopé. You must learn to tell the truth without fear of consequences. You would like to see Janni grow up brave and truthful, like an English boy—like what I hope Harold will be?"

"I should not like to see him grow up a fool," said Danaë smartly. Then she was frightened by what she had said. "O, my lady, you are right, and I am very ungrateful. Make my little lord what you please; it can only be good. And I will try to mould myself as you wish, but do not talk of separating me from him, for he is my very life."

The instinctive suppleness of the Greek nature revolted Zoe, but she said no more, hoping that the girl felt more than she would allow. As a matter of fact, Danaë was consoling herself with the reflection that once Janni had received a general education suitable to his birth—such as he would gain in Harold's company—it would be quite easy to add any little extra polish in which he might be deficient. Nothing could be farther from her wishes than that he should grow up with the conscientious scruples which beset these extraordinary English. She felt herself wasted as a spy upon them, and nothing but the conviction that they could not possibly be so open and sincere as they seemed kept her from boredom. Sooner or later she would discover that the Princess Eirene, at any rate, was engaged in some intrigue against Prince Romanos, involving her husband and his family, and this would justify her watch. Then would come that magnificent moment, the goal of her aspirations, when, in gorgeous European clothes provided by her own exertions, Danaë would appear at her brother's palace, leading Janni, a noble stripling, by the hand, and it would burst upon the astonished Prince Romanos that he possessed not only a promising heir, but also a sister eminently qualified to preside over his court. Few people would have considered that very second-rate and rather Bohemian assemblage as an abode to be desired, but to Danaë the dream of leading it, intriguing in it, and initiating Janni into its devious ways, was perfect bliss. As for the English, it might be convenient to have them for enemies, and she did not object to them as private friends, but as allies they were emphatically not to be desired.

About this time her acquaintance with the despised race was extended by the arrival of a visitor at the Konak. As she was helping Linton to prepare the guest-rooms in the old part of the building on the ground-floor, she gleaned some interesting information about him beforehand. He was Lord Armitage, little Harold's godfather, and—so she learned with extreme interest—a former suitor of the Lady Zoe's.

"But why did she not marry him?" she demanded. "You say he was a Milordo, and rich, with a whole ship of his own, and the Lord Glafko is poor."

"Because he wasn't the man for her," returned Linton sharply. "She could turn him round her little finger."

"Then he has not cruel eyes, that seem to pierce you through, and a mouth that shuts like a trap?" inquired Danaë curiously.

"That he hasn't. But"—as Linton realised suddenly what the question implied—"if you mean that the Colonel has, it strikes me you are forgetting your place, my girl. The Colonel is a real gentleman, and it's not for you to pass remarks on him. Lord Armitage is pleasant and well-spoken, with a kind word for everybody, but a sort of boy that will never grow up."

"Oh, holy Antony!" groaned Danaë despairingly, "these English! They are all children—all that I have seen. And now here is one coming whom the English themselves call a child! Does he bring a nurse with him, to put on his pinafores and feed him as you do the Lord Harold?"

"I suppose you think that's funny?" demanded the irate Linton. "You take my advice, Kalliopé, and curb that tongue of yours, or it will get you into trouble, and serve you right too. His lordship brings his secretary and his body-servant, as any nobleman would, and very likely some armed guards, as he comes by land. Though what he wants a secretary for is beyond me, for I should say he doesn't write many more letters in the year than I do."

"Perhaps he is like me, and can't write on paper, but only on walls or the ground," suggested Danaë, and was much pleased when Linton merely muttered angrily and would not deign a reply.

Two days later she was playing on the verandah with the children, when a young man came up the steps with a light springy step. Seeing her, he took off his hat hastily, and she saw to her surprise that he was not as young as she had thought. There was even gray in his hair. She rose politely and faced him.

"Good-day, lady," he stammered, and Danaë was wickedly delighted to detect that he blushed.

"Good-day, lord," she responded, hoping fervently that Linton was not within earshot, to come forward and point out that she had no right to be called 'lady.'

"Colonel Wylie—the Lord Glafko—told me to come up here—that I should find Princess Zoe——" he said confusedly.

"The Lady Zoe was here just now, but she has been called away," said Danaë, with great composure. "I think you will find her downstairs, lord."

"Perhaps she will come back," he said—evidently gaining courage, she thought. "I must speak to the little chap now I am here. I say, I didn't know there were two! How awfully queer not to have let me know!"

"The little lord here is ward to the Lord Glafko," explained Danaë. "This is the Lord Harold."

The newcomer took Harold into his arms in a dazed kind of way, said he supposed he had grown, and really his eyes were exactly like Wylie's. Then, apparently growing desperate under Danaë's solemn gaze, he murmured something about some sweets which were in his luggage, and went down the steps again.

"Who is the island-princess you have got up there?" he demanded eagerly when he met Zoe downstairs.

"The nurse-girl, I suppose you mean—Kalliopé?"

"A nurse-girl? Nonsense! But all the islanders are kings and queens, of course."

"What makes you say she is an islander? Has she told you anything?"

"Not about herself. Is she given to lavishing confidences on strangers? She hardly said a word to me."

"She is particularly gifted in the matter of supplying information," said Wylie, who had joined his wife. "Unfortunately it varies with time and circumstances."

"No, no; we must not prejudice him against her," said Zoe. "But do tell me why you decided that she must come from the islands?" she asked eagerly of Armitage.

"Her face! What more could one want? That blue-black hair and marble complexion, and the peculiarly pure profile—it is the very finest island-type. You get it nowhere else, and it degenerates horribly easily, even in individuals, under the influence of city life. Think of our friend Romanos. As a youth he must have been a perfect example of the type. Now he might stand for a rather battered Athenian of the rackety sort."

"Prince Romanos! Why, that is the person Kalliopé is like, and little Janni too—I see it now!" cried Zoe.

"That is the type, of course. They may even come from the same island. I noticed a suggestion of dialect in her speech which I have caught much more faintly in his."

"You have made good use of your opportunity for studying her, old man," said Wylie jokingly.

"Who could help it? Considered purely as a picture, she is the most beautiful woman I ever saw in my life."

"Now why do you say 'purely as a picture'?" asked Zoe quickly.

Armitage rather looked embarrassed. "The soul is not there yet, you know. But when it comes it must be a beautiful one, to look out through those glorious eyes."

"That's just what I feel about her," said Zoe—"that she has no soul, I mean. But she is such a fine creature, I long to see the soul appear. Perhaps she is really a sea-nymph, not a girl at all."

"But the nymphs could gain souls," said Armitage.

"By taking them from other people?" said Wylie meaningly. "Don't build up too much of a romance about the girl, old man, for whatever may be the truth about her soul, it's absolutely certain that she has no conscience. We'll tell you all about her—'ways that are dark and tricks that are vain'—after dinner, and how she foisted herself and the child upon us."

"I have an old man of the sea too," said Armitage, "and much less attractive to look at than yours. It is old Lacroix, as he chooses to call himself, my secretary. Poor old chap, he has a sad story—at least, I can't help fearing it will turn out to be sad—but he shall tell it to you himself. He wants your advice, and I shall be glad to know what you think. I've taken an awful fancy to the old fellow, and it really is rough on him——"

* * * * * * * *

"As much of a boy as ever!" said Zoe to her husband when they were alone together.

"Every bit as much. I suppose you are prepared for his falling in love with Kalliopé, Zoe?"

"Do you think it's very complimentary to me to suggest that he will fall in love with a nurse-maid—with *my* nurse-maid?"

"Nonsense! here he is with an empty place in his heart, and you throw him into the society of 'the most beautiful woman he has ever seen.' Ah, the thought has occurred to you, I see! What do you propose to do—get rid of the girl?"

"How can we cast her adrift? No, what I should like to do, if he really cared for her, would be to educate her—train her for him."

"My dear Zoe, isn't that idea just a little high-flown? Do you recollect that Armitage is a peer of the realm, with a certain amount of position to keep up—even in these degenerate days—when you calmly propose to promote his marriage with a young lady of unknown parentage and confused views of right and wrong? Do you even think it would be fair to him?"

"Most unfair, unless he could awaken the soul in her. If he could——"

"If he could, then all the worldly objections might go hang? Well, I am not the person to object, since Princess Zoe stooped to marry me."

Zoe put her hand over his mouth. "You were never to say that!" she cried.

"But it is a fact. Well, then, we are to further this preposterous affair, are we? I suppose we shall know if Armitage is really smitten, because he will want to paint her portrait."

CHAPTER IX.
ON THE TRACK.

DANAË was much exercised in her mind by the fact that Prince and Princess Theophanis dined with the Wylies that evening, and that after the meal, when they all repaired to the verandah, Maurice and Wylie made a careful inspection of the surroundings, evidently to see that there were no eavesdroppers at hand. They were plotting something at last, she was sure, and she crouched in the corner of the nursery window, which was as near to them as she could get, and listened eagerly to the scraps of conversation that reached her ears until disgust drove her away. She could hardly have expected that they would speak in Greek for her special benefit, but she felt distinctly injured when she found they were using, not English, which she had begun to pick up, but French. This was for the sake of Armitage's secretary, M. Lacroix, a soldierly-looking elderly man in a threadbare dress suit, who had sat almost silent throughout the meal. Now, on the verandah, Armitage brought him forward, and insisted on his taking a chair in the midst.

"Before my friend says anything," he said in his pleasant boyish voice, "I must tell you that he is really not Lacroix at all—nor my secretary at all, for that matter. May I present the Cavaliere Onofrio dei Pazzi?"

"Ah!" said Zoe sharply. Then, as the rest looked at her in surprise, she laughed with some embarrassment. "I think we must have met a relative of yours at the Dardanian court three or four years ago, Cavaliere—Donna Olimpia Pazzi? She was maid of honour to the young Princess of Dardania."

"That was my daughter, madame—and it is of her that I am come to speak." He rose from his chair and stood before them, as though to give himself more freedom. "Highnesses, and my kind host, Colonel Wylie, you will hear the story I have to tell, and give me your opinion on it? May I be pardoned if I first say something of myself?"

"Whatever the Cavaliere Pazzi has to tell us we shall be delighted to hear," said Maurice courteously.

"Highnesses—" the old man spread forth his hands deprecatingly—"it is not for me to recall to your minds the War of Liberation, nor the fact that the hero-king, Carlo Salvatore, took from his own breast the cross of St Eustace and St Martha and pinned it on mine, after a day in which we had fought side by side. Suffice it that the royal house of Magnagrecia has been pleased to regard me with continued favour. I have never been rich, but while my wife lived she made our small income provide amply for our needs. But she died"—he wrung his hands—"leaving me with an infant daughter, and the money, Highnesses—" he threw his arms wide—"it vanished! I am a soldier, not an economist—I confess it to my shame. My august sovereign and his gracious consort came to my aid, and provided for my child's future. She shared the education of the young Princess Emilia, and was one of the ladies appointed to her household when she was married to the Prince of Dardania. It was by no will of mine that my child went forth into that barbarous country, but I could give her nothing, and her royal mistress promised to find her a husband of suitable rank, and provide a dowry. My little Olimpia parted from me with the tenderest of farewells, and I lived—yes, literally lived upon her letters. But by degrees there came a change in them. The eyes of paternal love are sharp. I suspected a love-affair, and not a happy one. I entreated my child to treat me with frankness, and at length she revealed the truth. She loved a person whose rank was such that they could never hope to marry. I saw the danger of her position, and begged her to return to me. You will ask, Highnesses, why I did not insist, why I did not rush immediately to Bashi Konak and fetch her away. Alas! I was ashamed, afraid, to do so. Behold me living upon my pension—the only portion of my income that could neither be anticipated nor alienated in my more lavish days. A modest apartment provides me shelter for the night; in the day there is the restaurant, the club, the promenade. But what kind of life would that be for a woman young, beautiful, accustomed to courts, who would, moreover, forfeit all expectations from her royal patrons if she quitted the Princess? Without a dowry who would marry her? Therefore I sent her good advice, but—oh, blame me, Highnesses; you cannot blame me more than I blame myself—I allowed her to remain. Then I received a letter overflowing with the innocent joy of a romantic girl who believes that she has obtained her heart's desire. She was married. Her royal mistress wrote also, to assuage any anxiety that I might feel as to the marriage. It had been solemnised in her own private chapel, she herself and her mother-in-law had been present, every precaution had been taken to ensure its legality, but—" here came a tremendous pause—"it was to be kept secret for the present in view of the circumstances of the bridegroom. My daughter would remain with her mistress, and no difference would appear until Olimpia could be presented to the world as the bride of Prince Romanos of Emathia."

"Romanos!" cried Princess Theophanis, her voice rising almost to a shriek. "Maurice, Zoe, do you hear? He is married, and to a Latin!"

"I knew about it," said Zoe.

"My dear Zoe!" said her brother. "Was it fair to keep a thing like that from us?"

"I had no choice. She swore me to secrecy. It was on the day of his election—she was worried and excited—there had been some absurd idea among the people of his marrying me, you know—" she addressed the explanation to her husband—"and she could not stand it, poor thing. So she told me."

"And you kept it secret—depriving Maurice of his throne, endangering the rights of your own child!" cried Eirene.

"I tell you there was no choice. She made me promise. And the election was over. It is not as if this had come out first."

"What does that signify? They would have swept Romanos from the throne, sent him back to his beggarly Strio. It would have been the turning-point. Zoe, I can never, never forgive you. Maurice's future—the future of your house—was in your hands, and you deliberately cast it away."

"Pardon me, Princess," said Wylie. "It seems to me that my wife was not free to act."

"Most certainly she was not," said Maurice decisively. "When Prince Romanos and I submitted our claims to the choice of the Emathians, we pledged ourselves to abide by the result. When that had once been announced, we could not have taken advantage of Christodoridi's marriage to oust him, even if it had come to our knowledge."

"Oh, you are mad, all mad!" cried Eirene bitterly. "I, who sacrificed my child in the cause of the house of Theophanis, I cry shame upon you."

Maurice's face hardened. "We fought in Hagiamavra for the freedom of Emathia, Eirene, not for our own aggrandisement. And we are interrupting the Cavaliere Pazzi in his recital. Pray, monsieur, proceed."

The Cavaliere bowed. "At your Highness's gracious command. The news that the marriage had actually taken place threw me into a great difficulty, Highnesses. My first impulse was to cross at once to Dardania, and snatch my daughter from a position likely to prove so compromising. But cooler reflection assured me that such an action could only give rise to suspicions in the highest degree injurious to her. I wrote therefore—with all a father's authority, but I trust also with the natural sympathy of one who himself has loved—to desire her to obtain leave of absence from the Princess. A visit to her solitary parent would surely be the most natural thing in the world, and could be prolonged indefinitely until her husband found himself able to visit Magnagrecia and claim his bride from her paternal home. But alas! the love and obedience to which I had never appealed in vain in my child had turned traitor, and were now enlisted against me. My precaution precipitated the very evil it was designed to prevent. Olimpia's letters expressed the strongest reluctance to comply with my request. The fear of offending the Princess her mistress, of becoming a burden upon me—ah, well I perceived that these were only excuses; her true object was to remain as near her husband as possible. At last I resolved on the strong measures from which I had shrunk at first, and bade her be ready, for I was coming to fetch her. What evil fate caused the arrival of that letter of mine to coincide with a visit of Prince Romanos to the Dardanian court? When I received an answer, it was to tell me that Olimpia had accompanied her husband on his return to Emathia, though the time was not yet propitious for him to acknowledge her. Then, when it was too late, I hesitated no longer, and went in search of my daughter. I found her in the island of Thamnos, just outside Emathian waters. Her husband had been obliged to visit Czarigrad, and durst not leave her behind at Therma. There was no prospect of his acknowledging her at present, so that she could not go with him. Highnesses, our interview was a sad one—it tears the heart to recall it. I besought my daughter on my knees to return with me—to force the hand of the man who was risking her reputation for his convenience. She refused, she had cast in her lot with him. Then I begged her to permit me to remain and confront him, to urge upon him the absolute necessity of postponing no longer the step which he constantly assured her it was his firm intention to take in the near future. If he would call in the servants and the crew of his vessel, and declare before them that she was his wife—I would be content for the present with that. The state entry into Therma, the public recognition, might come later. But she refused to let me stay. Evidently she feared what might happen if we met. She assured me solemnly that if I declared my conditions she would take sides with her husband, and agree with him that the time was not yet ripe. She and he and her personal attendants knew that she was his lawful wife, and with that she was content. Highnesses, she was not content. I saw it in her convulsed face, heard it in her agitated accents, but the husband now took the first place, and the father must yield. Sorrowfully I left my child, and since that day I never seen her."

"You heard from her, surely?" cried Zoe.

"Did she remain in Thamnos, or accompany the Prince to Therma?" asked Wylie.

"I did receive letters from her, madame. The letters were posted in Therma, Colonel, and she gave me to understand that she was occupying a villa on the Prince's property, not far from the city. To its actual position she gave me no clue—doubtless fearing that I might again attempt to see her. The first letter I received after our unhappy parting begged me very earnestly to make no further allusion to the question of her recognition, but to think of her as an ordinary wife, married to a private person whose business obliged him to be a good deal away from her. She had perfect confidence in her husband, feeling sure that he would acknowledge her at the earliest possible moment, and in the meantime she lived a rather lonely but by no means unhappy life. She amused herself with gardening and the study of the Emathian languages and her husband spent with her every moment that he could snatch from the cares of state. At length she referred of her own accord to the subject she had begged me not to mention. If her child should be a boy, she was sure the Prince would take that opportunity of acknowledging her. The child was born. It was a boy, and it was baptised John, after the last of the Emperors, by the Greek rite. Olimpia assured me continually of her husband's delight in his heir, but there was no word of recognition. At last I lost patience, Highnesses, for what could happen that could provide a more favourable moment for the announcement? I wrote to my child then that the Prince's perpetual postponement of his promise absolved me from my engagement of silence, and that I was intending to take steps to announce the marriage on my own account."

"That was a dangerous thing to do, monsieur," said Wylie.

"It was, Colonel. I recognise it now, but it was at the time that rumours of an alliance between Romanos and a Scythian Princess were freshly mooted. I desired to cut the ground from under his feet, in case he should actually be meditating any baseness of the kind. But, Highnesses, I endeavoured to mitigate any harshness which my proposal might seem to imply. I was about to visit Therma, I told Olimpia, and then I would lay before her husband a fact which would go far to remove any objections his subjects might be expected to entertain to the marriage."

"And pray, monsieur, what was that?" demanded Eirene, her pale face flushed, and her eyes glowing.

"Simply, madame, that in the poverty-stricken veteran before you, you behold the great-great-grandson of Maxim Psicha."

"Maxim Ghazi?" cried Wylie. "But why not have used that weapon before, Cavaliere?" For the name of the great Illyrian hero of the eighteenth century, who had built up a short-lived Christian state in his native highlands, and but for his early death by treachery, would probably have succeeded in driving the Roumis from Illyria, was one to conjure with among both Greeks and Slavs in Emathia.

"I was not aware of its value, Colonel. It is only the changes of these later years that have taught the world there is any Illyrian question at all. The formation of one Balkan state after another, and finally the emergence of Emathia from Roumi tyranny, have revived in the Illyrians the national feeling that has slumbered for generations, and which the Roumis did their best to stamp out by promoting local and tribal feuds. I have of course always been aware of my descent from the son of Maxim Psicha, whose mother fled with him to Magnagrecia on her husband's murder, and who married an heiress of the Pazzi and took her name, but it was not until last year, when a deputation of Illyrian notables visited me in my humble lodging, and invited me formally to place myself at the head of their struggle for freedom, that I recognised it had any bearings on present-day politics."

Wylie looked across at his brother-in-law with raised eyebrows, and Maurice spoke.

"You may not be aware, monsieur, that I myself was offered the crown of Illyria at the beginning of last year, and invited to negociate a British protectorate over the country when I refused it?"

"I was informed so, Highness, but you will permit me to say that it was your British birth, to which the Greeks in Emathia object, and not your Greek descent, which has no interest for the Illyrians, that led to the offer. When you referred the deputation to Prince Romanos and the Assembly at Therma, they turned their thoughts from you to the descendant of Maxim Psicha."

"Another opportunity lost!" cried Eirene.

"But you would have objected strongly to their adopting me on any other ground than as the heir of John Theophanis," said Maurice. "At any rate, it is satisfactory to know why the offer collapsed so suddenly. But I cannot imagine, Cavaliere, why Prince Romanos did not jump at your news. His subjects would not have objected to his marrying anyone who brought with her as a dowry the future adhesion of Illyria."

"Alas, Highness! the news was never told. I received an urgent letter from Olimpia, entreating me to write what I had to say, but on no account to come to Therma. The moment was most unpropitious, and my visit might do irreparable harm by setting people talking. I could well understand that the moment was unfortunate for my son-in-law, for the rumours of his impending marriage were becoming more definite. As you have no doubt seen, his photograph and that of the Grand Duchess Feodora were published together in the papers, and it was positively, though not officially, announced that they were engaged. I did not wish to embarrass Olimpia by insisting on visiting her against her wishes, but I wrote very strongly pressing my point, and refusing to commit my news to paper. I have had no reply to that letter, Highnesses—no further letter of any kind from my daughter."

His auditors were silent, and looked at one another. The inference was obvious, but no one liked to put it into words. At last Maurice spoke.

"Pardon me, Cavaliere; do I understand that you have had no news of Donna Olimpia from that day to this?"

"If they can be called news, I have had one or two brief notes from her husband—assurances that Olimpia could not write, but sent her love and implored me not to be anxious, and above all not to come to Therma. Nothing in her own writing—not even a pencilled signature. I wrote again urgently, demanding definite tidings of the nature of her illness, the opinion of her doctors—above all, some word from herself, failing which, I should start for Therma at once. What did I receive, Highnesses? A long letter purporting to be written by Prince Romanos at his wife's dictation. Why do I say 'purporting'? Because it was never dictated by Olimpia. It was not the letter which a loving, ailing woman would send to the fond father who was breaking his heart for her at a distance. It was the letter of a poet trying to put himself in such a woman's place, full of images that would not occur to her, of words that she would not dream of using. Highnesses, when I received that letter, my mind was made up. I also have a soul capable of stratagem. I left behind me letters to be posted at my usual weekly intervals, and started for Therma by sea."

He paused, to deepen the impression, then hurried on, his words seeming to overflow one another. "I said, Highnesses, that I possessed a mind capable of stratagem. To that let my proceedings on approaching Therma be witness. I sent my old soldier-servant on shore with my passport, and wearing clothes of mine, while I remained on board the steamer. No sooner was the name on the passport perceived than he was detained, and refused permission to proceed into the city. At the police-office he was photographed, his physical measurements taken, as though he were a criminal, and he was reconducted on board, informed that he would not be allowed to land. My worst suspicions were confirmed, but I have one consolation. Neither the photograph nor the measurements thus obtained will help the Therma police when they have to deal, not with old Filippi, but with me."

"I think you are very wise, monsieur," said Wylie. "I understand also that Prince Romanos has never seen you? You decided, then, to make your next attempt to enter Therma by land?"

"No, that was my idea," said Armitage proudly. "We met at Trieste, and the Cavaliere heard I was bound for Therma, and asked me to take him in the yacht, but I thought it would be much safer to get in by the back door. So I got him a brand-new passport, and they let him pass the frontier without the slightest suspicion as Lacroix and my secretary. I thought he might go on to Therma to see about rooms for me, and make inquiries on his own account, and then when he has found Donna Olimpia, we can bring the yacht up and get her off in it."

"But what do you think has happened to her?" asked Maurice.

"Why, that she's imprisoned somewhere, of course."

"Not likely," said Wylie. "Unless she has altogether broken with her husband, he would have been able to get her to write to her father and beg him again not to come. No, I'm afraid it's worse than that——" Zoe pinched his arm, and he changed the form of his sentence suddenly. "But after all, it's quite possible that she has refused to be bamboozled any longer, and he has shut her up somewhere lest she should spoil his matrimonial projects."

"Do you think he can have carried her off to Strio?" said Zoe. "Don't you remember that stagey old ruffian of a father of his? He said to me so evilly that Strio had dungeons as well as palaces, when he thought I aspired to the honour of being his daughter-in-law."

"But they are on the worst possible terms," said Armitage.

"Do you know, I should say that Professor Panagiotis would be the best person to enlist on your side, Cavaliere," said Maurice suddenly. "He is very keen on the Scythian match, but he can have no idea of the harm he has been doing."

"No, wait," said Wylie. "Imagine the Professor's feelings when he finds out that he has been tricked all along—that the Scythian match can't take place, and never could have done. I don't think it would be for Donna Olimpia's safety for him to make that discovery, and I am sure it will lose Prince Romanos his throne."

"That last consideration would have no weight with me, Colonel," said the Cavaliere. "Whether my son-in-law retains his position or not is a matter of indifference. My sole object now is to rescue my daughter from his clutches, and to carry off her and her child into safety—if it is not too late. After that forged letter I could believe him capable of sinking to any depths of baseness. And if it is so, if he has repaid Olimpia's confidence with treachery, then I will unveil his iniquity and hound him from his throne, if I have to tramp barefoot through Europe."

Eirene crossed quickly to where he stood. "Be it so!" she said, holding out her hand. "We are united. We will make it clear what he really is, and drive him from the throne he has usurped."

CHAPTER X.
THE PORTRAIT.

THE Cavaliere Pazzi had gone on to Therma, as what Armitage called his "advance agent," to find out the best hotel and take rooms for him there, and discover which of the public buildings of the new city were worthy of being immortalised by Milordo's brush. Happily the people of Therma were not likely to guess that their lofty stucco palaces were anathema to the artistic mind, which would have infinitely preferred the tumble-down Roumi relics they replaced, so that the Cavaliere would be able to pursue his private inquiries under cover of his architectural researches. Maurice and Wylie were much occupied with a vexatious matter which was disturbing the extreme north of their territory, at the point where it touched the Debatable Land. A Pannonian scientific expedition, duly authorised by the Therma Government, which was conducting a geological survey of the district, had contrived in some way to excite the dislike of the inhabitants, who declared that the members were looking for hidden treasure. Natural cupidity combined with race-hatred to make the search as difficult as possible, and the Emathians put so many obstacles in the explorers' way, and dogged their steps with such persistent malignity, as would have stirred even the mildest of scientists to revolt. These particular scientists were young and fiery, and demanded effectual protection for themselves and their pursuits, under the threat of holding up the North Emathian administration to the execration of Europe, sending a deputation to Klaustra to argue the case against the representatives of the peasants. Wylie would fain have hurried at once to the disputed area, and settled the difficulty on the spot, but this suggestion did not meet the learned men's wishes. They wanted, not police protection, but a definite edict to secure them from molestation, and deprecated the untoward importance which would be attached to their mission if Wylie carried out his intention. The peasants were equally determined that the strangers' proceedings ought to be stopped at all costs, and brought up relays of witnesses to prove that they were impiously and callously interfering with all manner of time-honoured landmarks.

The game of accusation and contradiction went on merrily, wasting time day after day, and Armitage was left to his own devices and to the society of the ladies for entertainment. Thus forsaken, he conceived the idea of occupying his leisure by painting Danaë's portrait, and to Wylie's intense delight asked Zoe's leave to do so. True to her first resolution, Zoe consented, hoping to discover, during the hours occupied in the task, some clue to the enigma of the girl's personality.

As for Danaë herself, she was highly flattered by the request, having long admired in secret the large painting of Zoe which the artist had presented to her and her husband as his wedding-gift. Her ideas on the subject were not exactly in accord with Armitage's, however, as was made evident when she presented herself for the first sitting robed in Linton's best black gown and a stiffly starched white apron, with her hair strained back from her face and piled into a kind of helmet on her head, in distant imitation of Zoe's coils. Zoe and Armitage gazed at her in speechless horror as she displayed herself with much pride, and were devoutly thankful for the sudden irruption of Linton, who had discovered the unauthorised use made of her Sunday gown, and lost no time in proceeding to recover it. Zoe herself presided over the transformation of the European into the everyday Kalliopé, a change which had to be effected almost by force, for the girl was sulking furiously. She resented particularly the restoration of her hair to its usual massive plaits, for the uncouth pile secured with stolen hairpins had been a special triumph. The Lady Zoe was obliged to do her hair loosely and fluff it out to make it look at all well, whereas she, Danaë, had so much that she could hardly get it all up even when it was twisted as tightly as possible! Her face was like a thundercloud when Zoe led her back at last, and Armitage, welcoming the gay dress and long plaits in place of the grotesque array which had affronted his horrified vision, had no chance of doing more that first day than obtain an excellent attitude for an embodiment of disgust.

Things improved afterwards, though it was several days before Danaë could be induced to appear save with an expression of restrained protest, and Armitage made one sketch after another, trying to find the best attitude for bringing out the points of the beautiful face and form. Danaë was in no wise shy. To her mind the Christodoridi were the equals of any of the royal houses of Europe, and the conviction lent a stately assurance to her manner that puzzled Zoe and roused Armitage to fresh admiration. Pursuing her plan of training her handmaid for a loftier future, Zoe gave herself some trouble in the matter of choosing subjects for conversation during these mornings. She had thrown herself of late so completely into the actual life that surrounded her that Armitage was rather surprised to find how keen her interest in literary and artistic matters still remained. But he was fresh from London and the circles in which she had shone before her marriage, and he found it quite easy to believe that a brilliant woman of her achievements might find the society of Emathian country ladies, and the duty of leading them in the way that they should go, pall at times. Therefore he talked of books and pictures and historical events, following her lead, and Zoe watched Danaë's face to see how it affected her, and tried to draw her into the discussion by asking her the right word in Greek for such and such a thing. But the result was disappointing. The girl had no foundation of general knowledge on which to build. Names which would have brought a glow of enthusiasm to the cheek of most of her countrywomen had no meaning for her, and history was represented to her mind by the rude chronicles of the sordid and bloodthirsty squabbles of her Christodoridi ancestors with the other island chiefs. When she could be induced to recite one of these metrical romances, then, indeed, her eye kindled and her voice became almost inspired, but to her hearers the matter was hopelessly inadequate to the emotions it evoked. They could not tell that she felt she had justified her descent from these rather unheroic heroes, and that the barbaric crimes and virtues which they supposed her to admire in her rulers were honoured family characteristics to her.

After the sittings had lasted for a week, Zoe came upon Armitage turning over his portfolio with a perplexed face. It was full of sketches of Danaë of all sorts and sizes—whole-length, half-length, three-quarters, full face, profile, face turned away, some worked up almost into pictures, others the merest record of a moment's pose.

"Not satisfied yet?" she asked him, smiling.

"How can I be?" he demanded, viewing with frowning brow a pencil drawing of Danaë recounting with immense gusto the tale of a particularly black piece of treachery practised against an enemy by Prince Christodoridi's father. "There's no soul in anyone of them, and it seems a kind of desecration to paint that face without it."

"How can there be?" demanded Zoe in return. "She hasn't got one—at least, that's what I am beginning to think."

"She has, she has!" cried Armitage stoutly. "I have caught glimpses of it—the merest glimpses—and it was gone again."

"They must have been the very merest glimpses, for I have been watching most eagerly, and have never seen a sign," said Zoe. "Why, even in this—" she took up a sketch of Danaë looking down on Janni and Harold playing at her feet—"in which she looks really sweet, there is not a hint of anything more than a kind of wild affection. She would go through right and wrong without a qualm to get Janni anything he cried for."

"Or Harold either. She has a very real liking for you and Harold both, I believe, though in your case it is mixed with a good deal of—of lack of comprehension."

"Why don't you say contempt at once? That is what she feels, I know perfectly well. And no doubt we are all of us miserable failures according to her savage code—and Maurice, as the best of us, the worst failure."

"No, I am the worst failure, I think. Prince Theophanis does at any rate rule, and with a strong hand when necessary. I potter about the world in a yacht, ready enough to help my friends, but without sufficient grit to annex a principality for myself. Oh, I have seen it in her eyes, I assure you, and it sets me wondering what exactly she would expect me to do on the lines of the villainous Despots she admires so much."

"Oh, murder us all, and Romanos too, and seize Emathia, I suppose— regardless of the effect on the Powers," said Zoe. "And yet you still think the soul is there?"

"I tell you I have seen it. But I can't say the look is characteristic. Still, I know exactly how it would change the whole face. I could paint it now."

"Then do it," said Zoe, with a sudden inspiration. "Paint two pictures of her, one as she is and one as she ought to be—as you and I would like to see her. That one I will put away, and when we are old and gray-headed we will look at it and see whether she has developed in accordance with it or not."

"But you would not let her see it?"

"Certainly not. One doesn't want to add hypocrisy to the poor child's obvious faults, and that would be a kind of temptation to it. No, she knows she must not look at the picture until it is finished, and you can keep the second one out of sight. When she sees herself in all her glory, she will be quite satisfied, and in no danger of finding fault with the expression."

Armitage took the advice thus tendered him, and to Zoe there was something very pathetic about the smaller picture which grew under his hand in the neighbourhood of the large one. The splendidly handsome face, with its firm lips and scornful eyes, seemed to look down with contempt on its neighbour, into which, Zoe thought pitifully, the artist had painted the reflection of his own kindly soul rather than that of his sitter. If Kalliopé had a soul, it seemed to be buried deep beyond all means of reaching it; there was no way of getting at the girl herself. These thoughts were in Zoe's mind when she came to the sitting one morning, to be met on the way by Armitage, who was carrying his large picture with some difficulty owing to a letter in one hand.

"Wait one moment, Princess," he said. "Kalliopé is not there yet, and I have just had a letter from the Cavaliere. You will like to hear what he says?"

"Oh yes!" cried Zoe. "Has he discovered anything?"

"He thinks so. He says he had little difficulty in finding the villa where his daughter used to live. The people all knew that Prince Romanos had prepared it for a lady, who lived there in great retirement, and never went out. He used to visit her frequently, but of late his visits had entirely ceased, and the old woman who once did the marketing had also disappeared suddenly. Also the sentries who used to guard the house on the outside had been removed—and all these things happened at the same time, five or six months ago. Of course it might mean merely that Donna Olimpia had gone to live somewhere else, but the Cavaliere made up his mind that she had been murdered—and really you can't wonder, after what he told us about her letters. He managed to get into the grounds one night with the help of a rope-ladder, and explored the whole place thoroughly. The house was clean and tidy, and there were no stains of blood, which was what he had feared to find, nor was there any grave in the garden. But everything indoors looked as though the inhabitants had gone away suddenly, without having time to pack properly. The furniture was all awry, and Donna Olimpia's gowns were hanging up in her wardrobe. In the nursery the little boy's toys and things were all left, and as far as he could tell the servants' clothes were all in their rooms too. What should you think it pointed to?"

"It looks as though they had been seized and carried off somewhere without being allowed to take anything with them," said Zoe. "Can it be Strio after all? But it seems such needless cruelty on the Prince's part not to let them take their things."

"Well, I should almost have thought they must have been abducted by some one else who objected to the way in which the Prince spent his time; but why they should take all the servants I don't know," said Armitage. "It seems unnecessary trouble, for if it was merely to ensure secrecy, I don't suppose they would have stuck at killing them. But the Cavaliere seems to have agreed with you. He was remarkably lucky, for just as he was coming out of the house, he saw some one in the garden. It was a tall man, wandering up and down on the lawn in front, throwing his arms about and groaning. He guessed immediately—which is more than I should have done—that it was Prince Romanos, tormented by remorse, and he went for him at once, and demanded what he had done with his wife and child. It really was Romanos, and he seems to have behaved rather well, all things considered. He didn't appear to mind Pazzi's dropping in upon him, and explained, with suitable expressions of grief, that all the inhabitants of the house, Donna Olimpia, the baby, and three servants, had been carried off by diphtheria in the space of two days. How does that strike you?"

"As remarkable, to say the least."

- 88 -

"So the Cavaliere thinks. He tried to corner Romanos in every possible way—about the letters especially. But he stuck to it that the first few were really written during his wife's illness, and contained her messages. The long one, which was supposed to have been dictated, he gave up at once, confessing that he had made it up in terror lest the Cavaliere should insist on coming to Therma, and add a public scandal to his private grief. Well, it seemed so impossible to shake his story, and he displayed such a friendly wish to keep his father-in-law in sight while he remained in the city, that the Cavaliere smothered his suspicions and accepted the story. They even visited Donna Olimpia's grave together the next day, and Pazzi might have come away satisfied if Prince Romanos had not made a bad slip. Something he let drop suggested to the Cavaliere that there was some uncertainty about the child's death, and he nailed him there and then. Bit by bit it came out that the little boy had not died with his mother. His nurse had snatched him up in a fit of delirium and carried him off, and was believed to have thrown herself and him into the harbour from the quay that same night. Their bodies had not been recovered, but a woman with a child in her arms was known to have drowned herself, and if those were not they, where are they?"

"You know," said Zoe inconsequently, "that I see a likeness in little Janni to Prince Romanos. What if he and Kalliopé were the missing child and nurse?"

Armitage started. "If it could be!" he said. "But no. You remember, Princess, that you thought Kalliopé also was like the Prince. But there is nothing to account for that. And the Cavaliere says somewhere that the nurse was an elderly woman—a Roumi, by the description he has of her."

"It is a most curious coincidence," said Zoe.

"But nothing more, I imagine. Well, do you wonder it made old Pazzi suspicious? However, he didn't show it, but the moment he could shake off his affectionate son-in-law he went straight to Professor Panagiotis, who has promised to get at the rights of the matter by hook or by crook. So now the fat's in the fire."

"This may be very dreadful," said Zoe, after a pause of dismay. "I don't think the Cavaliere ought to have spoken to the Professor before consulting us. Maurice and Graham would have gone to Therma and helped him to bring Prince Romanos to book. He would probably tell the truth when he found they knew so much, and were only anxious to help him. But now— oh, do warn the Cavaliere to take no open steps, whatever he may discover, before letting Maurice know. One can never tell what Professor Panagiotis will do. I suppose he has an ideal in his mind, and goes straight for it, he cuts off so many corners that anyone else would have to go round. I only hope the Cavaliere's letter has not been read on the way. We never consider the post here safe, you know."

"Pazzi waited until your brother's own messenger was coming out, and sent the letter by him. That accounts for our not having heard from him before, I suppose. Oh, I will warn him till all is blue, but I should doubt if Prince Romanos will come through this time."

"Personally, one could hardly wish him to escape," said Zoe, "for however much poor Donna Olimpia was to blame, he must have treated her shamefully. You can't wonder at her coming to Therma, for she knew only too well that she could not trust him out of her sight. Do you remember how lovely she was when we were at Bashi Konak? That must have been when they first met, of course, but she had changed very much when she told me about her marriage. And she was really devoted to him, poor thing!"

"The man ought to be flayed alive!" muttered Armitage, in a tone so ferociously at variance with his usual sunny kindliness that Zoe was betrayed into a laugh. He looked ashamed, and took up his picture again. "Well, Princess, we have kept poor Kalliopé waiting a long time, but I thought you ought to know how matters stood."

"Oh dear, I hope she won't have looked at the other picture!" cried Zoe, hurrying up the steps, but she was too late. Danaë was standing beside the easel, contemplating her idealised portrait with a pleased smile.

"Am I really as beautiful as that?" she asked them as they came up, with a naïve frankness which betrayed no doubt of its answer. For the moment, in this softened mood, her expression was really not unlike that of the picture, Zoe thought. But as Armitage reached the top of the steps, she saw the second canvas in his hands.

"Ah, I thought this one was too small!" she cried. "Have you made two pictures of me, lord? But you might have let me wear the European clothes for one of them! Are they both exactly alike?"

In his perplexity, Armitage was still holding the larger picture, instead of placing it on the easel, and she came behind him and looked at it over his shoulder. Neither he nor Zoe ventured to say a word. Perhaps the girl would not notice the difference! But even as Zoe watched, a change came over the smiling face, and an angry sob broke from the beautiful lips. Danaë was at the easel again, her little dagger in her hand. Fiercely she drove it into the canvas, slitting it across and across and round the edge, then stood confronting them for a moment with stormy brow and heaving breast.

"You shall not mock me!" she gasped. More she would have said, but her fury would not let her speak. She snatched off her coin-decked cap and trampled upon it, caught up her apron and tore it into ribbons. Then the dagger which she had hurled from her caught her eye again, and Armitage sprang forward to seize it, fearing she would do herself an injury. His hand was actually on it, but she tore it away and struck at him as he tried to wrest it from her. Then, still in the same passion of silent rage, she hacked and hewed at one of her heavy plaits of hair, unheeding Zoe's entreaties, until it was severed in her hand, and flung it at their feet. Then the tension relaxed, and she pressed her hands to her eyes and fled sobbing.

"I ought not to have done it. How could she understand unless it was explained to her? Of course she thought I was trying to make fun of her," said Armitage, holding his wounded wrist.

"She had no business to look at the easel when she was told not," said Zoe practically. "You must let me tell Linton to bring some hot water, and we will tie up your arm. I am afraid she must have hurt you a good deal."

"Oh, I shall bear her mark!" he said, laughing, but Zoe thought that there was more in the words than a joke. Twisting his handkerchief round his wrist while she called to Linton, he stooped and picked up the severed plait from the floor. "What a pity!" he said.

"Yes, the naughty girl has effectually spoilt her appearance for some time," said Zoe. Armitage was smoothing the thick blue-black strands, and she took them from him with gentle firmness. "I shall keep this to make Miss Kalliopé a wig when she needs it," she said. "If she should take it into her head to cut off the other plait the next time she has a fit of temper, there will be nothing to fasten her cap to."

"Yes, indeed, ma'am," agreed Linton. "Anything more like a pig with one ear than that poor ill-tempered girl as she rushed past me just now I never did see. And to show such a wicked spirit, when his lordship was taking her picture so beautiful! I do hope, my lord, if I may make so bold, you'll paint her with the short hair showing, as a lesson to her to keep her temper in hand for the future."

"But that would spoil my picture," objected Armitage, who was an old friend of Linton's.

"And if it did, my lord, what's that to curing a fine handsome girl like that—and good with children too, as I must confess, though I wouldn't say as much to her—of her wicked ways?"

CHAPTER XI.
THE RETURN OF PETROS.

WHATEVER course Armitage might take with regard to his picture, Danaë was conscious that her outbreak of passion had set a barrier between her and the rest of the household. Even the children shrank from her in her black moods, and now Linton gathered them ostentatiously under her wing, requesting Danaë not to come near them until there was no danger of her doing them a mischief. This was the nearest approach to scolding that she received, for Zoe, without even alluding to the cause of the disfigurement, helped her to rearrange her hair in two smaller plaits so that it was as far as possible disguised. Armitage's bandaged wrist was a perpetual reproach to her, but she met with no reproof in words, though when she plucked up courage to apply to Wylie, who had found and confiscated her dagger, for its restoration, he refused without vouchsafing a reason. But though no word was said, and no punishment inflicted, she was surprised, and even irritated, to find that she felt her guilt much more keenly than on a memorable occasion when she had pushed Angeliké, then a child of four, off the fortress wall. Angeliké happily fell into a rubbish heap, and beyond being half-choked with dust, suffered no harm; but the incident roused Princess Christodoridi from her usual placidity, and she insisted that her husband should inflict a suitable punishment on his elder daughter, towards whom she suspected him of undue partiality. Struggling and screaming, Danaë was held fast by the women-servants while her hair was cut off by her father's dagger, and thereafter, a miserable little shorn object, she had been held up to every visitor as a model of juvenile depravity until her mother grew tired of the subject—the injured Angeliké meanwhile basking on the softest cushions, and enjoying the first taste of every dainty dish. The girl could recall even now the fierce thrill of resentment of the injustice that seized her when, just as her hair had almost grown again, her mother had rehearsed the whole story to a stray cousin from another island, though perhaps it was her father's injudicious sympathy that brought her at last to feel as if she was the injured party and Angeliké the aggressor. But now, assure herself as she would that Zoe and Armitage had mocked her cruelly and intentionally humiliated her, she could not bring herself to believe it, and the unaccustomed sense of guilt made her increasingly miserable. To use Linton's phrase, she "moped," and the household seemed to have lost sensibly in light and colour while she hung about in secluded corners. It was a relief when, after three days of morose inactivity, she asked sullenly for stuff and needles and thread, though she still sat solitary, making herself a new apron in place of the one she had torn up.

The end of the verandah, whither she betook herself, was quite remote from the usual living rooms, and she worked as if for a wager, undisturbed by either Zoe or Linton, who thought that a period of reflection would do her no harm. Hearing steps in the court below her, she set them down to one of the servants passing on an errand, until a low hiss and the word "Kalliopé!" reached her ears. Looking over the railing, she saw the guard Logofet, who had never forgiven her for the reprimand he had received on the occasion of their first meeting, standing below.

"Your uncle's here, Kalliopé," he said with a grin.

"I have no uncle," she cried angrily.

"Oh, that's all very fine. He told me to tell you that your uncle Petros was here, waiting to speak to you, and that it would be the worse for you if you didn't go."

"It's a lie. I have nothing to do with him."

"Oh, come now!" Logofet assumed an air of virtuous reproof. "Didn't I hear him myself ask the Prince to find you a place, and the Prince wouldn't have you without his leave? You take my advice, and don't tell any more lies, which no one believes, but just go and speak to him, for he won't go away without seeing you."

"But how can I speak to him? They won't let me pass through the gate at this hour."

Logofet winked. Danaë had already suspected the source of his excessive geniality, and now she was certain of it. "*They* may not, my dear, but I will," he said, "and I go on guard at the small door in a few minutes. Just cough three times when you come round the corner, and I'll turn my back. If the Lord Glafko expects me to see in the dusk like a cat, why, he'll be disappointed! So be a sensible girl, and do as you're told."

He stalked away with exaggerated steadiness, and Danaë wondered for a moment whether she durst claim the protection her employers had promised her against Petros. But after what had happened, her pride rebelled. And after all, he might only have come to assure himself that she and Janni were in safe keeping, and not to take them away. When the dusk had quite fallen, therefore, she slipped down the nearest staircase, which led into a smaller courtyard at the back of the main block, and seeing Logofet's figure dimly as he stood on guard, gave the signal coughs. The bulky form at the gate became intensely interested in a gleam of light from an upper window, and she turned the well-oiled key and slipped out. Under the wall was waiting a man wrapped in a thick dark overcoat or *kapota*, and as Danaë approached him he struck a match, revealing the face which had been the terror of her dreams for months. When he saw her, he chuckled irrepressibly.

"So it's true that you cut off half your hair!" he said. "I wondered whether I should find you tamed, my lady, with the Lady Zoe making such a pet of you, and the English lord putting you into a picture, but I see you're the Despot's true daughter still."

"I suppose you have been drinking with your friend Logofet," said Danaë icily. "Say what you have to say, and go."

"That's easily done, my lady. I want the little lord."

"What do you mean to do with him?"

"To restore him to his anxious father, of course," with a chuckle.

"I don't believe it. You want to kill him, as you did his mother. I won't give him up."

"Oh yes, you will, my lady, and without making any fuss about it, because if you don't, I shall simply go to Prince Theophanis and tell him the truth about both of you. Then the Lord Janni will go back to his father, and you to yours. Of course, if you are longing to get back to Strio, I have no objection, but it's for you to say."

Danaë shivered. Strio was bad enough to look forward to, but what she shrank from more was the prospect of her story becoming known. That the nature of all the lies and evasions and subterfuges she had employed should be publicly exposed, that she should stand forth as an impostor, the accomplice in a murder, the deceiver of her own brother and her kindest friends! She pressed her hands together in agony, and Petros spoke again, insinuatingly this time.

"It's not my business, lady, I know, and the Despot would kill me if he guessed what I am saying, but there's no need to go back to Strio if you don't wish it. The Lady Zoe will surely find you a husband if she has taken such a fancy to you, and you won't catch me letting out anything. I'm only asking you to do what will benefit us all. The Lord Romanos is mad to get his son back, I see my way to something handsome for myself if I take him back, and you will be able to stay on here. Isn't that fair?"

"My brother wants Janni back?" Danaë spoke in a dazed tone. "But then how is it you have not come for him before?"

Petros laughed with some little confusion. "Must I keep you here in the cold while I explain everything, my lady? Isn't it enough for you to know that the little lord is badly wanted, and to hand him over?"

"I will do nothing unless I know why you want him, and why you have waited so long."

"Holy Nicholas, lady! you are your father over again. Well, then, the first thing the Lord Romanos thought of on the Lady's death was to keep everything quite secret. If he had lost his love, he need not lose his people's good opinion as well; you see?"

"You are insolent!" flashed out Danaë. "The Lord Romanos acts as a wise man acts."

"Then surely, my lady, there can be no harm in his servant following in his footsteps? At any rate, that is what he has tried to do. For when the Lord Romanos remembered the little lord, and found that he had disappeared, he was torn between his paternal affection and his fear of discovery. He longed to trace his son, but he durst not bring the police into the matter, lest they should find out too much, and therefore he entrusted the matter to me. Now, lady, knowing that you and the little lord were safe where I could put my finger upon you at any moment, could I really be expected to bring the search to an end before it had begun? That is not a wise man's way."

"You allowed the Lord Romanos to believe that his son was dead?"

"Lady, although I am not a father, I can enter into a father's feelings. I watched my lord carefully, and brought him the news of a wretched woman—a Roumi whose husband had taken another wife—who had drowned herself and her child in the harbour. If the Lord Romanos had accepted the tale as a convenient ending to the matter, it should have ended there, but he displayed so much grief in thus losing the child as well as the mother that I gave him a little hope. The bodies had not been found, and there was no proof that they were yours and the little lord's. And that hope, my lady, I have cherished cunningly ever since, bringing my lord news of clue after clue, and investigating them at his command until they have turned out false. I must have sampled the *mastika* of every wineshop in Therma since I saw you—'gathering information,' the police call it."

"And I suppose my brother is tired of false clues, or you would have visited the wineshops all over again?"

"You don't think so poorly of me, lady, as to imagine I would let his Highness learn that he had been deceived? No, I could have gone on as long again, as you say. I had even satisfied my lord your father by sending him word that after everything had fallen out exactly according to his wishes, it had been necessary for you to take a situation in the country, to avert suspicion, and I had several new and very fine clues ready to go on with. But we were interrupted. The Lady's father came to Therma."

"What! had he heard what had happened?" cried Danaë.

"I know not, my lady, but I think he had made up his mind that the Lord Romanos had had her removed because her presence was become dangerous. I know only that my lord called me, and said, 'Friend Petraki, I am ruined for ever unless we can find the little lord at once. If I have been a good master to you all these years, stand by me now.' Could I think any longer of my own advantage then, lady? No, I did not hesitate to renounce my pleasant task of investigation, and naming only the reward I desired, I set forth to follow up the clue that led hither."

"And what was the reward?" asked Danaë, unmoved by the devotion so pathetically displayed. Again Petros appeared a little confused.

"Why, lady, you must see that I have felt myself in considerable danger these last few months. A man can never be quite certain that he has covered all his tracks. At any moment my lord might discover that I had some connection with the Lady's removal, and I know him well enough to be sure that, without any chance of telling tales, I should pay the forfeit, though I followed him when he left Strio twenty years ago. My price is a full pardon, therefore, and so I told my lord, confessing that I had killed an old woman in a quarrel. He swore by the All-Holy Mother that if I brought him back his son I might kill every old woman in Therma—provided I did it in decent seclusion—and I started at once."

Danaë laughed in the darkness. "Every old woman in Therma, do you say, friend Petraki? There is pardon for that, but not for killing one Kyria Olimpia."

"Lady, it is you who mistake." Petros spoke slowly and meaningly. "In that deed I had no part, and can invoke without fear the most awful of all curses upon the villains who took part in it. You yourself heard the orders the Despot gave me, that the Lady who was leading his son astray was to be brought alive to Strio, there to be imprisoned where she could do no more harm. Those orders I did my best to fulfil, and I laid no hand on her. It was those with me—strangers whom I hired to help me carry out the Despot's behest, and who I now think must have been also in the pay of some one whose interest it was to get rid of the Lady—who slew her. That I struck down old Mariora I have confessed—she had often given me the rough side of her tongue, and she was going to raise the alarm, and I was afraid she would call me by name."

"I see," said Danaë. "Far be it from me to destroy your confidence in the Lord Romanos."

"Lady, I am not one to tempt my lord to break his promise. When I quit this place with the little lord, you will not find me going straight to Therma.

I shall leave the Lord Janni in a safe place, while I go forward and acquaint my lord of his recovery. I know a wise man—a lawyer whose father was a priest—and he has drawn me up a paper for the Lord Romanos to sign, calling down upon himself if he breaks his promise such curses as no man living would dare to face."

Danaë's attention had wandered. "Friend Petros" she said quickly, "how can the little lord save his father from ruin?"

"I cannot tell, my lady. It seemed to me that perhaps the old man, the Lady's father, desired to have the child and bring him up. Then he would promise to leave my lord undisturbed, and keep the story secret, taking the Lord Janni away with him, so that it might never be known whose son he was."

"If that is it——" she paused a moment. "You must have him, Petros, if it is to save his father, but I shall come too."

The reply was not flattering. "Holy George! you will ruin everything, my lady. Why should you come?"

"Because I cannot stay here without him. The grandfather will only know that I am his nurse, and I shall beg him on my knees to take me with him. Then I can bring up the little lord in the right ways, as befits the son of John Theophanis. If he will not take me, perhaps I can manage to follow them somehow, and if not, I can but go back to Strio. That would be better than staying here and telling fresh lies——"

"It is for you to command, my lady, but I knew not you loved the island-life so much."

"It is not for you to judge my doings. See, friend Petros," desperation made her conciliatory, "you will be glad to have me to take care of the little lord on the journey and when you leave him. And I can support you, as you said, if it is necessary to swear that you had no part in the Lady's death."

"That's true," said Petros doubtfully; "but I meant to take the child under my arm and ride the first stage to-night. Now I shall have to see about another pony or a mule, and it's too late to do anything. I shall have to waste another bottle of good *raki* on that beauty Logofet, too, to get him to let you pass to-morrow evening. But it's quite likely I shall bring in the Lord Janni in better condition with you than without you, so I'll make the arrangements, and send you word by Logofet where to meet me. But mind, my lady, no playing me false, or you will be sorry you tried it."

"I wish you had said that in Strio!" burst from Danaë. "The Despot would have sent you to feed the fishes."

Petros caught her wrist. "You may be as high and mighty as you please, my lady, but I warn you once more not to trifle with me. I have too much at stake, and I swear by the All-Holy Mother and all the saints——"

She tore her hand away. "You forget yourself, dog! If I choose to make use of your escort on my journey, it should not lead you to presume. I shall be ready when you send me word."

She coughed three times outside the door, and it opened with a suddenness which suggested that Logofet must have been straining his ear at the keyhole. He tried to kiss her as she slipped in, and only his unsteady condition enabled her to escape. She hurried up the staircase quivering with rage and shame—not even able to account for the feeling which bade her choose an ignominious return to Strio rather than a fresh campaign of falsehood to enable her to remain at Klaustra. Everything was gone now, the new friends whom she had liked in her own curious way, the European culture she had been acquiring at such pains, the hope of a wider and freer life than Strio and a future Striote husband could offer, the half-acknowledged pleasure she had begun to take in Armitage's gentle manner and frank boyish face. With a return of her old vehemence, she ran frantically along the verandah and burst into the nursery, where Linton was much embarrassed by the difficulty of giving both the children their supper at once. The spoon which was approaching Harold's open mouth landed a dose of bread and milk on his pinafore instead, as Danaë rushed in and threw herself on the floor, burying her face in the folds of Linton's gown.

"Oh, Sofia, I am the most wicked and miserable girl that ever lived. I am worse than a beast!"

"There, there!" said Linton with creditable sympathy, "don't take it to heart so much as all that, Kalliopé. It's well that you should see it for yourself, but there's no use making a fuss about it. Show your repentance by doing, not by talking, is my motto. And you may as well help me with these precious lambs, for I can't so much as hear myself speak with Master Johnny screeching fit to take your head off."

Janni was loudly demanding food of Nono, and Harold was dissolved in tears over the untoward fate of Nin-nin's last spoonful, so that the needs of the moment were pressing, and when the meal was over Danaë helped to put the children to bed as usual. She seemed to have slipped back into her ordinary place after her three days' exile, and Linton was too much relieved by her docility to do more than lecture her in general terms as she put on her spectacles to hem the sides of the new apron. Zoe glanced at them with delight as she stole in for a look at the babies after dinner, and laid a kind hand on Danaë's shoulder in token of renewed confidence. To her surprise, there were depths of tragedy in the eyes the girl lifted to her face. Danaë saw, not the cheerful nursery, with its red curtains and its brazier and lamp, but the chill autumn evening and rough roads for which Janni and she must to-morrow exchange all this comfort and safety. But as no words followed, Zoe interpreted the glance as one of penitence, and felt nothing but pleasure in recalling it.

The next day everything seemed to conspire to make it easy for Danaë to fulfil her compact with Petros. Linton trusted her with the children as though she had never expressed a doubt as to her treatment of them, and Harold and Janni found their dear Nono at their service for uproarious games all day long. The games kept Danaë from thinking, and they made the children tired, so that Linton swept them off to bed half an hour before the usual time. They both went to sleep "like angels," as she observed, and then, leaving Danaë to watch over them, she hurried off to help Zoe in dressing for dinner. She never forgot that her real and original status in the household was that of ladies'-maid, but it was not often that her nursery labours allowed her to return to its duties. As soon as her mistress's door had closed behind Linton, Danaë knew that the moment was come. She took Janni out of bed, and dressed him without his even waking, then put on her own outdoor coat, twisted a shawl round her head, and went out on the verandah. The tipsy voice of Logofet greeted her immediately.

"Kalliopé, pretty little Kalliopé, I thought you were never coming. Your dear uncle is waiting for you and your brat round the third turning on the left—no, the right—no, it was the left, I'm sure of it—opposite the small door. You won't find me there, because I'm just going to sit down quietly and rest a bit, but you can let yourself out and in—no, you won't want to get in again this time, ha, ha! Take care not to run across the Princess. She hasn't come in from the hospital yet."

Hugging affectionately a large bottle, Logofet lurched away, and Danaë, with a sick feeling at her heart, went back into the room and fetched Janni and the bundle of clothes she had put ready. She felt as if she did not care whom she met, but she instinctively shrank into the corner of the staircase as the back-door opened and Princess Theophanis came in, attended by a servant with a lantern. Danaë could not tell whether she had been seen or not. It seemed to her for a moment that she caught the glance of cold dislike with which Princess Eirene always regarded her, but there were other things to think of.

"Where is the sentry?" asked the Princess sharply. "He must have left his post. Light me to the door, and then go and report his absence to the Lord Glafko."

She passed in at the house-door, and Danaë seized the opportunity to slip out. Once outside, she hurried in the direction of the third turning on the left, expecting to find Petros there, fuming and swearing. But he was not there, and though she waited some time, in deadly terror of passers-by, he did not come. Then there occurred to her, with a fearful shock, Logofet's maudlin uncertainty as to the turning, and she ran back into the main street, panting over the cruel cobbles until she had passed the Konak and reached the third turning on the right. There was no one there either. For a moment she waited, hardly able to believe in her good fortune. Petros had repented, or changed his mind, and was not waiting for her at all. Then with swift reaction came the thought that the summons might be a trick of Logofet's to get her shut out, and she ran back to the door in fresh terror. But the handle turned easily, and she burst in, to the intense astonishment of the man now on guard, who seemed disposed to detain her for explanations. But she was the Lady Zoe's favourite, and therefore not to be roughly handled, and muttering something about an errand, she brushed hastily past him while he was locking the door. She was almost at the end of her strength, but she staggered up the stairs with Janni and the bundle, along the verandah, and into the nursery. Could it be possible she had been gone so short a time that Linton had not yet returned from her chat with her mistress? Quickly, in the dim light of the shaded lamp, she took off Janni's wraps and laid him in his cot, careful not to wake Harold, sleeping close by. Something strange about his crib attracted her attention as she turned from tucking Janni up, and she lifted the clothes. The bed was empty. Harold was not there.

CHAPTER XII.
MISSING.

DANAË sank upon the floor by the empty cot, literally unable to stand. Wildly she sought for an explanation of Harold's disappearance. Had Petros carried him off in revenge, believing she had deceived him, or had Harold, and not Janni, been his real object all along? But what good could the possession of Harold do him, unless he meant to take him to Therma and pass him off as Janni? Prince Romanos was not likely to jeopardise his own safety by proclaiming the substitution, even if he realised it, and to his father-in-law one child was as good as the other. That must be it. Somehow or other she had missed Petros in the darkness, and he had made his way in and seized Harold, possibly believing him to be Janni. But here was Janni, sleeping peacefully, and Harold would be carried off to Magnagrecia, where his parents would never find him. For—and Danaë saw it clearly—if she gave the alarm and accused Petros, matters could not stop there. The whole story must come out, for Petros in his anger would unmask her as he had threatened to do. And in the few moments of relief she had enjoyed after the blissful discovery that he was not waiting for her, her present home and all its ease and comfort and safety had become doubly dear. No, she could not now renounce it by her own act. She would do all she could to help in recovering Harold, short of telling what had actually happened, and if the worst came to the worst she could always confess Janni's true parentage, and leave her employers to take what steps they thought best.

"Why, Kalliopé, whatever in the world are you doing on the floor?" demanded Linton's hushed voice. "My lady couldn't keep me with her to-night, because of letters just come from Therma, so I just popped down to the kitchen to see what Artemisia was going to send us up for supper, and to ask about her son that was ill. But get up, girl, do! What's the matter?"

Danaë's eyes met hers in the dimness like those of a hunted creature. "The Lord Harold is not here," she murmured.

"Not here? Who's taken him?"

"I don't know. I—I found him gone."

"You found him gone? Why, you bad girl, you don't mean to say you left those blessed children alone, and me just turning my back for a minute?"

"Some one called out to me that my uncle was here and wanted to speak to me, and I ran down to see, but there was no one there. I was not gone long."

"Not long—I know what that means! And that precious child screaming his little heart out, no doubt. Of course his papa heard him—the darling!—and came and carried him away to the drawing-room, giving him his death of cold, as likely as not. I'll fetch him back at once; but you mark my words, Kalliopé, I don't trust you with the nursery again in a hurry."

In the Wylies' drawing-room an informal council was being held over the letter Armitage had just received from the Cavaliere Pazzi. Prince and Princess Theophanis had come in, for the news it brought was startling. Armitage translated roughly as he referred to the paper in his hand.

"After all, there's no doubt that the poor old chap acted wisely, from his own point of view, in going to Professor Panagiotis," he said. "The Professor seems to have found out more in three days than he did by himself in a month, and things certainly look very black against Prince Romanos. According to the Cavaliere, these are his principal points:— There was no notification of the existence of an infectious disease at the villa, at a time when the Prince declares all its inmates were mortally ill with diphtheria; no doctor was summoned there until the day registered as that of the death of Donna Olimpia and two of her servants; no nurses were seen coming or going, and no medicines or disinfectants appear to have been purchased."

"But look here," said Wylie; "let us give the devil his due. This absence of doctors and nurses and so on doesn't necessarily imply that there was no diphtheria, but it does account for its being so fatal. According to the story in the last letter, there must have been five people ill of it, and no one to nurse them."

"Except Prince Romanos himself on his daily visits, when he went in and out without apparently taking any precaution against infection. That seems to be proved by the evidence of the sentries," said Armitage. "The Professor certainly doesn't do things by halves. Imagine his convicting the Prince out of the mouths of his own soldiers! But, Wylie, don't you see the Cavaliere's point? Even if the deaths were really due to diphtheria, and not to violence, the poor creatures were practically murdered by being left without care and medical attendance. They couldn't get out to ask for help, I suppose they couldn't even cook for themselves—why, they must have starved to death. It's worse even than if he had had them killed. Can you conceive the callousness of a man who could see five people—his own wife and child among them—dying by inches day after day, and do nothing to help them?"

"No," said Zoe decisively, "it is inconceivable. I have no particular kindness for Prince Romanos, but cruelty of that sort would be impossible to him. He is a poet, you must remember. If he had contemplated a crime of the kind, he would never have gone near the place, either then or afterwards."

"Then we are thrown back on the hypothesis that he had them murdered," said Armitage, "and what makes it look very likely is that on the very day the deaths took place a number of men in the uniform of the Prince's guard were seen by the sentry to enter the grounds of the villa. He had been informed that an additional guard was to be placed round the house itself at night, owing to the Prince's absence from Therma, and seeing these men enter, apparently by means of a key of their own, without knocking for admittance, he thought it was the detachment detailed for that duty. They were there some time, in fact, until after the old woman-servant—mark this; she died of diphtheria that very day, you will remember—had come in from her marketing, and then they marched out again, just before the sentry went off guard. Most unfortunately, the man who relieved him cannot be found. He took his discharge from the army shortly afterwards, and all trace of him has been lost. But it is known that the Prince visited the villa that afternoon, and sent off in hot haste for a doctor. The doctor has also disappeared. He was a foreigner, and having signed the certificate that Donna Olimpia and the two servants died of diphtheria, which was required by the municipal regulations before the bodies could be buried, he returned presumably to his own country—but no one knows."

Maurice rose from his chair in uncontrollable emotion. "Don't go any further, Armitage. We have no right to push this inquiry without giving Romanos a chance to defend himself. Certainly it looks like a dastardly murder, but there may possibly be some explanation. We know that the man is a brave soldier, and I can't believe it of him."

"Just let me finish," pleaded Armitage. "If he is innocent, it is most unfortunate that he has made away with another witness whose evidence might have helped to clear him—or at least acquiesced in her disappearance. Don't you remember the nurse who, according to his revised story, ran away in a fit of delirium and drowned herself in the harbour with the child in her arms? Well, in Pazzi's last letter, which I read to you, Princess—" to Zoe—"he said that the missing nurse was a Roumi, and rather elderly than not. That description, according to the evidence of eye-witnesses, exactly fits the woman who threw herself into the water—some of them knew her. But now the Cavaliere has unearthed a letter of Donna Olimpia's in which she speaks of the nurse as a rough handsome girl from Strio."

The rest looked at each other, and Armitage went on hurriedly—

"Her name was Eurynomé Andropoulos, and she was the niece of the Prince's servant Petros. Donna Olimpia wrote that she had always disliked Petros, and would not have had a relation of his in the house, but her husband had a fancy for the child to be brought up on the Striote nursery tales and songs."

"How long ago exactly did Donna Olimpia die?" asked Maurice.

"Janni calls Kalliopé Nono," murmured Zoe.

"She told us that Petros would say he was her uncle, but he denied it as earnestly as she did," said Wylie.

"Then that child is a descendant of John Theophanis, after all!" said Eirene. "But his mother—his mother was a schismatic! There is no need to fear him."

"Fear him—a baby like that!" said Maurice, with a mingling of scorn and affection in his tone. "My dear Eirene, would you propose to turn the poor little chap out in the cold, if we had reason to fear him, as you call it?"

"We ought to be thankful that we have been able to save anyone from such a wholesale murder," said Zoe.

"Wait!" said Wylie suddenly. "Please remember, all of you, that we know nothing yet for certain. We do know enough of this girl—Kalliopé or Eurynomé or whatever else she may call herself—to be sure that if we have her in and cross-question her she will deny everything without a qualm, and probably seize the first opportunity of taking the baby and running away somewhere else. She may be in the pay of Romanos—paid to keep out of the way until the story of Donna Olimpia has died down—or she may have been merely mad with fright when she told us her rigmarole of contradictory stories at first. Or—she may even not be the girl we are thinking of at all. At any rate, we have her here safe, and the child too. I should advise very strongly that we say nothing whatever to her at present, but that we get old Pazzi up from Therma, and spring the thing upon her in his presence. I doubt if we shall get the truth from her even then, but there's just a chance of it."

"Then I think Romanos should be asked to come as well," said Maurice, "and perhaps Panagiotis too. There is so much at stake that we ought——"

"Please, ma'am, may I have Master Harold?" Linton's voice, reproving at first, became insensibly frightened as she looked round the room and failed to see her charge anywhere.

"Master Harold, Linton? Why, you told me yourself he was in bed an hour ago!" cried Zoe.

"And so he was, ma'am, but I made sure Master had heard him crying and brought him down here. If I've said so to myself once as I come down from the nursery, I've said it on every stair. And where is the precious lamb if he isn't here, may I ask, ma'am?"

"Why, in bed, of course," said Wylie, while Zoe, with a scared face, ran out of the room.

"No, sir, that he isn't, begging your pardon, and if any of you gentlemen are playing a joke on me, I take the liberty to say it's not what I should have expected of you. Oh, do tell me where my little lamb is, anybody that knows!"

"We don't know, Linton, any more than you do," said Maurice kindly, "but we will come upstairs and help you look for him. I suppose the little rascal might have crept out of bed and be hiding somewhere, or even have walked in his sleep?"

"How could he, sir, and me fastening him safe into his crib before I left him? But if you can find him I'll take him back thankful, and no questions asked."

It was clear that Linton still believed herself and Harold to be the victims of a practical joke, as she toiled up after the rest to the nursery, where Zoe had Danaë in a corner, and was questioning her fiercely.

"You think some one must have come up while you were away? Graham! Maurice! she says she went down into the courtyard to speak to her uncle, and when she came back Harold was gone."

"How long ago was this?" asked Maurice.

"Excuse me one moment," said Wylie. "Armitage, will you go to the sergeant in the gatehouse—he speaks Greek—and tell him to go the round of the Konak and see that no one, man, woman, or child, is allowed to leave? After that he is to parade his men ready for duty. Linton, go into all the rooms on this floor, and see whether the child is hidden anywhere, and call out to Parisi and Markos to do the same downstairs. Now, Kalliopé!"

"Lord, I know nothing," moaned the girl.

"That we shall see. You were left in charge of the nursery. What made you leave it?"

"Some one called to me from the courtyard that my uncle was there, lord."

"Who was it? Who called?"

"Lord, I cannot tell. One of the men, I think." She durst not mention Logofet, lest he should be questioned, for he knew too much.

"Who did he say was there—your uncle Petros?"

"I—I suppose so, lord."

"Why? Had you any reason to think he was in the neighbourhood?"

"I thought I saw him one day, lord—in the street."

"Did you speak to him then?"

"No, lord. I was frightened." Falsehood came as easily as ever to Danaë now that she had deliberately returned to it.

"Why were you frightened?"

"Lest he should have come to fetch us away, lord."

"Did you think he had come to steal the Lord Harold?"

"No, lord, there was no reason why he should. That is what I cannot understand. If it had been my own little lord——"

"Then you do think Petros has taken him? Why?"

"Lord, I do not know, except that he is an evil man."

"Well, you went down to look for your uncle. Did you find him?"

"No, lord; there was no one there."

"Where did you look for him?"

"In the great courtyard, lord." Princess Theophanis was looking at her, and Danaë knew at once that she had been seen as she crouched in the darkness on the stairs. She held her breath and waited for the words of denunciation, but they did not come. Wylie was speaking again.

"Did you come up again at once when you did not find him?"

"I stayed and sought him a little while, lord; then I came up. The nursery looked just as it had done when I left it, and the children seemed to be sleeping. But when I straightened the clothes, the Lord Harold was not there."

"And did you give the alarm at once?"

"Alas, lord! I fell to the floor in my terror, and lay there."

"That is so, sir," put in Linton, who had returned unsuccessful from her search. "I found her laying on the ground like a dead thing, crying out that Master Harold was gone."

"Think," said Wylie sharply. "Can you imagine no reason why Petros should have carried off the child?"

"None, lord. Except," as a bright idea occurred to her, "that there was a reward offered for a little boy who was lost at Therma, and he may be hoping to gain it."

"Ah, and how did you hear that, if you have not seen him?"

Danaë realised her danger. "I—I heard it, lord," she murmured.

"And you have no idea why he should come so far to fetch a child who had nothing to do with it?"

"None, lord." She looked up with such evident innocence that Wylie was puzzled. Maurice's old theory that she had come among them as a spy, with possible designs upon Harold in the interests of some unknown enemy, had naturally been revived by the event, and the girl had undoubtedly blundered badly in her last answer. But it seemed hopeless to go on cross-questioning her in the hope of eliciting further admissions which led to nothing, and it was something to have gained the suggestion that Petros was presumably on his way to Therma. No more time must be lost, and he turned quickly to his wife.

"Well, Zoe, this gives us some sort of clue. Maurice and Armitage and I will search the town at once, and send parties out on all the roads. If the fellow has passed, we can catch him by the telegraph at a dozen points on the way to Therma. You and Linton had better make a thorough search of the Konak, upstairs and down. Here are the keys of all the storehouses. Perhaps the Princess will kindly let you look in all her rooms, for no one can tell where the child may have been hidden. Take Parisi and Gavril with you when you go across to the stores. And don't be frightened. Between us we ought to be able to get the little chap back all right."

Wylie spoke more hopefully than he felt, for the apparent purposelessness of the abduction made it difficult to deduce any conclusions from it. He had left Zoe plenty to do, and she and Eirene, tucking up their evening gowns under thick cloaks, began a systematic search of the whole rambling assemblage of buildings which constituted the Konak. Attended by the guard Gavril, armed to the teeth, and the stout Greek butler, carrying a lantern, they hunted again through all the Wylies' rooms, then through those of the Prince's house and the range of storehouses on the left of the courtyard, and even the barracks of the guard on either side of the gateway. The small courtyard at the back, and the garden, damp and dismal in the cold autumn night, were not forgotten, but when they came back with haggard faces, utterly exhausted, they were still unsuccessful. Most of the servants were weeping helplessly in the passages, but Linton had stirred up her friend Artemisia the cook to subdue her grief sufficiently to prepare some soup, which she coaxed her mistress to take. Zoe refused to go to bed, and Linton remained with her, leaving Danaë on guard in the nursery; and so that dreadful night passed, first one and then the other dozing off for a minute or two, then springing up in terror, and running to search in some place which might have been forgotten. It was not until morning that Wylie came stumbling uncertainly up the stairs. One glance at his worn face told his wife that his quest had been as vain as her own, but she forbore to put the fact into words.

"Dearest, you are tired out," she said, with a tenderness that rarely found verbal expression from her lips. "Come and sit down here, and have something to eat. Linton, you kept some soup hot on the nursery stove as I told you? No, Graham, don't talk till you have had something. You had no dinner last night, you know." Her mouth quivered involuntarily as she remembered how Linton had broken in upon the party in the drawing-room with her terrible news. "Now here is the soup. Take it to please me."

Utterly spent, Wylie obeyed, and not until he had finished would she let him tell his tale.

"We have sent the police through the whole town, Zoe, and searched all the inns. No one at all resembling the description of Petros has passed on any of the roads. We have telegraphed to all the places on the line, and sent out messengers where there is no wire. The people are awfully sympathetic, and they are all enlisted in the search."

"And anyone who found him would know who he was, because of his blue eyes," said Zoe, trying to speak cheerfully. "And no one could have the heart to hurt him, could they, Graham? when they saw his dear little face."

"No, of course not," said Wylie hoarsely. "Maurice and I have made plenty of enemies, no doubt, but I don't think any of them are such curs as that."

"Oh no, they couldn't," agreed Zoe. "Some one is sure to bring him back to us soon, looking so naughty and happy and smiling—Oh, Graham!" she broke down and hid her face, sobbing, on his shoulder— "Graham, if they don't!"

"My dear, my dear!" said Wylie brokenly, and as he put his arms round her Danaë, who had been watching through the half-open door, fled away in tears. The words she could not understand, but she knew the meaning of the tones, and no amount of arguing with her conscience could assure her that she had nothing to do with the scene. She had at first entertained wild hopes that Petros might be intercepted and killed, without being able to compromise her by anything he said, but then she remembered that unless he was able to return to Therma and produce Janni, or a child representing him, her brother had declared that he would be irretrievably ruined. He must be allowed to reach the city, then, but as soon as sufficient time had elapsed for Prince Romanos to be secured from whatever danger was threatening him, Danaë would declare her charge's true parentage to her mistress. Then everything would be set right, but in the meantime the sorrow around cut her to the heart, and she and Linton mingled their tears over Janni's solitary breakfast and his irrepressible inquiries for "Aa-aa."

CHAPTER XIII.
THE CULPRIT.

NEITHER his personal sorrow nor his sleepless night could be allowed to relieve Wylie from the pressure of his daily duties, and after less than an hour's rest he was presiding at an inquiry into the conduct of one of his military police, who had quitted his post without leave on the preceding evening. This was Logofet, who had awakened from deep dreams of peace to find himself in durance, and could not imagine how he had got there. The report of the man who had escorted Princess Theophanis to the hospital made it clear that he and his mistress had entered at the small door of the Konak by merely turning the handle, and had found no one on guard within, and this rendered it probable that Logofet's remissness had permitted the entrance of the kidnapper to whom the night's misery was due. Nothing was said of this, however, though as many of his comrades as could find any excuse to be present crowded the room where the prisoner, alternately defiant and lachrymose, confronted his Colonel.

"Drunk, lord! I have not been drunk for ten years," he blustered, happily unconscious that he had been found fast asleep, with the empty bottle by his side.

"The witnesses will prove that you were drunk last night. Where did you get the spirit from?"

Into Logofet's bemuddled brain darted an idea and an impulse of revenge. Witnesses? Then the girl Kalliopé had betrayed him. Very well, then he would betray her.

"Do you really wish to know where the *raki* came from, lord?" he whined.

"Certainly." Wylie expected to hear as usual the name of one of the wretched Jewish spirit-sellers, duly licensed by the Therma authorities, who were a thorn in the side of the rulers at Klaustra, and seemed to have a special predilection for corrupting the police.

"Then don't ask me, lord; ask little Kalliopé. Ask her who gave me a bottle of *raki* two evenings running, so that I should turn my back while she slipped out at the little door."

Ignorant as he was of the night's excitement, Logofet was astonished at the sensation produced by his words. Wylie pushed his chair back abruptly, his face perfectly white, and the spectators exchanged glances and whispers and exclamations of surprise. After his first stunned silence, Wylie rose.

"I cannot inquire into this case; it must go before the Prince," he said. He was too much shaken to give the necessary orders, but an eager messenger ran to bear the news to Maurice, and the scene of the inquiry was quickly changed to the broad verandah before the Prince's house. Eirene sat beside her husband, with a curious watchful look on her face, and Zoe, whom they had wished not to disturb, seemed to divine in her restless sleep that there was news, and woke and came as well. With an instinctive sense of drama, messengers and servants alike had combined to prevent the news from reaching Danaë, and when she was sent for she came unsuspiciously, expecting, indeed, further cross-examination, but nothing worse. It was not the lowering countenance of Logofet that first warned her of the crisis, but the look on Armitage's face as he leaned against the side of the doorway. One glance he gave her—a quick inquiring glance, as though to assure himself that she was unjustly accused—then he deliberately turned his eyes away.

"I have sent for you, Kalliopé, because what Logofet has to tell concerns you," said Prince Theophanis. "Sit down beside your mistress, and when he has spoken we will see what you have to say."

Danaë sat down on the doorstep, conscious as she did so that Zoe, as if mechanically, moved her chair a little farther away, and Maurice signed to Logofet to speak. The prisoner had managed to learn the state of affairs by this time from the conversation going on around him, and was correspondingly elated. He spoke with a certain soldierly bluffness, which left entirely out of sight the fact that he himself was anything more than a witness.

"I am a plain man, lord, and cannot tell a long story. Two days ago I met Kalliopé's uncle in the town——"

"Wait; how did you know he was her uncle?" asked Maurice.

"Why, lord, he said so; besides, I saw him outside Therma the day that this ill-omened girl first thrust herself into your house. He said he wanted to speak to his niece, and asked me to let her pass out and come in again. He had some good *raki* with him, and I consented. That evening she went in and out quite properly, though rather in a hurry, so I thought little of it when he asked me to do the same for him again the next night. She was an obstinate piece of goods, he said, and wouldn't do what she was told, but I was to tell her to bring the brat this time, or it would be the worse for her——"

"You said 'your brat.' You know you did!" burst from Danaë.

"To bring *the* brat, or it would be the worse for her," corrected Logofet, with the air of an honest man unjustly aspersed; "and thinking that she was about to relieve you, lord, and the gracious lady your sister, from the maintenance of herself and that foundling she brought with her, I thought it an excellent deed. So he gave me another glass of spirits—which I swear to you, lord, must have been drugged, for after giving the message to the girl I fell down insensible, and knew no more."

"Now, Kalliopé, what have you to say?" asked Maurice. "You told the Lord Glafko last night that you had not seen your uncle at all, except at a distance, that the message you received merely told you he was here, and that you went down into the great courtyard to look for him, but could not find him."

"And it is all true, lord," cried Danaë desperately. "This man is lying, having hated me since the day your kindness brought me to this house. I have spoken no word to the man Petros, who calls himself my uncle, and I went nowhere last night to look for him, save into the great courtyard."

"Lord," said a voice from among the police on the steps, "I admitted this girl Kalliopé by the small door last evening from the street." Maurice looked at Danaë.

"Lord, he also is lying," she cried. "These Slavs of yours all hate me, who am a Greek."

Princess Theophanis leaned forward in her chair, and spoke slowly and distinctly. "I saw Kalliopé hiding on the stairs near the small door when I came in from the hospital," she said. "She had a great bundle in her arms, which might have been a child. I remember thinking at the time that it looked like one."

"Oh, Eirene, why didn't you say this before?" cried Zoe, in agony. Her brother raised his hand for silence.

"Kalliopé, you will do better to tell the truth. Two witnesses have proved your story to be false. You were in the back courtyard, you went out and in at the small door, you took out with you a bundle resembling a child. Had she the bundle in her arms when she returned?" he asked suddenly of the guard who had spoken.

"I could not see, lord; there was no light. She was very much wrapped up, and she may have been carrying something."

Before anything more could be said, Zoe tore her hand from her husband's, and flung herself on her knees before Danaë.

"Oh, Kalliopé," she sobbed, "give him back to me! He was so sweet, and he never did you any harm. I have tried to be kind to you—if I was ever unkind, I ask you now for forgiveness. Only tell us what you have done with him. You shall not be punished in any way—you shall have anything you can ask, if you will only give him back."

"Lady mine, I have done nothing with him," sobbed the girl. "I call the All-Holy Mother of God to witness that I had no hand in stealing the Lord Harold. If I could tell you where he is at this moment, I would do it gladly."

Wylie raised his wife gently. "My dear Zoe, the girl is hardened. It is no use appealing to her. Wouldn't it be as well to continue this inquiry in private?" he asked of Maurice, who replied by remanding Logofet to the cells, and dismissing the police spectators. The hunted look was in Danaë's eyes again as she faced her judges, but Maurice spoke with studious gentleness.

"Kalliopé, you have been in this house for some months. Don't you understand yet that your mistress has always meant kindly towards you, and done everything in her power for your good? She can't believe, and I can't believe, that you could repay her kindness in such a way. Tell us the truth now, and I will pledge myself that as soon as the child is recovered you shall be sent safely back to your own home, and no punishment inflicted on you."

"You will not believe me, lord, if I do tell you the exact truth," cried Danaë defiantly.

"If it is indeed the truth, we will," he replied.

"Then hear the truth, lord. I did go out and speak to the man Petros two nights ago, and I did pass through the back courtyard to speak to him again last night, carrying a child in my arms. But he was not at the place he had appointed, and the child was my own little lord, and not the Lord Harold. When I did not find Petros, I carried my little lord back into the house. I knew you would not believe me!" she cried angrily, looking round at the faces of the rest.

"How can we believe you, Kalliopé?" asked Maurice. "You would have us believe that you took little Janni out and brought him back again, and that this had nothing to do with the Lord Harold's disappearance. Now, be honest. Did you hand over the Lord Harold to Petros by mistake for Janni?"

He realised the futility of the question even before the dark cloud gathered on Danaë's brow. "I mistake another for my little lord!" she cried, in supreme disdain.

"Then did you try to deceive Petros by giving him the wrong child, hoping to keep Janni here?"

"No. I was going with him myself. But of course you will not believe me. Do you believe me, lady?" she demanded suddenly of Zoe. For the moment the impulse to tell the truth from the very beginning was upon her.

"Oh, Kalliopé, how can I? You have told us so many falsehoods!" moaned Zoe. Danaë cast upon the rest a look of mingled scorn and reproach, and turned to go in at the door. But as she did so, Armitage stepped forward and took her hand.

"Lady Kalliopé, I believe what you have told us to be true. Now be brave, and you shall prove your truth to all. The Lady Zoe will joyfully acknowledge that she was wrong when she receives her child back. There must be more that you can tell us which would throw light upon his loss and help us to find him. Don't let your pride make our grief deeper."

Again Danaë wavered, with confession on her tongue, but a scandalised whisper from Eirene, "Lady Kalliopé, indeed!" turned aside her intention. She drew her hand away from Armitage. "I have told the truth, lord, and it is not believed. Now therefore I will take my little lord and depart from this place."

"You will do nothing of the kind," said Wylie sharply. "You have shown pretty plainly that you are not fit to have the charge of a child, and Janni will remain in your mistress's care. Remember that you are under the very gravest suspicion. Go back to the nursery and try to redeem your character."

Danaë shot a furious glance at him, and swung through the doorway with a swagger that would not have disgraced her father. This unfortunate experiment in telling at any rate part of the truth had left her absolutely convinced that she was an injured victim, and her employers cruel oppressors, but she was not going to allow them to see that their injustice could make her unhappy. When she was gone Wylie turned to his brother-in-law.

"I am sorry to have taken the words out of your mouth," he said, "but that girl's effrontery simply sickens me. You don't think I was too severe?"

"Not if she was really telling lies," said Maurice, "and if she wasn't, she has only herself to thank for our not believing her. And most certainly she must not be allowed to take the other child away. In fact, I don't know that it wouldn't be wise to restrict her movements a little—forbid her to leave the upper floor of your house, for instance."

"No, that wouldn't do. Don't you see, if there was any truth in the story that Petros really wanted Janni, he will come back and try to get him? He can't very well do it without communicating with her, and if she is regularly watched while she imagines herself to be going about freely, we shall catch them both. Zoe, you had better come back and lie down."

Zoe obeyed submissively, and Armitage went with them, trying to imbue Wylie with his own belief that Kalliopé had really told the truth at last, and they had missed a great opportunity by not recognising the fact and encouraging her to go further. When their voices had died away, Maurice turned to his wife, who was gazing straight before her.

"Eirene, I cannot imagine why you said nothing last night of seeing Kalliopé on the stairs. You can't really mean that you thought at the time she had a child in her arms."

"Why not? I thought, as the man Logofet did, that she was going to relieve us of her presence and that child's, and I was not sorry."

"But when you heard Harold was lost, it must have struck you——"

"Oh, my dear Maurice, don't cross-examine me as you did that wretched girl! It did strike me, of course."

"Then why didn't you tell us? I can't understand why you should have kept back a fact like that."

"No, I suppose you could not understand. The reason is not one that would enter a man's mind, very likely. Oh, Maurice, does it really want explaining? Zoe has her child, and I have lost mine; isn't that enough?"

"But she has not got hers—that's just the trouble."

"No, but she has had him, and I—I thought, 'Why should she not know for a little what I have to bear always?'"

"But, Eirene—Zoe has never done you any harm, has always been the kindest of sisters to you."

"I told you you would not understand. You can go and play with Harold, and talk of adopting Janni. I can't forget my own child."

"Forget him—do you imagine I ever forget him? Eirene, why will you always behave as if the loss was yours alone? God knows it was bad enough for you, and I have tried never to make it worse by any word of mine. But you can't think anything will ever make up to me for Con."

"It is different with you. You only think of him as the child you played with, but to me he was the hope of the future, the heir of the Empire, before whom that upstart Romanos would fall headlong. I should have been content for your life and mine to be uneventful, even unsuccessful, if it had meant that he would one day wear the diadem in Hagion Pneuma. But now—what do you think it means to me to go through this farce of empire-building in a country town, visiting hospitals and schools and being gracious to a set of schismatics, with the knowledge that even when Romanos is expelled, no child of yours and mine will take his place? But you don't see it. I tell you, that girl Kalliopé would understand what I feel better than you do!"

"Ah, poor wretched girl!" said Maurice thoughtfully. "We must see that the letter we were discussing last night is sent to Romanos, to say that his son is probably here."

Eirene sprang up from her chair, her eyes blazing. "That is you all over, Maurice! You can think of the usurper even when you are blaming your wife for not showing sufficient consideration for your sister. You may be a saint, as Zoe thinks, but you are not the man for Emathia. Do you imagine that if Romanos had been in your place, Kalliopé would have left his presence without being made to tell what she knows?"

"If I am not the man for Emathia, at least it was not my own choice that took me there," said Maurice. "But if you are right, Kalliopé at any rate has reason to be thankful I am here."

It was without any realisation of her good fortune in this respect that Danaë repaired to the nursery on her dismissal from the inquiry. She entered the room with a certain hesitation, which was immediately justified, for Linton rose in defence of Janni like a ruffled hen.

"You dare to come back here, you wicked girl?" she cried. "Not a step do you set in my nursery, or my name isn't Sophia Linton. And as for letting you lay a finger on the blessed lamb that's left—why, I would sooner trust one of the girls out of the kitchen! You be off, and don't show your face again this side of the door, or I'll teach you something!"

Danaë might have pleaded Wylie's order as a reason for remaining, but her fiery spirit was roused. She went straight to her own room, and took up the bundle she had prepared the night before. She would go and search for Harold herself, and when she brought him back, they would be forced to acknowledge how unjustly they had judged her. She went down the stairs, crossed the great courtyard, and would have passed out at the gate, but the man on guard there barred her way with his rifle.

"Not this way just yet, my dear," he said with a grin. "The back-door is more your style, isn't it?"

"Let me pass!" said Danaë. He laughed in her face.

"Got another baby in that bundle, Lady Stealer-of-Children?"

"Will you let me pass?" she cried, furious.

He became serious. "No, my girl, I won't. You're not to be allowed to leave the Konak. We are too fond of you to let you slip away like this," with a return to jocularity. "When we can exchange you for our little lord, then you may go, and welcome. Back with you!"

She looked at him for a moment as though gauging the possibilities of a struggle, and he bore the scrutiny with a display of white teeth and a pleasing consciousness of the armoury of weapons in his belt. Then she turned without a word, and marched in her stateliest manner across the courtyard. Once back in her own room, she took off the good clothes which she had bought out of her wages during her sojourn at Klaustra and her coin-decorated cap, and put on the worn and dirty garments in which she had come from Therma. Unfastening her hair, she deliberately rearranged it in one long thick plait and one ridiculously short one, and twisted a handkerchief round her head. Then she walked down the stairs again and into the kitchen, and presented herself before the astonished eyes of Artemisia and her underlings.

"I am come to work here," she said.

Amazement checked Artemisia's utterance for a moment, but she made a gallant attempt to rise to the occasion. "Well, this is an honour, and an unexpected one!" she remarked slowly. "The gracious Lady Zoe did not tell me she was going to give me more help, or I should have asked her to send anyone rather than a child-stealer from the islands. Oh, don't eat me, please, Lady Kalliopé! I am not a baby, you know." A snigger from the underlings. "I suppose the Lady Zoe thought there were no children to steal down here. And you have come to work, have you? How sweetly kind of you, lady mine! But they don't do any work in the islands, do they— except robbing guests and murdering them?"

"Let the islands alone," said Danaë gruffly. "If you were a guest there, you would be safe even after saying that."

"Until I had crossed the threshold, I suppose? Once I was outside I might expect a knife in my back. What are you girls laughing at?" with a change of subject disconcerting to the group of gigglers. "Don't you see that the Lady Kalliopé has come to show us all how to work? Give her that bowl of onions, Sonya, and let us see how they peel them in the islands."

After that, Danaë would have suffered tortures rather than resign the bowl of onions to anyone else. The tears ran down her cheeks, but she persisted in the task, and when it was over received an ironical compliment from Artemisia, and was set to clean saucepans. While this was being done, Linton appeared at the kitchen door, with rather a scared face.

"So that's where you've got to, you naughty girl, giving me such a turn, thinking you'd made away with yourself, as you well might!" she cried, catching sight of Danaë. "What's taken you down here I don't know, but you come straight away upstairs again. My Lady says you can sit in your own room and have your meals there, and I'm to find you some needlework."

Danaë raised her black eyes, sombre enough now, and looked straight at her. "I stay here," she said.

"Oh, very well!" cried Linton, with suspicious readiness, "I'm sure I've got no objection. If Kalliopé prefers your company to mine, Artemisia, I hope you're more flattered than I should be. You keep an eye on her, that's all. Don't let her give you the slip."

"Not I, my most beloved Sofia," responded Artemisia. "She'll get a crack on the head with a rolling-pin if she tries it."

"Ah, if only we had sent her straight down here when she first came, what a lot of trouble it would have saved!" lamented Linton. "You know how to manage her, you do."

And she retired from the kitchen in a frame of mind that was almost cheerful, to assure her mistress that that bad girl Kalliopé was now where she belonged, and that it would do her a lot of good to be put back in her place after having so much notice taken of her. Zoe, discovering that the change was a voluntary one on Danaë's part, was puzzled. Was it a kind of penance the girl was imposing on herself for her share in Harold's disappearance, or was it more in the nature of an act of moral suicide? Danaë herself afforded her no help in deciding, for when they came across one another she met Zoe's eager, entreating look with one of blank stolidity. From whatever motive she had chosen her present position, she was making full acquaintance with its disadvantages, for all the heaviest and most unpleasant tasks were by unanimous consent awarded to her. They were many, for the kitchen arrangements at the Konak were patriarchal, dinner being provided every day for the guards as well as for their superiors, and Artemisia had a sarcastic tongue and a heavy hand if everything was not done to her satisfaction. Danaë made no complaint, spoke to no one unless she was asked a question, and went through her work with a silent contempt for her surroundings which her associates found extremely galling. But in her own room at night she was preparing a suit of boy's clothes, clad in which she might elude the vigilance of the guards and fulfil her purpose of escape. For the shirt, loose jacket, and heavy outer coat, her own clothes would do well enough, and the cap and long leggings were easy of manufacture. To make the linen kilt she had recourse to one of the sheets from her bed, cutting the other in two so that Linton's eagle eye might not see that anything was wrong, and for a night or two she practised wearing the new garments, so as to accustom herself to walking in them.

CHAPTER XIV.
A RESCUE EXPEDITION.

DANAË had been three or four days at her new work, conscientiously returning scorn with scorn, when one afternoon the sound of music drew the servants out into the courtyard. A band of gipsies with a dancing bear had obtained admittance, affording a welcome distraction to the suitors waiting their turn to be heard by Prince Theophanis, and Artemisia and her subordinates hastened to take part in the fun. Danaë alone remained in the kitchen, morosely determined to accept no lightening of the penalty she had imposed on herself, though the many-stringed fiddles of the gipsies sounded very pleasant in her ears, and she had a great curiosity to see what a bear was like. She stood with her back to the door, pounding corn, and trying to keep the great pestle from beating time to the music, which made her feet long to dance, and the soft tread of moccasined footsteps failed to reach her ears until, looking up suddenly, she found one of the gipsies close beside her. Before she could scream, he threw back his hooded cloak and revealed the features of Petros. She stared at him aghast.

"So you have come down in the world, my lady!" he observed genially. "But so much the better for me, for I might have found it difficult to speak to you upstairs."

"What are you doing here? You should have been at Therma before this," cried Danaë, finding her tongue.

"Without what I came for, my lady? Besides, the roads were not safe. I had to wait here for a day or two, and it has given me this second chance."

"But what do you want?" she asked, bewildered.

"Why, the little lord, of course. Yourself too, lady, if you insist upon it, but the Lord Janni at any rate."

"But you took the Lord Harold. You can't want both!"

"Oh, can't I?" Petros grinned. "The Lord Harold has a value of his own, my lady. I own that I meant at first to make him serve both purposes, but now you might sooner carry a pet dog through the streets of Czarigrad than a blue-eyed child through the ranks of Glafko's police. He must stay where he is for the present, but you and I and the other can get through all right with the help of the gipsies. They know something about disguises."

"So I see," said Danaë absently, glancing at the skilful alterations made in his appearance by the dark dye on his face and the ferocious horns of his moustache. "Bring the Lord Harold back, and I will come at once."

"Not so, lady. I have said I want both."

"And I have said I will do nothing to help you until he is here."

"Will you ruin your brother, my lady?"

"No, it is you who are ruining him, wasting your time here, and raising the country against you for no good."

"That is for the Lord Romanos to say," muttered Petros mysteriously. "But if I have to go to him at Therma without either child, who will bear the blame then, lady mine?"

"You!" cried Danaë. "As you will when the Lord Glafko has you up before him in a minute or two."

She had been edging gradually sideways, so as to bring the large kitchen table between herself and him, and now she made a dash for the door. But before she reached it, his voice arrested her.

"Betray me if you like, my lady, but that will not restore the Lord Harold. He is where no one can find him, though the police have been closer to him than I am to you, and the gipsies will no more give him up than I would. If necessary they will kill him rather than that he should be discovered in their hands."

"But you have confessed to me that the gipsies are hiding him!" cried Danaë triumphantly.

"True, lady, and you may tell it to the Lord Glafko. But when the gipsies swear that they have no knowledge of him, and the strictest search fails to discover him, is your word of such power that it will be believed in opposition to theirs?"

The hit was a shrewd one, and it told. All the misery of the loss of confidence of the last few days returned upon Danaë. No, her word would not be taken.

"Kalliopé!" Artemisia's voice broke into her indecision from the courtyard. "Where are you, girl? Bring out that plate of honey cakes. The Tzigany says the bear likes them."

She caught up the cakes from the table, but paused at the door. "Go to Therma, then, without the Lord Janni, for you shall not have him. And if any harm comes to the Lord Romanos by this delay, be sure he shall know who is to blame for it."

She was out in the courtyard in a moment, and making for the stalwart form of Artemisia, whose presence would be an effectual protection against any further argument on the part of Petros. The performance having come to an end, and the gipsies reaped their reward of small coins, somebody had suggested that the bear also deserved something.

"Are you sure he likes them?" asked Artemisia doubtfully, with the plate in her hand. "I thought bears ate people and sheep."

"Try him, lady; he would do anything for a honey cake," said the leading gipsy. "If you knew how to hold it, he would dance for it."

"It's all very well to say 'try him,' but what if he prefers me to the cake?" The question was received with a chorus of dutiful laughter by Artemisia's satellites.

"Ladies," said the gipsy, "you seem to think this is an ordinary wild savage bear. I assure you that he is most civilised and polite. Far from eating human beings, he prefers honey cakes to any meat you could offer him. Now if the chief lady will throw one when I say the word——"

The bear opened his mouth at the word of command, and caught the cake which Artemisia threw. After that, amid screams and giggles, the kitchen-girls took their turn, until the cakes were gone. The gipsy smiled superior.

"Now, ladies, I hope you are satisfied. You should see this old fellow playing with the children—never a scratch nor a bite! And his kindness to a little cub we have got——"

"Why, where did you get a bear-cub at this time of the year?" asked a forester standing by.

"Found him in the woods, of course—eight or nine months old now, I suppose. Anyhow he's there, and anyone who likes can come and see him. Does any lady or gentleman want a nice handsome young bear for a pet? We are open to an offer, for he scratches and bites like a little fiend—has to have a muzzle on whenever he sees company. Would the gracious Prince like to buy him, do you think? He would make a fine ornament to this courtyard, chained to a good strong pole in the middle." Fresh screams, and vehement exclamations of dissent from the feminine part of the audience. "Well, you are not very encouraging, I must say, but if anyone can get me into the Prince's presence, and he buys him, I can promise a handsome commission."

The women-servants called down loud maledictions on anyone who might venture to influence the Prince in the desired direction, but Danaë was silent. When the gipsies and the bear moved towards the gateway, to give another performance for the benefit of the guards in their quarters, she followed in the crowd, and observed minutely the various words of command. Princess Theophanis, standing on the verandah of the Prince's house, pointed her out to Armitage.

"That girl is absolutely heartless," she said. "Look at her enjoying that wretched creature's antics!"

"I should be inclined to believe that she hoped to slip outside with the gipsies, and so escape," he said. "But I don't think any of us really understand her yet."

"At any rate, there will be no harm in warning the guard at the gate to be on the alert," said Eirene, "since the Prince seems to think it is important to keep her here."

A servant was summoned and took the message, and her safe custody assured, Danaë passed out of Armitage's thoughts for an hour or two. Then, as he was passing the unused ground-floor rooms on the way to his own room in the dusk, a voice spoke to him out of a doorway. "Lord!" it said, and looking round, he saw a figure crouching against the door.

"Lord," it said again, "were the caves where the gipsies live searched when the Lord Harold was lost?"

"Yes, that was one of the first places where the police went. We all thought of the gipsies, and the caves were searched most thoroughly. I'm afraid there's not much hope in that direction, Kalliopé."

"Lord, would you like to find the Lord Harold?"

"Like to find him? What are you thinking about? Of course I should!" cried Armitage indignantly.

"Well, lord, if you would like to discover him yourself, and with your own hands restore him to the Lady Zoe, will you go out shooting to-morrow, taking my cousin Sotīri as guide, and saying that you will be away all night?"

"Your cousin? I didn't know you had one here. Who is he?"

"He is a very good boy, lord, who can walk far over the mountains. He will carry your gun and food, and show you good sport. Also he will guide you to where the Lord Harold is hidden."

"Kalliopé!" said Armitage, grievously disappointed, "is it possible that you have known where he is all this time? If so, come with me at once to the Lady Zoe, and restore him to her yourself. You can't think that I want the credit instead of you—especially at the price of two more days' unhappiness for her. But no, I can't believe you lied to me the other day."

"No, lord, I spoke the truth, though you alone believed me. And I have known nothing till to-day, nor do I indeed know now. But I guess. If a great force of police went to the place, the people might kill the child or carry him farther away, but seeing only a Milordo and a boy, they will feel no fear. I will tell my cousin Sotīri all that I think, so that he may lead you. And if the child is not there, then the blame is mine and I am deceived. But if he is there——"

"If there's a chance of his being there, it's worth trying. When are we to start, and what is there to shoot?"

"You must start about mid-day, lord. Holy Vasili! I know not what there is to shoot. Wolves? bears?"

"I hope your cousin will be a better guide than you are," said Armitage drily. "How am I to know what gun to take?"

"Lord, your wisdom is great, you know what it will be best to say. Only tell me, that Sotīri may say the same. Shall it be wolves?"

"Bears, I think. They haven't begun their winter sleep yet, and their skins are better. On the whole, I think it will be enough if you say one particular bear."

"Oh no, lord!" she cried in a panic for which Armitage could not account. "I will tell him bears. Then when you are ready, and waiting at the gate, will you call out loudly and angrily for Sotīri, and he will come?"

"Certainly I shall be very angry if he keeps me waiting," said Armitage, with great gravity, and bidding her good-day, went on. His evening was a cheerless one, with Zoe and Wylie, both haggard with hope deferred, each trying to keep up for the sake of the other. As he had said, if there was the slightest chance of relieving their anxiety, it was worthwhile following up the slenderest clue. That Kalliopé believed she had hold of one was evident, but to him, remembering the close search that had been made already, the probability of success seemed but faint. And Danaë herself, now that she had taken the desperate step of enlisting Armitage's support was little more hopeful. Petros was at present among the gipsies, and might be expected, since she had declined to help him in securing Janni, to have left them to-morrow on his way to Therma; Harold was also concealed among them, and in a hiding-place so cunningly contrived that the police had passed quite close to it without suspecting his presence. That was all she had to go upon—that, and the idea which had darted into her mind that afternoon, as she listened to the talk in the courtyard; an idea monstrous, incredible, but just possible.

Armitage was conscious of a disconcerting suspicion that he was a fool when he found himself at the gate the next day, laden with his gun, a thick coat, and a basket of provisions. He was quite certain that the man on guard thought him one.

"I am looking for a Greek boy who was coming with me, Gavril. Sotīri is his name. Have you seen him?"

"There are plenty of the young rascals about, lord, but I don't know all their silly names. What should a Greek know of our mountains? Better take an honest Slav. I myself, if you would ask leave for me from the Lord Glafko——"

"That must be another day. The boy shall have his chance. He has promised to show me a bear. Sotīri!"

"Take care that he isn't a brigand spy, lord, hired to lead you into an ambush. The ransom of a Milordo——"

"Well, if I am not back by this time to-morrow, you must come and look for me. Sotīri! I shall not wait any longer."

"Here, lord, here!" cried a panting voice, and a handsome boy in Greek dress dashed across the courtyard. His *kapota* was rolled up over one shoulder, but he seized the basket and Armitage's gun. "My cousin kept me so long talking. Let me carry your coat too, lord. It can go over my other shoulder."

"I will carry the basket, then. Be careful with the gun," and Armitage passed out, followed by his henchman. They went through the streets of the town, exchanging greetings with the people they met, but Armitage noticed that Sotīri did not seem to be known personally to the Greeks who saluted him, for though his dress was a passport to their sympathies they looked curiously at his face. On the other side of the town the mountains frowned close above the houses, divided by a gorge down which flowed the torrent which provided the water-supply, and in a series of caves, natural or artificial, in the sides of this gorge the gipsies had sojourned from time immemorial. When they reached the foot of the path which led to the caves, Armitage stopped and called up the boy, who had managed to make himself almost invisible under his load of coats.

"Now, Sotīri, tell me what your cousin's plan is. We are not to march up to the first cave we come to, and demand the Lord Harold, I suppose?"

"No, lord, we cannot hope to recover him till night. But we can find out where he is. Will you graciously ask to see the bear-cub that the gipsies offered for sale at the Konak yesterday, and offer to buy him? My cousin does not think they will be willing to sell him, but it is important we should see the cave in which the bears live."

"Very well. Your voice is curiously like your cousin's, Sotīri. You had better give me the gun while we are going up hill. It is too heavy for you."

"Nay, lord, rather do you give me the basket. You must not judge my strength by Kalliopé's," cried the boy, with a gay laugh. "I have carried far heavier loads up worse hills than these. And it is unkind to compare my voice to a girl's."

"So it is, Sotīri. I beg your pardon. Well, in a year or two you will be able to laugh at the idea. Meanwhile I will stick to the basket. And be sure to stand where I can see you when I am talking to the gipsies, in case you want to make any sign to me."

"As you will, lord." Sotīri dropped behind again respectfully, and presently Armitage received confirmation of certain suspicions that had occurred to him. Missing the sound of the labouring breath behind him, he turned suddenly, to discover coats and gun on the ground, while with frantic haste Sotīri was twisting up a long plait of hair which had escaped from beneath his cap. Not having been seen, Armitage allowed himself a smile, and went on a step or two.

"Do you find it too heavy, Sotīri?" he called out, without turning round.

"No, lord," replied a hasty voice. "I dropped my cap, and had to go back for it."

"Better keep close to me here," said Armitage, as they turned the corner of a rock, and came out on a narrow platform of stone which appeared to form the centre of the social life of the gipsy community. The moment they showed themselves, every hole and cranny in the cliff seemed to disgorge humanity, and they were quickly surrounded by a crowd—old women offering to tell their fortunes, young women rolling bold eyes at them, children pawing their clothes with dirty hands, and all begging shrilly in a dozen different languages. With great wisdom Armitage addressed himself to the oldest, ugliest, most withered and most generally witch-like of the women, and presenting her with a handful of small coin for general distribution, asked if he could speak to the head of the tribe about the bear-cub he had to sell. The old woman looked doubtful. She was not sure whether the tribe would sell the cub after all. It had brought them good luck, and they thought of keeping it and training it to perform with the other bear. Armitage expressed so much disappointment, however, and hinted at such a good price, that the old woman hobbled off at last to the cave where the chief, who turned out to be her son, was sleeping, and woke him. With him a dozen swarthy, cunning-eyed rapscallions were added to the group, and listened greedily while Armitage made his offer. But the chief was adamant, though for a different reason from that given by his mother. The cub had been sold that very morning—a murmur of resentment rose from the women—to a rich Pannonian gentleman who was going to present it to the Zoological Gardens at Vindobona.

"This is most disappointing," said Armitage. "I wanted to make a sketch of him, and then to present him to Prince Romanos, who is establishing a natural history collection at Therma. Would you mind showing him to me, that I may see whether he is larger than another I have heard of?"

"There's no objection to that, if the gracious gentleman quite understands that the creature is not to be bought," said the chief. "The bears are kept here."

They moved towards another cave, and two men went in. One led out the dancing bear, which shambled blinking into the light, the other, standing just inside the entrance, showed a brown furry body in his arms.

"We dare not bring him out, lord, lest seeing a stranger he should begin to scratch and fight," explained the chief. "He is muzzled already, as you see."

Armitage looked critically at the little bear, while Sotīri, at his side, gazed with awestruck eyes into the gloomy recesses of the cave. "A fine little beast! Do you think you could get him quiet if I came here to sketch him another day? I would pay, of course."

The chief seemed doubtful. The creature had a very uncertain temper, but if the gracious gentleman cared to take the trouble of coming again, and run the risk of disappointment—— Armitage reassured him, and arranged to come again the next morning, in case the purchaser of the cub should wish to take him away soon. Then, guided by a gipsy who was to lead them to the top of the gorge, and show them the way into the woods, he and Sotīri went on. When they had parted with their guide, he turned eagerly to the boy.

"Well, Sotīri, is it all right? Did you find out what you wanted to know?"

"Yes, lord, I found what I expected to find."

A light broke upon Armitage. "You mean that they have the child hidden in the bear's den?" he cried.

"Yes, lord, he is hidden in the bear's den. And now, with your gracious permission, we must go a long way into the woods, in case the gipsies send after us, and then we must come back to this same place."

Armitage took out his compass and made the necessary observations, and then he and Sotīri plunged into the forest and walked on till they were tired. Dusk was beginning to fall, and retracing their steps was a long and painful process. It was quite dark when at length they arrived again at the edge of the wood, at a point where, by going a few steps further, they could look down the gorge, and see the twinkling lights which showed where the gipsies were cooking their supper in the mouths of their caves. Sotīri helped Armitage into his coat, unfastened the straps of the provision-basket, and retired to a respectful distance. It was a mild night, and the withered beech-leaves made a comfortable couch. Armitage ate and drank, and then reflected that if Sotīri were as hungry as he was, the share of food which he had given him on his horrified refusal to sit down and eat with his employer must be quite insufficient. He called to the boy, in a low voice at first, then louder, but no answer came. Following the direction he had taken, he came upon him, wrapped in his *kapota*, fast asleep, with the untasted food by his side. Armitage stole back to his place without waking him.

"They may say what they like, but that is a fine creature!" he said to himself.

CHAPTER XV.
THE ACME.

AFTER smoking a cigar or two, Armitage fell into a doze, from which he tried at first to rouse himself by spasmodic efforts, but reflecting that in any case it must be hours before they could safely approach the gipsy settlement, he allowed himself after a time to yield to the drowsiness that was overpowering him. From this he was roused at last by an anxious voice.

"Lord, where are you? Lord, lord!" and almost simultaneously some one stumbled and fell over him.

Armitage sat up. "Gently, Sotīri, gently! What's the matter, lad?"

An embarrassed laugh answered him out of the darkness, where Sotīri was presumably picking himself up. "I don't know, lord; I think I must have been dreaming. I woke up and was frightened to find myself in the forest in the dark, and then I went the wrong way to look for you and could not find you, and I thought you had gone away and left me——"

"To storm the gipsy caves by myself? Hardly. Stand in front of me, boy, while I see what the time is."

Sotīri obeyed, and Armitage struck a match and looked at his watch. "A quarter past twelve. Better not start for an hour or so, for no one will be awake in the town, and we don't want to have to wait about when once we have got the child. We will have something more to eat, Sotīri—lighten the basket a little."

Sotīri laughed again. "I have not eaten nearly all you gave me, lord. I think I must have gone to sleep in the middle. I will go back and finish it."

"Get another nap, and I will tell you when it is time to start," Armitage called after him in a low voice, and then moved nearer the edge of the cleft, whence he could look down the gorge, and see the few remaining fires dying out one by one. Here, away from the shadow of the trees, he could just distinguish the time without striking a light, and he sat and shivered, restraining his impatience manfully, until two o'clock. Then he went back to the wood and called Sotīri, who appeared shamefacedly.

"I did not think I could have gone to sleep again, lord, but if it had not been for your voice I believe I should not have waked till morning. Then we may really start now? I have everything ready here."

From the recesses of his coat he produced two parcels, at which Armitage glanced in surprise. He unfastened one.

"Honey cakes for the bear, lord. They are what he likes better than anything. Holy Nicholas! how Artemisia must have cursed when she found half her batch gone! That was really what made me late in starting—Kalliopé was getting them, you see. And this—" indicating the other parcel—"is meat for the dogs."

"To keep them quiet, of course—I never thought of that. But then you and Kalliopé have kept me so entirely in the dark as to what we were going to do that I had not much chance. It is a pity she didn't tell me about the dogs, for we might have sprinkled something on the meat that would send them to sleep."

"Oh, is there something that will do that?" asked Sotīri in dismay. "I am sorry, lord; I—we did not know."

"Well, we must hope the meat alone will be enough. Now, before we start, tell me exactly what we are going to do."

"This is my plan, lord. I will go on first, if you please, my moccasins making little noise on the path, and give the meat to the dogs. You will follow, and when we reach the ledge of rock you will graciously take from me the gun and the coats, so as to leave me quite free. Then I will go into the bear's den, and fetch the child out."

"You go into the den alone? Nonsense, I won't hear of it!"

"Lord, the bear will not mind me. I have the honey cakes for him, and I know the words the gipsies use to bid him be quiet. Kalliopé has told me them all. He may not even wake when I go in, but the noise of your boots would rouse him at once."

"I don't like it," said Armitage reluctantly. "However, I shall be there with the gun, if he turns nasty. Look here, give me the things to carry now, boy; I insist upon it. You must have your hands free to cope with the dogs."

"As you will, lord," and they started, Armitage keeping his eyes on Sotīri's white kilt as a guide. When they had nearly reached the ledge, they heard the uneasy bark of a dog in front, which was answered by a chorus of others, dying down gradually as no further suspicious sound was heard. The boy held up his hand, and crept on alone, Armitage following very slowly and with great caution. Looking along the ledge, he could discern Sotīri surrounded by a horde of curs, which he was feeding with discrimination on choice morsels from his pockets. When the dogs were all occupied, Armitage judged it safe to advance, and they merely favoured him with a snarl as he approached them. Sotīri had left them to their feast, and crept into the dark mouth of the nearest cave. Armitage, waiting in intensest anxiety with his gun cocked, heard a menacing growl, which made him step forward, but a peremptory low voice uttered a word of command, and the clatter of a chain followed as the bear retreated. Then Sotīri hurried out, with something in his arms, and without a word led the way along the ledge, past the other caves, Armitage following.

"You have got him all right?" he ventured to ask, when they were on the descending path once more, and he had uncocked his gun.

"Yes, lord, all right," with something like a giggle. "I think he is asleep."

A feeble cry from the burden contradicted this, and Sotīri clasped it closely to his breast, and crooned over it in tender accents, which drew another smile from Armitage. At the foot of the hill the boy turned to skirt the town, instead of passing through it, and Armitage in his mind applauded the wisdom of the course. If the gipsies should discover what had happened, and pursue them in force, they would certainly expect them to take a straight line for the Konak. They plodded on wearily when the expectation of immediate pursuit had passed, and in the faint lightening of the darkness which preceded dawn, Armitage received a shock.

"Sotīri!" he cried, running forward regardless of his load, and grasping the boy's shoulder, "you have brought away the bear-cub, not the Lord Harold at all!"

Sotīri laughed—a weary little laugh, but one full of amusement. "And yet it is the Lord Harold, lord. Here is a thick bush; you can strike a match safely."

Standing in the shelter of the thicket, Armitage obeyed. There before his horrified gaze was the furry form of the little bear. But as he looked, Sotīri tilted the upper jaw back like a cap, and exposed Harold's dark head and blinking blue eyes.

"You don't mean to say they had the cheek to keep him dressed up like that?" cried Armitage.

"Yes, lord; that was the secret," said Sotīri demurely.

"Good heavens—Princess Zoe's child! It's too disgusting. Now mind, boy, his mother mustn't see him like this. It would give her an awful shock. We must get hold of Linton somehow, to dress him properly."

"Why, lord, will she care what he wears, so long as she has him back?" asked the boy. Armitage frowned.

"Of course not, really, but one has a feeling—— You don't understand, but it's a horrible idea."

"Very well, lord, I do not understand. I will see whether I can find Sofia." The boy spoke so meekly, but with such an undertone of pain, that Armitage had the unreasonable feeling that in some way he had been a brute. He said no more until they came in sight of the Konak, and then he called Sotīri back.

"See here, lad; I have been thinking it's not necessary to bring Linton into this. Call your cousin instead. The whole credit of getting the child back is due to her, isn't it? Very well, then; she ought to have the pleasure of giving him back to his mother, and she shall."

"Thank you, lord," said Sotīri joyfully. Then his face fell. "You say the whole credit is hers, lord. Don't you think I helped at all—even when I went into the bear's den? I was really frightened."

"I think you are an impudent young rascal, boy," was the reply, given with much severity. "Even if you were frightened, you ought to be swaggering about now, and pretending you weren't. You'll never make a man at this rate—a Greek man, anyhow. And as for trying to do your cousin out of the credit which belongs to her, I tell you it's a shabby trick. Why, you know what trouble she is in at present, and if you and I, by sinking our share in the business, can help her to get back to her former position, doesn't she deserve it?"

"You are right, lord. I am a beast," was the subdued reply, and as Sotīri walked mournfully on ahead, Armitage suffered agonies from suppressed laughter. "I don't know whether I'm standing on my head or my heels," he said to himself.

Arrived at the gateway of the Konak, Armitage knocked authoritatively, and though the guard on duty refused vehemently at first even to entertain the idea of admitting them before sunrise, he yielded when he heard who was outside. Harold in his furry disguise was wrapped in Sotīri's *kapota*, and completely hidden, which excited wild curiosity on the guard's part as to the results of the expedition. Armitage imposed silence on him by means of a gift, and they hurried across the courtyard to the colonnade outside the unused rooms, where he had spoken to Kalliopé two nights before. Harold was suddenly thrust into his arms, as Sotīri said hastily, "One moment, lord!" then turned back to say with great emphasis, "Since we started, lord, my cousin has been hiding in one of these rooms. So anxious was she for the child's recovery that she could not bring herself to remain among the servants, but sought refuge here, that I might bring her the news as soon as we returned."

"Poor thing! she must indeed have been anxious," said Armitage gravely, and the boy disappeared. When a step was next heard on the stone pavement, it was Kalliopé who approached. She lifted her eyes silently to Armitage's face, and he saw that there were black circles of fatigue surrounding them which stood out clearly in comparison with the whiteness of her cheeks, but inconsistently enough, he found her more beautiful than even the first day he had seen her. She took his hand and kissed it, lifted Harold from his arms, and was gone. Armitage felt a sudden sense of flatness, an uncertainty as to what ought to be done next, which was disconcerting after the crowding events of the last eighteen hours. Then he surprised himself in a tremendous yawn, and very wisely found his way to his room and went to bed.

He was awakened after what seemed about a minute's sleep by a vigorous knocking, followed by the unceremonious entrance of Wylie, who burst in, and seizing his hand, shook it with such energy that Armitage cried for mercy.

"My dear good man," he nursed the released hand ostentatiously, "what in the world is it?"

"Oh, nonsense, don't try to shirk! We know it's all owing to you, old man. Kalliopé has been telling us all about it, though we can't make head or tail of her story. Who is this cousin who went with you? We never heard of him. But what does it signify, when you've brought the boy back? I tell you I thought I was dreaming, when I felt a tug at my moustache—something like a tug, too—and heard a little voice saying 'Da! da!' but when I opened my eyes there was Zoe with the child in her arms. Old man, you can't conceive what it is to get him back. Hurry up and dress. Zoe wants to thank you herself. She and Linton and Kalliopé are all on their knees at this moment baby-worshipping, with a shifting audience of women from other parts of the place. I'm going on now to tell Maurice. We can never thank you enough."

"Don't thank me at all," said Armitage. "The whole idea was Kalliopé's, and she provided in her cousin a highly efficient instrument for carrying it out. I only obeyed orders. By the bye, I hear she was in hiding all day yesterday. Did you find it out?"

"We thought she had slipped through our fingers, of course, and there was a good deal of mutual recrimination among the servants. Where she hid I can't imagine, for we thought we had hunted everywhere. Well, poor girl, she has heaped coals of fire upon our heads—in a sort of way, for there are a lot of suspicious things about her still. But be quick and get dressed."

When he was gone, Armitage obeyed, and in due course found his way to the verandah, where Harold, fresh from a most necessary bath, and dressed by the rejoicing Linton in his Sunday frock, was the centre of attraction on his mother's knee. Zoe looked up with eyes full of tears.

"Oh, we can never, never thank you enough!" she cried. "Harold, give Uncle a kiss and say 'Ta' to him for bringing you back." Harold obeyed solemnly. "I don't think he looks any worse, except perhaps a little thinner—do you?" she went on anxiously. "Isn't it horrid that he can never tell us how they treated him, because he will have forgotten all about it when he is able to talk? But I really believe he hasn't had his face washed all the time he has been gone. Still, if there's nothing worse than that, we may be most thankful. What is it, Parisi? Breakfast? How can one think of breakfast now? If you really had the fine feelings you expect me to credit you with, you would have put some food unobtrusively on the table over there, and left us to discover it when we remembered we were hungry."

Parisi smiled respectfully. He was a highly cultured person, having once edited an Athenian newspaper, but he could never see a joke when it was against himself. Having duly acknowledged Zoe's attempt at wit, he repeated in a soft murmur, "The gracious lady is served," and stood aside to allow her to pass downstairs.

"Oh dear, I suppose we must go!" groaned Zoe. "But Harold must come, and sit in his high chair beside me. And Janni had better come too, poor little fellow! for he feels himself quite eclipsed. Do you know, he is really most frightfully jealous—after having Linton all to himself, of course. We must all take particular notice of him to-day——"

"If we can, in the presence of this conquering hero," said Armitage, holding out his arms for Harold. "Let me carry my god-son downstairs, Princess. I see Prince Theophanis is coming across with Wylie to pay his respects, so this youngster is highly honoured."

"Now do tell me," began Zoe, when they were seated at breakfast, and Maurice had presented his own and Eirene's most hearty congratulations, "how you managed it. Oh, and where is this wonderful boy Sotīri? He seems to have turned up just when he was wanted, and disappeared without waiting to be thanked. But I must thank him. I can't be happy until I have done it. Surely you must know where he is?"

"I'm afraid I am partly to blame for his disappearance," said Armitage. "It struck me that he was a little inclined to insist on his share in the exploit and belittle his cousin's, and I let him know that I didn't think it quite fair. I'm sorry if I hurt his feelings, though, for he did well. What do you think about your cousin, Kalliopé?" he turned to Danaë, whose face was a study as she stood behind Janni's chair, and spoke in Greek. "Has he run off because I scolded him?"

She responded with eager haste. "Oh no, lord, it is nothing of that kind. He has done what he came for, and is gone. You will never see him again. He would wish you to forget him. To be thanked and praised is a thing he would detest."

"Then Kalliopé must act as his representative, and take his thanks and praise as well as her own," said Wylie.

"Yes," said Zoe. "Kalliopé, what is there that you would really like? You understand that nothing the Lord Glafko and I could do for you would be in the slightest degree the measure of our gratitude, but we should like to give you something tangible at once, which would show the servants what we thought of you."

The girl's eyes glowed, then gloomed. "Something that I should really like, lady mine?" she asked breathlessly.

"Yes, whatever you like best," Zoe assured her. "Don't be afraid, Kalliopé. Tell me what it is, and if we have not got it here we will send for it at once." She expected to be asked for a watch and chain, of the showy kind that Artemisia and her like loved to display upon the velvets and satins of their feast-day attire, but Danaë fell upon her knees, and breathed out the desire of her heart in scarcely audible accents.

"Lady—oh, lady mine, if I may indeed have what I should prize most in all the world, let me for this one evening wear European clothes, and eat at your table as if I were a European like yourselves!"

The grotesque nature of the request, and the passion with which it was urged, took Zoe aback. "But, Kalliopé, that is rather a foolish wish, isn't it?" she asked kindly. "Wouldn't you rather have something real, that you could keep and show, and take away with you, when you go?"

The girl rose to her feet, her eyes heavy with tears. "I knew it was too much. I have no other wish, lady. Give me what you will."

"Oh, let her do it, Zoe!" cried Wylie sharply.

"I will bring Eirene to dinner to meet her," said Maurice.

"Let her do it, Princess," said Armitage. "She deserves it."

"Of course you shall do it, Kalliopé, if you really wish it," said Zoe, her momentary hesitation overborne. "I will lend you one of my gowns—you shall choose whichever you like—and I will do your hair for you myself. I won't trust even Linton. There! will that please you?"

"Oh, lady mine, you give as a king gives—with both hands full," cried Danaë, with a half-sob, as she knelt again and laid Zoe's hand on her head. "Never, never will I forget your goodness to me!" and she burst into tears.

"She is tired out," said Armitage—rather to Zoe's surprise when she thought about it afterwards. "Better let her have a good rest, Princess. Must have been pretty wearing—hiding away all yesterday and not knowing whether we should come back successful or not," he observed to the others, when Zoe had led the sobbing girl out of the room.

No one saw anything more of Kalliopé until the evening, when Linton, divided between gratitude for her achievement and acute disapproval of the method of its reward, woke her that she might choose her gown. To the maid's indignation and Zoe's amusement, she picked out unhesitatingly the most magnificent thing in the wardrobe, a Parisian creation of glittering golden tissue which Zoe had worn at the court ball that formed the culminating point of the series of splendid festivities before the departure of the allied fleets from Therma, by which Prince Romanos had signalised his own election and the wedding of his rival's sister. Linton almost wept when she was bidden to alter the hooks a little to allow for the Greek girl's classic development of figure, and Zoe was glad she should be spared the further pang of seeing her mistress acting hairdresser to this upstart. But when the thick blue-black locks, still disconcertingly short on one side, were ready for manipulation, Danaë turned suddenly, and took the comb out of Zoe's hand.

"Lady, I must tell you—perhaps you will not think me worthy of all this honour when you have heard—I have no cousin. It was I who put on boy's clothes and went with Milordo yesterday to find the Lord Harold."

"Kalliopé!" Zoe exclaimed in dismay, but the anxiety in the girl's eyes moved her. "It was very brave of you, and I can only thank you all the more," she added hastily.

"Then you don't mind, lady?" with incredulous joy.

"No-o, not for this once. Not that you are to think that I want you to go about in boy's clothes at other times," firmly. "You are never to do it again."

"Not unless it is necessary. I have done it once before—in Strio," she added quickly. "Lady, did Milordo guess?"

"I really don't know," said Zoe. Then, reviewing what had been said at breakfast, she decided in her own mind that he very certainly had guessed. "But if he did, you may be quite sure that no human being will ever hear a word of it from him," she added.

- 136 -

"Thank you, my lady," said Danaë soberly, and they turned again to the hairdressing. Presently Linton brought back the gown, and Zoe and she refused to let the girl see herself until the transformation was complete. Then, as Linton wheeled forward the large cheval-glass, there was a simultaneous gasp from the three women. Kalliopé in this guise was superb—there was no other word for it. The masses of dark hair, the alabaster complexion thrown up by the gold of the gown, the splendidly moulded arms and shoulders, made her a matchless picture. Danaë herself was the first to speak.

"Lady, you will let me wear that?" pointing to a great boa of fluffy white ostrich feathers. "I—I am not accustomed——" Zoe threw it round her shoulders, and sighed.

"I shall never dare to wear that gown again, now I have seen how splendid she looks in it," she said in English, and Linton replied—

"Well, ma'am, I don't deny I was against it, but this I will say: it would have been a sin and a shame for the girl not to be dressed properly once in her life."

"It suits you magnificently, Kalliopé," said Zoe in Greek, as she caught the anxious glance the girl was directing from one to the other. "Now walk about a little, while Linton dresses me, and learn to manage your train."

"Lady—" Danaë paused to enjoy the effect of her dark head rising out of the creamy feathers—"don't you think Milordo will want to make a picture of me now?"

"I don't know," said Zoe, rather taken aback. "We will ask him, if you like."

Danaë assented joyfully, and Zoe found her eyes on her continually during the evening, which really went off very well. The difficulty Maurice had found in fulfilling his promise to bring his wife was known only to himself, but since he had argued her from her first flat refusal, through the assertion that the mere request was an insult, to the position that the whole thing was a mad joke, and never to be presumed upon afterwards, he felt he had reason to be satisfied. Having submitted, Eirene made up her mind to do so with a good grace, and if she had known Danaë to be a young princess she could not have treated her more graciously. The girl showed by her behaviour that she had used her eyes to good purpose since her arrival at Klaustra. Her mistakes were wonderfully few, and she repaired or ignored them, as seemed most advisable at the moment, with a natural dignity that left nothing to be desired. Small-talk she was not an adept in, but Armitage found her a promising pupil, and after all, it was not necessary for her to talk—merely to sit and allow herself to be looked at.

Nevertheless, he was curiously disconcerted when Zoe came up to him in the drawing-room afterwards, with the stately beauty following her like a shadow.

"Lady Kalliopé wants to know whether you will paint her portrait in this dress?" she said lightly, but the girl's eyes were tragic with entreaty. Armitage frowned.

"Certainly not. Think of the incongruity!"

"It would please her very much," Zoe urged.

"You do not like me this evening, lord?" asked Danaë mournfully.

"I like you better in your own dress," was the stout reply.

"Oh no, lord—not in those common clothes!"

"Just to please her—she has deserved it," said Zoe.

"Well, look here," said Armitage in desperation. "May I take this sheet of paper, Princess?" He went to the writing-table, and using the blotter as a sketching-block, drew rapidly for two or three minutes, with swift glances at Danaë. When he handed the paper to Zoe, there were two figures on it, each expressed with the utmost economy of strokes—Danaë in her present dress, all train and long gloves, with a coronet of hair emerging above a fluffy mass of ostrich feathers, and Danaë in her native costume, standing on a cliff looking out to sea, one hand shading her eager eyes, vitality in every line of her form. "Now which of those do you like best?" he asked triumphantly.

"Oh, this one, lord!" was the fervent reply, as Danaë laid her hand affectionately on the one representing her at the moment. Armitage laughed, but not very heartily.

"I am beaten," he said. "Well, as the Lady Kalliopé pleases."

"It is really a caricature," said Zoe, in a vexed tone. "You can hardly see anything of her."

"No. After all, it is a picture of the gown that is wanted, isn't it? Why, think; I shall be able to paint the whole thing without the sitter's being in the room—or even in the neighbourhood." Armitage did not guess how prophetic the words would seem to him later.

Danaë was satisfied. When she came to Zoe's room that night to restore her borrowed plumes, she smiled happily as she pulled off her gloves.

"Oh, if only every day were like this evening, lady mine, how good I could be!" she sighed.

CHAPTER XVI.
J'ACCUSE.

THE glow of that wonderful evening had faded into the light of common day, and the conquering beauty in gold tissue was Cinderella again in her despised national dress. But for the present the memory was enough, and Linton's caustic comments were forgotten in the glorious fact that Kalliopé, the underling, had for once associated on equal terms with Linton's employers. These employers were too much occupied this morning with their own affairs to have much thought to spare for their guest of the night before. The post, which was not by any means a daily, or even a regular occurrence, came in before breakfast was over, and Armitage tore open one of his letters with considerable excitement.

"Old Pazzi!" he said. "He's on his way here—ought to get in to-day. Says he had just had my letter telling him we thought we might be able to give him news of his grandson, and was starting at once."

"Poor old man! How nice it will be if Janni really is his grandson," said Zoe.

"Will it?" asked her husband. "In that case Janni would also be the son of Prince Romanos, you must remember, and we should find ourselves in a dilemma between them."

"Why, Maurice!" cried Zoe, rising to greet her brother. "Have you come to breakfast? Do sit here."

"No, thanks; I have breakfasted. Is there any news from Pazzi? Here is Romanos writing to declare himself the most unfortunate and worst treated man in the world, and casting himself upon us for advice and help. He is coming here privately, and is due to arrive to-day. The queer thing is that he is bringing Panagiotis with him."

"Had he got your letter about Janni?" asked Wylie quickly.

"Evidently not. I didn't mention Janni, you know—put it very carefully, that circumstances had come to our knowledge intimately connected with his private affairs, and it was possible we might be able to throw some light on them—but he makes no allusion to it. Besides, he must have started before it could have arrived."

"Well, Pazzi is on his way here, and is also due to-day."

"You don't think they are travelling together? No, one of them would surely have mentioned it. And where does the Professor come in?"

"I should say he is at his favourite game—acting as friend of both parties. He and Romanos have discovered that Pazzi is on his way here, and they are afraid of revelations. So they are coming too."

"Which party will get here first?—or will they arrive together? Well, I suppose we shall get some light now on many things. Zoe, I think it would be well not to tell Kalliopé who is coming."

"I shouldn't dream of it. There will be nothing startling in the Cavaliere's returning to his duties, of course, and as Prince Romanos is travelling incog., there is no reason to mention his name at all."

As it happened, the Cavaliere Pazzi was the first of the travellers to arrive. Armitage was out sketching, and Maurice and Wylie were busy administering justice when he reached the Konak, so that he was ushered at once to the verandah where Zoe was sitting with the children and Danaë. The old man's face looked pinched and worn, but his eyes gleamed with youthful fire.

"You have news for me, madame?" he said eagerly. "It cannot be, as I have once or twice in my hurried journey been tempted to fear, that you have held out a false hope to allure me back from Therma?"

Zoe spoke in Greek to Danaë. "Bring me the Lord Janni, Kalliopé." The girl obeyed, and Zoe took the child and set him on the old man's knee. "So far as we can tell, that is your grandchild, Cavaliere."

"This, madame? Ah, I think I can trace in him something of my lost Olimpia, though more of her treacherous husband. Is it not a misfortune, that I cannot behold even this relic of my child without recalling her murderer?"

"Can you not be satisfied to rejoice that he is alive, without blaming him for what he can't help?"

"His nurse snatched him from destruction, I suppose?"

"So we believe, but she told so many contradictory stories at first—owing to terror, perhaps—that we have really left off questioning her about it. Now look at him, Cavaliere; isn't he a dear little fellow? Kiss your grandfather, Janni; he loves you very much."

Janni had maintained his position only by dint of being forcibly held there, for the Cavaliere's piercing eyes and beaklike nose made him a formidable person, but now he looked up into his face, and apparently reading there some encouragement, put his arms shyly round his neck. The old man was much moved.

"Blessings on thee, my Giannino!" he cried. "And it was this little angel, madame, that his unnatural father tried to murder!"

"Ah, that we cannot be sure of," said Zoe earnestly. "The Prince is coming here, and must tell his own story."

"Coming here—that villain? Madame, I entreat you, let me take this child, and the faithful woman to whose devotion I owe it that he is spared to me, and seek safety before he is exposed to fresh dangers."

He stood up, with Janni in his arms, and seemed ready to start at once. Zoe was at her wits' end.

"But after all, Cavaliere, he is the Prince's son as well as your grandson," she pleaded. "We cannot let him go away till his father has seen him."

"And succeeded in killing him?" with a grim smile.

"But we don't know that he did try to kill him. And it's quite certain that he won't try to do it here. Besides, don't you see what a good thing it will be for you and the Prince to thresh matters out together on neutral ground, so to speak? You don't want to go on believing such a dreadful thing as that poor Donna Olimpia was murdered by her own husband if it isn't true?"

"I think, madame, that it will take a cleverer tongue than even my son-in-law's to persuade me of his innocence."

"Well, then," urged Zoe desperately, "if he did do it, perhaps he will let you keep Janni rather than have the scandal made public. And if he did try to kill him, surely he won't want him now?"

"Will you pledge yourself that your brother and husband will not give up the child to him, madame?"

"How can I? If he can clear himself, I suppose it is natural he should have him back. But if not, then I think I can promise that at any rate we shall keep Janni in our own charge for the present."

She saw with much relief that this suggestion was acceptable, for the old man's mien had been so determined as to make her fear it would be necessary to send for Wylie to prevent his carrying off Janni bodily forthwith. Now he replaced him gently on her knee.

"You have given me fresh life, madame, in restoring to me this little child. I see myself returning to my modest dwelling with a new interest in place of that of which I have been so cruelly deprived, concealing from the lad the sad story of his parentage, and bringing him up as a worthy descendant of Maxim Psicha. Even in the materialistic and impoverished Magnagrecia of to-day, there will be a place in the army for the grandson of a veteran of the War of Independence, and in the meantime my pension will suffice for us. The girl there is the deserving young woman to whom I owe the preservation of this precious life?"

"Yes; but, Cavaliere, you have asked her no questions—merely taken for granted that Janni is your grandson. Would you like me to interpret for you?"

"No, madame, I will ask her no questions now, lest it should be charged against me that I have put words into her mouth. I will question her in the presence of her late master—and I entreat you to bring it about that I may do so as soon as possible. I am an old man, and I have travelled fast, but I cannot rest until I have unmasked the villain."

"I hear sounds as if some one was arriving," said Zoe, rising. "If it is the Prince, and he is willing, we might talk about things after lunch. But will you not put it off till to-night, and rest a little first?"

"I cannot, madame. I am my daughter's avenger."

They went down the stairs together, leaving Danaë a prey to intense curiosity and apprehension. The Cavaliere's treatment of Janni had at once recalled to her mind the words of Petros respecting the arrival of the Lady's father at Therma. But if this was the man, how much did he know, and how much did her employers know? She was racked with anxiety, for the lies which had once come so glibly to her lips were now harder to frame, and moreover, they had landed her in such a tangle that she did not know how to extricate herself. Even if she gave the lie to everything she had said already, she and Janni and their relations with Petros must still be accounted for—and she had no means of discovering how much or how little of the truth it would be expedient to make known. She walked restlessly about, trying to decide what to do, and as her gaze fell casually into the courtyard, she was electrified to see her brother crossing it in company with Prince Theophanis. Next to Petros, Prince Romanos was the last person she desired to see at the moment, and she dropped down behind the parapet, but not before he had caught a glimpse of her. The moment before, he had been walking wearily, like one tired and depressed, his shoulders bowed, his very moustache drooping. But the merest sight of a handsome girl acted as a challenge, and he drew himself up, squared his shoulders and twisted his moustache. Then, to the intense amusement of his sister, watching him from between the railings, he pretended to have dropped something and induced his host to go back with him a dozen yards or so to look for it, that he might swagger past again, casting furtive glances up at the verandah in search of the face he had seen.

"You should wear a kilt, lord—not European riding-clothes—if you want to show off properly," Danaë addressed him mentally, veering unconsciously towards Armitage's views on costume. "But what are you doing here? and what is Friend Secretary going to do? What has been discovered? How much does anyone know?"

Questions very similar to these were in the minds of all those who met at the luncheon-table of Prince and Princess Theophanis. Wylie and his wife and Armitage were there to meet Prince Romanos and Professor Panagiotis, and in the presence of the servants nothing important could be discussed. It struck most of the English party as quaint that Prince Romanos, whose whole future, so far as could be judged, hung upon the result of the forthcoming conference, was very much at his ease—almost as if he had transferred his burden to the shoulders of his friends, and it was no further concern of his. He even remarked to Zoe that she had a remarkably pretty girl in her household, but unfortunately very shy, and she reflected that years did not seem to have wrought much change in him. When they moved into the drawing-room, however, there was a general feeling that something was going to happen, and the almost instant appearance of the Cavaliere Pazzi showed that it was not to be long delayed. He and his son-in-law bowed to one another coldly.

"I heard that you were ahead of me, monsieur," said the Prince.

"I thought it probable that you might follow me," was the reply, given with studious lack of formality. The Prince's sallow face flushed darkly, and Maurice interfered in haste.

"You may be surprised by our claiming acquaintance with your private affairs, Prince, but as a matter of fact, your wife confided the news of your marriage to my sister very soon after it occurred."

"She could not have found a better confidant," said Prince Romanos politely, but Zoe found his eyes fixed gloomily upon her. He was clearly asking himself whether it was possible that she could have kept this damaging secret—known, no doubt, to her husband also—so long without making use of it to injure him?

"It did not occur to her to connect the two events," Maurice went on, "when, five or six months ago, a girl from the islands, in charge of a little child, sought refuge with us. But perhaps you see a connection?"

"How long ago?" asked Prince Romanos excitedly. "A girl from the islands, you say? Was the child a boy?"

"The exact day was that on which Wylie and I left Therma—when you were to have joined us, but were prevented by—by severe personal bereavement."

"Exactly. But what should have taken the girl to you?"

"We found her running away in terror from your servant Petros and she implored our help. Her first story was that her sister had been murdered by her husband——" Maurice paused involuntarily, struck by the ominous coincidence of the words, then hurried on—"and she was escaping with the child. Petros was anxious to claim control over her, but she denied frantically that he had any right to it, and we did not think he was quite the person to take charge of a young girl. We agreed to produce her if she was wanted in any legal proceedings, and meanwhile promised to find a place for her here. My sister has employed her in the nursery, and brought up the little boy with her own child."

"Princess, accept the thanks of a father who thought himself bereaved of wife and son in one day," said Prince Romanos, kissing Zoe's hand. "Then the discerning eye of Zeto detected the son of John Theophanis under the mean disguise?"

"Don't flatter me too much," said Zoe, laughing with an effort. "Janni was just the age of my own Harold, and made a delightful companion for him. Besides, the girl very soon informed us that he was not her sister's child, but some one immensely superior. But can you be quite sure that he is your lost child?"

"My heart tells me so, Princess. Janni? his very name! The day of his adoption, that on which I lost him. The anxiety of my faithful Petros to recover him—by the bye, the rascal has been leading me a pretty dance since. All-Holy Mother of God! he must have known where the child was the whole time! The nurse-girl is his niece; they must have made up the plot together."

"Surely it would be better to have the girl here at once, and let her bring the child for you to see?" said Maurice, and Wylie called to one of the servants outside and gave him the order. Prince Romanos looked slightly disconcerted.

"I could wish to have embraced my recovered treasure first in private," he said to Zoe, with the faintest hint of reproach in his tone.

"And to have given instructions to the nurse in private also?" inquired the Cavaliere sarcastically.

Meanwhile, the receipt of Wylie's order caused commotion in the nursery. Danaë declared that she would not go down; she was tired, she was ill, she was terrified; Linton must take Janni. They wrangled over the whole process of getting him into his best frock, and were still fixed in their respective determinations when Parisi himself puffed upstairs to inquire what was the reason of this delay? Was the Lady Kalliopé waiting for the Lord Glafko to come and fetch her, or did she insist upon the escort of the gracious Prince himself? Danaë's elevation of the previous night had not met with approval among the servants, and she realised in time that they would like nothing better than to drag her by force, struggling and shrieking, into the presence of Princess Theophanis and her guests. Therefore she merely tossed her head in answer to Parisi's ponderous raillery, and seizing Janni, marched defiantly down the stairs and across the courtyard.

"Why, Eurynomé!" said Prince Romanos stiffly.

"I am she, lord," she responded. "You wished to see the little lord?"

The Prince's ill-humour melted as he held out his arms, and the watching grandfather noted jealously that the child went to him at once, and nestled confidingly against his shoulder. Danaë watched them with pride.

"What made you take the little lord away, Eurynomé?" demanded the Prince abruptly.

"You told me to, lord," was the answer, which produced a sensation. Was the Cavaliere justified in insinuating that Prince Romanos had suborned Petros and the nurse to remove the child and keep him out of sight?

"Nonsense, girl! Tell the truth."

"I am telling it, lord. Did I not bring you the little lord, to comfort you, when you were mourning over the body of the Lady, and did you not command me many times over to take him away?"

"I told you to take him to the nursery, of course."

"Yes, lord; and was he to remain there forgotten, until the murderers came back to kill him as they had killed his mother?" There was another sensation.

"Who were these murderers, Kalliopé?" asked Maurice.

She looked round desperately. All her instincts of loyalty bade her lie through thick and thin, if necessary, to support her brother, but she had no means of knowing whether truth or falsehood would profit him better. "If I could tell my lord about it alone first?" she faltered.

"No, no—no teaching the girl what to say!" cried the Cavaliere Pazzi furiously, and Professor Panagiotis turned a warning glance on Prince Romanos. He responded gloomily.

"No. Say what you know at once."

"It was a very hot day," began Danaë hesitatingly. "My lord had visited the Lady to bid her farewell, and old Despina had gone out marketing. The Lady was writing a letter in the shade of the wood, and I was playing with the little lord on the ground near her. We were just going to take him indoors for his sleep when we heard noises at the gate. Old Mariora came running to bid the Lady hide, because there were murderers there, and went to try to stop them. But the Lady bade me take the little lord and hide him, and she would speak to the murderers and give me time. Then I carried the little lord very quickly through the house and hid myself with him, and remained there a long while, and when I came out the Lady lay dead on the grass, and Mariora on the pathway, and Despina near the gate." She paused with something of pride. If she had said nothing that was false, she had at any rate exercised a judicious economy of the truth.

"Where did you hide yourself, Kalliopé?" asked Zoe.

"It was—up a tree, my lady." Formerly this would have been mentioned with pride, but now Danaë blushed.

"Could you see the murderers?" asked Wylie quickly.

Her eyes sought her brother's face anxiously, but in vain. "Yes, lord," she admitted with reluctance.

"What were they like?" asked Professor Panagiotis.

"They wore the clothes of the guard, lord," after another wild glance at Prince Romanos. Danaë knew by the demeanour of her audience that she must be establishing some very serious charge against her brother, but its nature she could not define.

"Was there anyone among them that you knew?" asked Maurice. Her lips moved, but no answer came.

"Was Petros one of them?" asked Wylie, with a sudden inspiration, and Danaë threw Petros to the wolves without a qualm. He was a good way off, and if he was discredited beforehand his recrimination might be robbed of its power.

"Yes, lord; Petros was there."

"Was that why you were running away from him afterwards?"

"Surely, lord. I feared that he would take the little lord and slay him."

"But why did you tell us so many lies about yourself and the child?"

"How could I do otherwise, lord? I did not know then the goodness of your hearts, and I desired to save the little lord until I could restore him to his father."

"Knowing that his father desired nothing of the kind?" demanded the Cavaliere. Happily he spoke in French, and Danaë did not understand him. Maurice interposed hastily.

"The girl had better go now, I think. We can send for her again if anyone wants to question her. Take the little lord back to the nursery, Kalliopé."

She vanished, with Janni in her arms, and delivered him duly into Linton's care. But having exactly fulfilled the order she had received, she returned noiselessly, and sat crouched on the verandah close to the window, with so little parade of secrecy that the guards below thought she had been told to return, and did not molest her. The conversation within was continued in French or English, as before she was sent for, and of course she could not understand it.

"I went through the roll of my guard that evening," said Prince Romanos wearily, "to satisfy myself; and with the exception of Petros, who was on the sick-list, they were all able to account for themselves."

"Naturally. They were on duty," snapped the Cavaliere.

"I suppose there is now no objection on your part, Prince, after what we have heard, to admitting that Donna Olimpia was murdered?" interposed Maurice.

"Yes, she was foully murdered," he groaned.

"Then why invent the diphtheria lie?" demanded Wylie.

Prince Romanos spread forth his hands helplessly. "I can see as well as you do to what suspicions I exposed myself," he said; "but I was simply not in a position to take up the matter properly. I could not afford to alienate my people by allowing my marriage to come to light at the moment, and as mother and child were both dead, so far as I knew, it seemed the wisest course to hush things up for a time, and inquire into them fully afterwards."

"It was undoubtedly the most convenient course for yourself at the time," said the Cavaliere, with deadly meaning.

"What do you insinuate, monsieur?" the Prince asked him sharply.

"I insinuate nothing, I accuse. At that time you were negotiating for the hand of the Grand Duchess Feodora. Unfortunately there was an obstacle;

you had a wife already. Your wife refused to be pensioned off or to allow herself to be repudiated. Therefore you sent a detachment of your guards to murder her, under the ruffian Petros, your confidential servant. To order the death of the child was too much even for you, but you drove him from you with his nurse, and Petros knew what he was intended to do. But for the meeting with Prince Theophanis and Colonel Wylie, neither nurse nor child would have been seen again. In intention you murdered them as truly as in fact you murdered your unhappy wife and her servants."

CHAPTER XVII.
THE USE OF FRIENDS.

THERE was a moment's hush of expectation when the Cavaliere had hurled his charges at his son-in-law. Prince Romanos met them characteristically.

"Princess," he said, turning to Zoe, "do you believe that I murdered my wife?"

"No, I don't," said Zoe.

"Then I am content. If one so skilled in the knowledge of the human heart—a woman, too—can acquit me, what more can I ask?"

"This is all very pretty and poetical," said Wylie impatiently, "but merely as a matter of curiosity, Prince, we should like to know what defence you propose to offer if your father-in-law publishes throughout Europe the accusation he has just made."

"Ah, there I am helpless. I put myself wholly into the hands of my friends. I did not murder my wife, but malicious circumstances have forced me into such a position that I realise it must appear that I did. The Cavaliere Pazzi has provided me with a motive, with instruments, with a deep-laid plan. How can I prove that I am innocent of this crime, which I abhor from my very soul?"

"You can hardly expect us to prove it for you, Prince," said Maurice, with unusual sharpness.

"Your Highness will pardon me." It was Professor Panagiotis who spoke, rising and coming forward impressively into the midst of the group. "I am here, at my own request, to represent the interests of Emathia, which would be gravely jeopardised if the Cavaliere Pazzi made his accusation public. I beg that it may not be supposed I have been in the Prince's confidence all along. I could wish it had been the case, but his Highness was otherwise advised."

"In other words," drawled Prince Romanos, "I was considerate enough to keep my marriage concealed from the Professor as well as from the public, knowing that it would disturb his tranquillity, and might lead him to disturb mine."

"From the Cavaliere's words," the Professor went on, "it would not be guessed that the proposal of an alliance with the Grand Duchess Feodora came, not from the Prince at all, but from the Scythian side. I welcomed it, I own, for it promised to guarantee the continuance of Emathian independence, and the establishment of a hereditary dynasty. Unfortunately, my master and I were working against one another, since he had the validation of the actual marriage in view, and I an entirely new one."

"But," cried Zoe, "the Scythian Government must have known all about the marriage. I know Donna Olimpia told me that the Dowager Princess of Dardania was present at it."

"That is undoubtedly the case, madame. The proposal of a more august alliance was merely a bait to entrap my master and his servants into complete subservience to Scythia. But it is only since the death of the lady concerned that the Scythian negociator has mentioned certain unpleasant rumours that had reached his ears, and asked for a definite contradiction of them."

"Aha, Mr Professor!" burst from the Cavaliere. "So you would transfer the crime from your master's shoulders to those of the Scythian Government, would you? Well, they are broad enough; but you forget that the murder was committed by members of the Prince's own guard."

"By men in the uniform of members of the Prince's guard," corrected the Professor. "No, monsieur, I should not be so foolish as to insinuate that the Scythians, any more than my master, were clearing the way for him to a marriage with the Grand Duchess. You have not the happiness of being Orthodox, but I appeal to those present who know something of our tenets. They will support me in assuring you that second marriages are looked upon with extreme disfavour by our Church, and in no case would one be contemplated for a member of the Imperial family."

"That's true. I had not thought of it," cried Maurice, while the Cavaliere sat stupefied.

"Then now you have merely to show who did commit the murder, Professor," said Wylie, in his driest tone.

Professor Panagiotis seemed unwontedly embarrassed. He wiped his brow, as though his forensic effort was proving exhausting, and played with a button of his coat. Then he spread forth his hands with a liberal gesture implying that now he was making a clean breast of everything.

"Your Highnesses, I approach this point with hesitation, since it must appear to you that you have been treated with insufficient confidence. But I ask you to consider my master's eagerness to see his marriage acknowledged and his dynasty established. In view of this, you will not be surprised to hear that the question of the construction of the Emathian railways became involved with the other negociation."

"Surprised? Not a bit!" said Wylie. "We all knew that there must be a *quid pro quo*. But I imagine that the Prince was not satisfied with only one bid. There is another Power interested in Emathian railways as well as Scythia."

"Exactly, Colonel," said the Professor, in a tone of relief; "and the present complications arise from my master's anxiety to obtain the best terms he could—the utmost in the way of recognition against the smallest possible concession. In this endeavour I am proud to acknowledge that I supported him—but unfortunately I was ignorant of the fact of his marriage, which was known to the Pannonian agents. He informs me that even before the unhappy event which we all deplore, attempts had been made to bring pressure upon him by threatening the safety of his wife."

The Cavaliere raised his haggard face with supreme disdain. "Bah! you are trying to lead us astray. Pannonia had no candidate in whose favour my daughter's removal was desirable."

"No, the plot was more subtle than that. According to my information, obtained by careful inquiry, the group of discreditable persons who were managing the affair in the interests—though without the ostensible support—of Pannonia plotted deliberately to murder the lady concerned and her child, and to cast the blame upon her husband. If he allowed himself to be intimidated, they would obtain all they could desire in the way of concessions; if he refused, they would denounce him publicly—not so much for the murder as for the heterodox marriage, and stir up the populace to revolt. Pannonian property would be damaged, Pannonian interests endangered, and Pannonia would demand from Europe a mandate to restore peace. Once in Therma, you may guess how soon she would quit it."

"Then Prince Romanos accepted the first condition, and granted the concessions?" said Maurice coldly. "You are surprised that I should know this?" as the Professor's eye wandered to his master's. "Colonel Wylie and I guessed that something of the kind was on foot when we discovered a few days ago that a Pannonian geological expedition, which had been giving us a good deal of trouble, was really surveying for a railway."

"The Prince temporised—nothing more," replied the Professor breathlessly. "With your Highness's assistance, we hope so to arrange matters that Pannonia gains only a very small portion of what she expected. I am about to speak frankly, for you will understand that my concern is for Emathia, and that if you, sir, had been elected High Commissioner instead of Prince Romanos, my endeavours would have been equally engaged on your behalf. It is quite open to you, I acknowledge it freely, to take your stand on the charges brought by the Cavaliere Pazzi, and claim that my master has shown himself unworthy of the confidence of Europe. It is extremely probable that if another election were held you would take his place. But I have received a friendly warning from Czarigrad, from a Greek occupying a very high official position there, that the present Liberal Roumi Government regards the semi-independent status of Emathia with keen dislike. A contested election, either now or at the end of my master's five years of office, would be the signal for a determined attempt to bring the country again under Roumi rule. There would be representative institutions, of course, such as they are, but Emathia, for which we have fought and laboured, to see her emerge triumphantly as a self-existent state, would once more be merged in the dominions of Roum. All the work of the last twenty years—of my lifetime—would be lost."

"This is very serious," said Maurice. "Do you think that if the election is not contested at the end of the five years things will be allowed to go on?"

"There would at least be no excuse for interrupting them, sir. If we could point to five years of peace and advance, and a contented people— but it demands sacrifices. And first of all, the Prince will make every amends in his power to the memory of the lady whom he so truly loved and so deeply mourns." The Cavaliere, who had been sitting sunk in his chair, looked up sharply. "The marriage, so unfortunately concealed, will be made public, and insisted upon in every possible way. The child whose life has been so wonderfully preserved will be brought forward as heir of the Christodoridi and his father's natural successor on the throne, and the body of his mother, whom I may now without offence style the Princess of Emathia, taken from its present resting-place and deposited with all honour in the vaults of the metropolitan church. Do you ask how we propose to face the public opposition? There will be none. Once it is known that Prince Romanos married the heiress of Maxim Psicha, and that their son unites in his own person the princely crowns of Emathia and Illyria, the match will be received with enthusiasm."

"And the murderers of my daughter?" asked the Cavaliere in a hollow voice.

Embarrassment returned upon Professor Panagiotis. "For the sake of Emathia, it is suggested that we all consent to certain sacrifices, monsieur," he said, after some hesitation. "It will be impossible, I fear, to extricate ourselves from the late negociations without conceding to Scythia and Pannonia an influence in our domestic affairs which we shall find very irksome. We look confidently to Prince Theophanis and his family for pecuniary help in making that influence as small as possible. My master resigns his natural desire for vengeance, since you will see that to accuse Pannonia of plotting the murder of his wife would precipitate instantly the crisis we hope to avert. Is it too much to ask you to exercise a like self-restraint?"

"In order that Romanos Christodoridi may be left in peaceable possession of the throne he has disgraced? I tell you, Mr Professor, I will tear him from it!"

"Will you ruin your grandson's future, monsieur?"

"Shall I buy a throne for my grandson at the price of his mother's blood? I would rather bring him up in a garret! No, I refuse your bribe!" he turned upon Prince Romanos. "Your plan is clear to me now. I will do you justice; you did not want to have to kill your wife. Her acknowledgment that your marriage was invalid would have been sufficient to clear the way to your Grand Duchess. But she refused to become a party to the dishonour you wished to bring upon her——"

"Pardon me, monsieur. The lady's honour is vindicated in the fullest possible way by my proposal," said the Professor.

"Yes, because she is the heiress of Maxim Psicha. But she was also my daughter, and she was foully murdered by her own husband's order. I can see it all—that last interview, the demand for her acquiescence in her own disgrace, her staunch refusal, the angry departure of the dastardly husband, the arrival of his bloodthirsty instruments! I see it, and as I see it Europe shall see it also."

"Europe will ask for proof," said Prince Romanos. "I may tell you that my wife and I parted the best of friends."

"Europe will ask for proof of that. Where is the letter that the nurse says she was writing when the murderers came?"

"I do not know. I saw no letter."

"No, and no letter will ever be seen. Shall I tell you what that letter contained? It was an appeal to me, her father, to come to her help, as I had offered to do, and take her away from Therma, where her life was not safe unless she consented to your repudiation of her. If that was not the letter, what was it?"

"Lady, what is the secretary man saying to the Lord Romanos?" Danaë had sat inert and uninterested while the Professor talked, but her instincts told her who was the man to be feared, and since the Cavaliere burst again into the fray she had been kneeling with her face pressed to the window watching his fiery gestures. Now, as his eager hands approached the Prince's throat, as though he would have torn a confession from him, she opened the window and stepped in. Her entrance broke the tension which held the listeners, and Prince Romanos smiled, not very naturally.

"Here is an unbiassed witness, at any rate," he said. "Why not ask her about the terms my wife and I were on?"

Professor Panagiotis responded eagerly. "Girl, what can you tell us about the Prince and his wife? Did he appear to be fond of her?"

"By no means, lord," was the prompt reply.

The Cavaliere laughed harshly. The rest gasped, and Prince Romanos sprang up and gripped Danaë roughly by the shoulder.

"Speak the truth, girl! Was I unkind to her?"

"Not unkind, lord, but you kept her in awe of you, as a wife should be kept. She trembled at the sound of your step."

He laughed as his father-in-law had done, and dropped back into his chair. "Go on. Perhaps I beat her?"

An affirmative was trembling upon Danaë's lips, but Zoe, out of pure sympathy and nervousness, threw herself into the breach, remembering the girl's earlier exploits.

"Think, Kalliopé, and tell us exactly how it was. Not just when they had a quarrel now and then, perhaps, but as it was generally. To us," with a gallant attempt to bring the matter home to her handmaid's mind, "what you have said is horrible, and makes us think the Lord Romanos one of the worst of men."

"Does it, lady?" in intense astonishment. "I said it for his glory. I could not bear any one to know how he was in thrall to her. But she bewitched him, one knows that."

"This seems a new view of affairs," observed Wylie. "He was not cruel to her, then?"

"Cruel, lord? If you had seen them as I so often saw them, he so mild and anxious to please her, and she frowning and ill-tempered! But that is always the way with witches. Only the unfortunate who is bewitched can see any beauty in them, but he pines away for love."

Danaë had carried the inquiry into such new regions that Maurice returned with difficulty to a previous question. "The Princess was writing a letter on the morning she was murdered, you say, Kalliopé; but it can't be found. Have you any idea what became of it?"

"I have it in my room, lord—hidden in my mattress." Again she had the pleasing consciousness of having caused a sensation.

"Go and fetch it at once," said Maurice, in a tone which sent her flying. Once in her own room, the letter was easily found, but as she pulled it out of its hiding-place, her fingers came in contact with one of the golden plaques of the Girdle of Isidora. A moment's pause, and she took it out also, fastening it round her waist under her apron, as she had done before. Things seemed so strange to-day that it might possibly be needed. Then, parrying Linton's questions, she went sedately back to the Prince's house, and handed the letter to Maurice.

"I kept it, lord, because I thought my little lord might grow up and none know who he was, nor believe me when I told them. But if I said, 'Here is writing in the hand of his mother,' they could doubt no more."

The proof seemed less obvious to her hearers than to herself, but Maurice took the paper gravely. "This is addressed to you, Cavaliere," he said, handing it to him. Seizing it eagerly, the Cavaliere read it through, arriving at the abrupt ending with obvious disappointment.

"I was wrong in one point, I confess it. It is clear that there was no open quarrel. My daughter was not offered the choice between death and disgrace. She writes to me that she is convinced her husband will soon acknowledge her openly. He had pledged himself afresh that very morning, accompanying the pledge with a gift of so much significance that she durst not describe it on paper, but hoped to show it me before long at the Palace."

"It was a piece of jewellery," said Prince Romanos hastily. "You will be at no loss to imagine what it was—since she received it as an earnest of her hopes? The crown which she was never to wear—alas! I had pleased myself with having it made for her to my own design."

"Did Petros know of it?" asked Zoe. "Because if he did, it might supply a motive for the murder."

"I have no reason to think he did. But stay—the drawer in which she placed it was broken open and the jewel stolen by the murderers. It certainly looks——"

"Kalliopé," interrupted Zoe, "do you think Petros can have murdered your mistress for the sake of the jewellery the Prince had just given her?"

"Oh no, my lady; he had no part in her death. And as for the jewel—— " she hesitated, and looked at Prince Romanos for guidance. "Am I to tell all, lord?"

"Most certainly. Always tell the truth," he said bluffly. To his utter stupefaction, Danaë unclasped the Girdle of Isidora from her waist, and laid it on the table.

"I would fain have spared you this shame, lord," she said sadly. "Lady," she turned to Zoe, "my lord gave this holy thing to the schismatic woman, and hailed her as Orthodox Empress. When she was dead, I took it from where I had seen her put it, and hid it, that it might be safe for my little lord's wife when he grows up."

"My girdle!" Danaë's voice was drowned by Eirene's shriek of joy as she sprang forward and seized the jewel. "At last, at last! Now we may hope for success!" she murmured, fondling the girdle and kissing it as if it were a living thing. Danaë's eyes blazed, and she threw herself forward to tear it from her. Prince Romanos pushed her back, not too gently.

"Be still, girl! That belongs to Princess Theophanis." Then to the rest, "There is some mistake. This girdle came to light in the course of the destruction of the old Scythian Consulate, after the visit which Prince Theophanis and Colonel Wylie and I paid to the operations. You will remember," he turned to Maurice, "that I was about to join you when this terrible event occurred. The girdle was handed to me just before I started, and I promised myself the pleasure of restoring it to Princess Theophanis with my own hands. My wife teased me to show it to her, and I allowed her to put it on, and left it in her charge till the afternoon. I thought it had disappeared with the crown, but now I see it was not so."

There was a moment's awkward silence, which Wylie broke abruptly. "Kalliopé," he said to the girl, who had stood looking with angry eyes from one to another while Prince Romanos spoke hastily in French, "why do you say now that Petros took no part in the murder? You told us before that you were afraid he would kill the child as he had killed the mother."

These were not Danaë's exact words, but she was too eager to answer to resent them. "I misjudged him, lord," she replied quickly, glad to put herself right as far as possible with regard to Petros. "He laid no hand upon the Lady. He has told me so himself since, and I ought to have known that he would not overstep his orders."

"His orders!" Everyone in the room seemed to echo the words, and Danaë stood aghast at what she had done.

"The orders of Prince Romanos?" asked Maurice.

"No, lord," very low.

"Whose orders, then?" There was silence.

"Kalliopé, you must tell us," cried Zoe impulsively. "Who gave these orders, and what were they? You can't mean that you knew of a plot against your mistress, and never warned her?"

"A plot, lady mine? There was no plot. My lord and——" she broke off hurriedly. "My lord's father heard of the schismatic woman who had bewitched my lord and was holding him in her snares, and he commanded Petros to bring her to Strio, where she would be kept safe, and do no more harm."

"And you knew of this?" cried Zoe.

"I came to Therma from Strio on purpose to help in the doing of it, lady."

"Kalliopé, you had a hand in this horrible murder!"

"No murder was intended, lady. The Despot desired only to put the woman where the Lord Romanos would not find her. But there was some mistake. Petros told me that among his helpers there were those who would willingly see her slain, and I warned him to do no more than he was commanded. He assured me all was well, and I helped to open the gate, not knowing that the evil men of whom he had spoken would be with him after all."

"Kalliopé!" There was such disappointment and misery in Zoe's cry that Prince Romanos sprang forward.

"Don't waste your pity on this wretched girl, Princess. She is trying to take us all in. Can you conceive a person of my father's standing initiating such a plot? It is preposterous, and she shall confess her falsehood on her knees."

In his excitement he had spoken in Greek, and now he tried to seize Danaë. She shook herself free from him with flashing eyes. "You know little of your father, lord, if you refuse to believe me."

"I know more of him than Eurynomé the nurse-maid. On your knees, girl! and confess that you have lied."

"But not more of him than his daughter. Yes, lord, I am your sister. Not Eurynomé the nurse-girl, but Danaë, daughter of the Despot Agesilaos Christodoridi and of the Lady Xantippe his wife."

CHAPTER XVIII.
EXPELLED FROM PARADISE.

THERE was a moment's astonished silence as the listeners gazed at the two handsome faces confronting one another, so much alike in their rage. Then Prince Romanos sprang at his sister like a tiger.

"You killed her? You and my father killed my wife?"

Wylie stepped between them just in time. "In Europe we do not strike women, Prince," he said.

Held back by the strong hand, Prince Romanos stood panting, his hands twitching and his face working convulsively. With an effort, he regained the mask of civilisation, which had fallen from him for a moment and revealed the fierce islander under the cosmopolitan exterior. With a gesture of the deepest contrition he turned to his father-in-law.

"Cavaliere, I can say no more. Do what you will; say what you will. Denounce me throughout Europe as the murderer of the woman I would have given my life to save. I will offer no defence; none is possible. I am her murderer—by the hands of my merciless father and of this fury who calls herself my sister."

"But is she your sister really?" gasped Zoe.

"I suppose so," he replied indifferently. "I know nothing of my father's present family, except that he has two daughters. Second marriages are held in low esteem among us, as you know. But from what I know of my father I imagine the story must be true."

Professor Panagiotis, unmoved by the storm raging around him, had been making notes on his papers. Now he looked up and spoke calmly.

"Your Highnesses, it seems to me that this revelation has come at a most opportune moment. I can hardly believe that either the Cavaliere Pazzi or Prince Theophanis will wish to take advantage of this surrender on the part of my master. His natural horror on finding himself betrayed by his nearest relations has made him forgetful of the interests alike of his son and of Emathia. Monsieur," he turned to the Cavaliere, "I imagine you are now convinced of the Prince's innocence?"

"I see a possibility of it," was the reluctant reply, "but his defence is very nearly incredible."

"Not if you were better acquainted with our people, monsieur. If the Lady Danaë will be so good as to tell us her story in detail, I think you will be forced to believe it."

He turned deferentially to Danaë, who looked at Zoe.

"My lady, shall I speak?" she asked.

"Certainly. The best thing you can possibly do now is to tell the whole truth," said Zoe bitterly. The girl ignored the bitterness, and addressed herself exclusively to her.

"Lady mine, I have deceived you in calling myself Kalliopé, as I deceived the Lady in calling myself Eurynomé. That I deceived you, I am sorry, but as for deceiving her, it was a good deed, and I do not regret it. I am the elder daughter of my father, who is called the Despot of Strio, and I dwelt there in his house until the early part of this year. Then there came to the island the man Petros, who had been summoned by my father on account of certain things he had heard, on which he desired Petros to assure him. But Petros could only confirm to him the truth of the rumours that had reached him concerning my brother, namely, that he was held in the toils of an evil woman, a schismatic by race, who had bewitched him so deeply that he scorned the daughters of all the kings of Europe for her sake. In the old days, my father would have commanded his son to repair to Strio, and would have taken from him this woman who called herself his wife, and put her to death before his eyes, after forcing her to release him from her spells, not permitting him to depart until an Orthodox marriage had been made for him—but those days are no longer with us. So my father gave Petros orders to bring the woman to Strio, where she should be safely kept, and made to set my brother free. Once she herself had released him, there would be no more danger. But it was necessary, since my brother guarded her so carefully, for one to be inside her house who should help Petros to enter, and I offered to be that one. Lady, why do you look at me as though I had done ill? I sought only to deliver my brother from the toils of a witch."

"How can I help it?" cried Zoe. "That you—you, who have been with us all these months, who seemed really fond of the children, should have helped to commit a cold-blooded murder, to kill your own sister-in-law— oh, it is too horrible!"

"She was not my sister-in-law, lady," with extreme horror. "She was a witch—even, perhaps," Danaë dropped her voice, "a vampire."

"She was the best and loveliest of women!" cried Prince Romanos; "and you, with your vile superstitions, are not fit to carry her shoes!"

"I thought she was a vampire!" said Danaë, with a certain gloomy satisfaction. "It is not enough to kill them; they retain their power when they seem to be dead, as you would know well, lord, if her spell was not over you."

"Kalliopé, be quiet; you make my heart sick," cried Zoe. "Don't—don't say you helped to do this awful thing!"

"You will not understand, my lady," said Danaë patiently; "I did not want her killed, for then the effect of her spells would remain, as it does now. She must be made to remove them of her own free will. You are too kind, lady. If you lived among us, you would know that it is wrong and foolish to be gentle with witches and vampires. You must make your heart hard, thinking of the victims who have to be delivered from them. That is what my father would have done, but his plans went wrong through the men whom Petros engaged to help him carry off the Lady."

"We shall get no sense out of this girl," said the Cavaliere gloomily. "Can't she speak the plain truth?"

"Look here, Kalliopé," said Maurice abruptly. "Were these men, whom Petros got to help him, intended to be members of the Prince's guard, or not?"

Danaë reflected a little. "Nothing was said about it, lord," she replied; "and I think Petros would have feared to broach the matter to them. He is servant first of the Despot, and then of my brother, but they are servants altogether to the Lord Romanos, and might have betrayed the plan to him. Surely they were dressed like the guard that they might be admitted to the villa without the sentry's suspecting anything?"

"That is possible. And you admitted them?"

"I put a little piece of iron, which Petros gave me, into the lock, lord, so that the key would not quite turn."

"And why did you hide yourself and the child, if you were sure no harm would be done to him?"

"The Lady bade me hide, lord, and I was frightened—old Mariora cried out. There was a panic upon me."

"Oh, Kalliopé, were you not sorry—not the least sorry—when you saw what you had done?" cried Zoe.

"I was a little sorry for Janni's mother, my lady—but not for the woman who had bewitched my brother."

Prince Romanos rose decisively from his chair. "Cavaliere, if you are not convinced, I am. Henceforth I live for vengeance. As for this wretched girl, I suppose she must enjoy the consideration she has denied to others. After all, perhaps her fittest punishment will be to send her back to Strio. I left it so young that I did not fully realise what an undesirable place it was to live in. I think—" he spoke in Greek, with intense meaning—"that we will send you back to Strio as a suspected witch, girl."

Danaë turned so deadly white that Zoe stepped forward to catch her. "Why—why should you say that, lord?" she murmured.

"You made your way into two households—mine first and then the Lady Zoe's—with false tales. Why should we have believed them if you had not cast a spell upon us? Through you my two servants lost their lives, I my wife, and Janni his mother. What harm you have wrought here I have not heard yet—but no doubt you have begun your evil work. You are discovered now, Lady Danaë, and you shall carry your fame home with you."

"Oh, lady, lady mine! You won't let them—" the words came brokenly as Danaë swayed and caught at Zoe. "You don't believe—— Am I really a witch?"

"Prince, how can you?" began Zoe, but Armitage took the shaking form from her arms, and turned upon Prince Romanos with honest indignation.

"You miserable hound! let the unfortunate girl alone."

"What! she has bewitched you too?" asked Prince Romanos, and with a shriek which rang in the ears of those present, Danaë swooned away.

"Oh, go out, go out and leave her with us!" cried Zoe distractedly to the men. "It has been too much—all this long strain—and this last thing, she thinks we believe it. Poor girl! she had no idea what she was doing."

"If I may trespass on your kindness to shelter her for one night more, Princess?" said Prince Romanos smoothly, as he went out. "To-morrow I will relieve you of such an unpleasant charge."

"Go, go!" said Zoe impatiently. Eirene had laid aside her recovered girdle for a moment, but there was a far-away look in her eyes as she brought water and restoratives and helped Zoe to lay Danaë on the floor. The moment the girl opened her eyes she left her and took up the girdle again, as though she feared being deprived of it.

"Better, Kalliopé?" asked Zoe kindly.

"Oh, lady, lady!" Danaë hid her face upon her mistress's breast, and clung to her trembling and shivering. "Is it true? Am I a witch?"

"No, nonsense! There are no such things. Lie down, or you will faint again." To Zoe's intense astonishment, the girl had pushed her away, and was trying to raise herself by a chair.

"Lady, it is true. I have bewitched you, and you don't know it. Let me go away, before I do you more harm. If I give myself freely to death, that will remove the spell."

"Lie still, and don't be silly. There are no witches now."

"There was one in Strio, lady—a girl only as old as I am—I knew her. She had no wish to do harm, but evil befell all those on whom she looked, and her lover fell ill and wasted away. Even the priest could do nothing, and when they took her to the festival of a very holy relic in another island, the roof of the church fell in, and killed several people. The day after she came back to Strio she was found dead at the foot of the cliff, and all said that she had thrown herself over so as to break the effect of her spells. And it was through me that the Lord Harold was lost."

"It was through you he was recovered. Now, Kalliopé, let us go back quietly, and you shall lie down in my room. I am not excusing you at all. You have done very wrong—worse than I could ever have believed—but instead of being sorry for that, you accuse yourself of being a witch, which is absurd."

"But you can be a witch without knowing it, my lady," the girl objected feebly, as they passed along the verandah. Zoe shrugged her shoulders deliberately, and made no answer until she had her patient established on the sofa.

"Now I am going to talk to you, Kalliopé—I can't call you Danaë yet. Why do you say your sister-in-law was a witch?"

"The schismatic woman? Because she was a witch, lady."

"I never saw anything like your obstinacy, Kalliopé. She was your sister-in-law, and she was not a witch."

"But, lady mine, she bewitched my brother!"

"There was no witchcraft about it. I knew her well. She was very beautiful and very loving, and I should have been surprised if your brother, being what he is, had not fallen in love with her."

"But to marry her, lady—forgetting all he owed to his house and to his faith!"

"That also was inevitable, unless he had deliberately cut himself off from her at once. But I should say rather that it was he who bewitched her to her undoing. It was madness in her to consent to a secret marriage, and so I told her."

Danaë's eyes were still obstinate, and Zoe spoke impressively.

"Well, I can't hope to convince you against your will. But your brother has far more reason to believe you a witch, and a malevolent one, than you had to think his wife one."

Again the trembling came upon the girl. "Oh, lady, why?"

"Because his wife brought him nothing but good—except what was due to his own concealment of the marriage—and you have done him the most dreadful harm."

Zoe turned away, and taking up a book, pretended to read, leaving Danaë to sob and shiver among the cushions. At last an inarticulate murmur called her back, and the girl seized her hand convulsively. "Lady mine, I am sorry; I wish I had not done it. But she was a schismatic, and they said she was a witch, and I believed it."

"Then don't believe anything so silly in future."

"But my brother, lady. He believes that I——"

"No, he doesn't. He only said it to frighten you."

"Oh, lady, then he will not send me back to Strio with that terrible message? You will make him have pity on me, so that I can stay here with you?"

"I should not let him send that message, certainly, but I am afraid he won't leave you here, Kalliopé. He means to take you away with him to-morrow."

"To be Janni's nurse at Therma?" hopefully.

"No, I don't think so. It wouldn't do. I am sure he means to send you home. But you love your island; you will be glad to get back."

For answer, Danaë flung herself off the sofa, and clasped her mistress's knees tightly. "Oh, lady mine, let me stay here! If you will not have me in the nursery, let me go to the kitchen again. Anything rather than go back to Strio!"

"But, Kalliopé, you must see that your brother could not leave you here as a servant. I should be very glad if he would let you stay, but you will be wanted at home. You are a great lady there."

"Oh, lady, if you knew what it was like! But you can't dream of it. Why, if you had been my father's wife when the Lord Harold was lost, do you think he would have taken you by the hand and spoken compassionately to you, as the Lord Glafko did? No, he would have beaten you till the blood came, for your carelessness in allowing the child to be lost."

Zoe sat aghast. "Well, it would certainly have been a warning against carelessness in future," she said, trying to laugh.

"There, my lady! you see what it is like. And I have seen now what it is like in Europe, where 'men do not strike women,' as the Lord Glafko said. How can I go back to it? Before I left Strio I knew of nothing better, but now that I have seen the Prince, and the Lord Glafko, and—and Milordo, and know how they treat women———"

"My poor girl, I see how hard it is for you, and I will do what I can. But I am afraid your brother is determined. Now go, and—and Linton had better help you to pack, in case———"

Zoe felt herself perfectly inhuman as Danaë turned great eyes of reproach upon her, but she durst make no promises. When her husband came in, she turned to him eagerly.

"Graham, you won't mind if I try to persuade Prince Romanos to leave that poor girl with us? It is a miserable prospect for her to be sent back to Strio."

"I shan't object, but I doubt if you'll get him to do it. And what have you in view for her exactly? Armitage doesn't seem to come up to the scratch."

"No, how could he? It must be a dreadful shock to find that a girl you have admired so much is practically a murderess. But I wish he would! It would be all right then. He could go away for a year's cruise, and I would take her thoroughly in hand. He wouldn't know her when he came back, and it would be so splendid introducing them!"

"But you don't think he might prefer to do the training and watch the transformation for himself?"

"Of course he might, but it's the dramatic effect I am thinking of. But I am afraid he has received too great a shock to want to have anything to do with her. And the Christodoridi are not a family that one would exactly choose to be connected with."

"That depends on your moral character. If you prefer a family that's bound to come up on top every time, you couldn't do better. Witness Romanos retiring triumphant from here with his attendant Professor!"

"Oh, you went on with your business, then. What has he got?"

"Freedom from pressure for the moment, and the prospect of establishing his dynasty permanently, which is what he cares about. His railway muddle he conveniently shoves off on our shoulders. Maurice consents to finance the proposed line between here and Therma, as the only way of keeping the port free, and retains the right of constructing a future extension from here through Illyria to the Adriatic, which may become very important. But Pannonia must be given the chance of continuing her line through the Debatable Land as far as this place, and we must square Scythia by letting her build one from Przlepka to Karajevo in Thracia."

Zoe was silent a moment, making mental maps of the proposed changes. "Perhaps they'll refuse," she said.

"I only wish they might, but they are too keen. They'll both trust to getting control of our part of the line in time. And it will be one unceasing fight on our part to keep them out. Romanos doesn't care, having secured his heir and avoided a European scandal, and found a way of slipping out of the partial promises he made to both Scythia and Pannonia."

"And he does nothing in return?"

"Oh yes; he makes us guardians to little Janni."

"I should have thought that was only another obligation. Do you mean regents in case anything happens to him?"

"No, he has sense enough to perceive that the child would never be accepted as High Commissioner either by the Powers or the people. It would be a case of Maurice or a return into the Young Roumi fold. But it is a handsome acknowledgment beforehand that if he comes to a violent end he believes we had nothing to do with it."

"Well, if that's all, I think he ought to be in a superlatively good temper this evening. I begin to have hopes."

But when Zoe seized an opportunity after dinner of pressing her wishes upon Prince Romanos, she was disappointed. He was firm in his resolution to send his sister back to Strio.

"But not with that accusation hanging over her?" said Zoe. "If it was so, I should refuse to let her go."

"No," he said reluctantly; "she well deserves it, but the result would probably be to disgrace the family still further. The best thing for her will be to retire into her original obscurity, and be forgotten here."

"But if you would only let me have her to train! She has such fine qualities, and she is so beautiful——"

"She is a beautiful savage, Princess, like all our women in Strio. They are no more fitted for freedom than an Arabian or Persian woman suddenly taken from the harem. Am I to let loose on Europe a being with the morals of the Dark Ages and the face and form of a goddess? Who could cope with her? In Strio we know what to do."

"She dreads it so much," urged Zoe; but as his face showed pleasure rather than sympathy, she tried another argument, which it ashamed her to have to use. "I really think she would be sure to marry well if she stayed here. Lord Armitage was very much struck——"

"I have too much kindness for my old comrade Lord Armitage, or any other civilised man, to inflict her upon him," he said, after a pause of consideration. "One of her own people, with old-fashioned views and a heavy hand, is the appropriate husband for her, and I shall make it my business to see that she is married quickly."

"It sounded to me as though he would have liked Lord Armitage, with his money and his beautiful new yacht, very much as a brother-in-law," said Zoe, when she was reporting her failure to her husband afterwards, "but he liked revenge better. I couldn't help wondering whether part of his anger came from the way she gave him away about the Girdle of Isidora."

"Princess Eirene is certainly not going the way to help him to forget his loss. Was it really necessary to wear it so conspicuously the very first night?"

"I believe she can't bear to lay it down. And didn't she look happy—quite young and blooming? I saw poor Maurice stealing puzzled glances at her every now and then. You know, she really thinks to-day is going to be the turning-point, that Prince Romanos will decrease and we shall increase. She is almost as superstitious in her way as Kalliopé in hers."

"Ah, that unfortunate girl! So Armitage didn't rise to the occasion?"

"No," very dolefully. "Oh, I quite see how much wiser and more prudent he is to remain silent, what a mistake it would be for him to fetter himself with a totally unsuitable wife, but I wish—oh, I wish that he had come forward! It would have been so chivalrous."

"So utterly foolish. Well, we can hardly——"

"No, he has sighed as a lover—perhaps not even that—sighed as an admirer and submitted as a peer of the realm," said Zoe flippantly. "I am just going to peep at the babies before I go to bed."

In the nursery Linton, with spectacles on nose, was busily engaged upon a cloth gown of Zoe's, which she had evidently been renovating and altering.

"I couldn't bear to let that poor girl go without some little thing to show there was no ill-feeling, ma'am," she whispered hoarsely. "She has been crying in bed fit to break your heart, and I thought it might comfort her a bit if we let her go off in European clothes. There's this dress of yours that the Master can't bear the colour of, as good as new, and she'll look a real lady in it, now that I've altered it to fit her."

"Thank you, Linton; it's very good of you to think of it," said Zoe, in a depressed voice. "How we shall miss her and Janni, shan't we? Poor things! how I wish the Prince would leave them with us."

"I'm sure I never thought to be sorry when they went—" Linton took off her spectacles and wiped them resentfully—"but there! you never know, as they say."

Zoe looked in at the two children in their cribs, bade Linton good-night, and went out. At the door a white figure with long black hair was waiting for her.

"Lady—oh, lady mine, will he let me stay?"

"I am so sorry, Kalliopé. I tried all I could, but he would not listen."

The girl wrung her hands wildly. "And last night—only last night, lady— I was so happy!"

CHAPTER XIX.
PATRIA POTESTAS.

DANAË was not to be allowed any mitigation of her hard fate; even the alleviations devised for her by her friends were forbidden. When her brother saw her in the European dress, he sent her promptly back to change it, and she travelled in his train not as his sister, but as Janni's nurse. For her own purposes she had chosen to leave Strio as a nurse-girl, and as a nurse-girl she should return thither. Her brother refused to own her. Petros, who was discovered at Therma, hanging about the Palace in a state of considerable embarrassment not unmixed with apprehension, since he did not know what his master had heard or what he would do, found himself treated as the person responsible for her misdoings. The very morning after her arrival, as soon as a respectable elderly woman had been installed to look after Janni, Danaë was summoned to the Prince's private room, and confronted with her alleged uncle, who was evidently extremely uncomfortable, and rather inclined to bluster. Some coins lay on the table.

"I won't take them!" Petros was asseverating. "You will accuse me of stealing next. I know you, my Prince."

"Take your wages, girl," said Prince Romanos coldly to his sister. "You will be expected to bring back something to add to your *proïka* [dowry] when you return from your situation. You had better take your niece back to Strio at once," he added to Petros. "Your passages are taken, and her luggage will be sent on board."

"But am I to go at once, lord?" Danaë ventured to ask.

"You will go straight from this room to the quay. And tell the girl's father from me," again he addressed Petros, "that he will do well to find her a husband at once, before she brings further disgrace on his house. And you may warn the husband to look well after her."

Flame flashed from Danaë's eyes at the words and the obvious glee with which Petros received them—for was not his master ranging him with himself against the Despot and the Lady Danaë?—but it was quenched by a sudden rush of tears. "O my Prince, you will let me bid farewell to the little lord?" she faltered.

"No," said Prince Romanos curtly. "I wish you had never come near him. I wish I had never set eyes on you!" he cried passionately. "I wish Strio and all upon it had been sunk in the depths of the sea a year ago, before you were inspired by the devil—" Danaë shivered at this plain speaking instead of the usual periphrasis—"to come and turn my life into a wilderness! To see you touch the child whose mother you murdered is an abomination; I will not hear of it. Go back to your accursed island, and may the fates repay to you and your accomplices the measure you meted out to the innocent! As for you, dog—" he turned suddenly on Petros, whose discomfiture on finding himself the object of his master's attention was very marked—"you cozened me out of a pardon, I believe?"

"I had your promise, my Prince," responded the delinquent, with an involuntary grin, partly due to nervousness.

"And you tried to place me under an obligation to you by stealing the Lord Glafko's son?"

"Why, lord, you were always lamenting that you had no way of bending the Lord Theophanis to your will, and when the chance offered I thought I would give you one."

"Unless your Pannonian friends held out the hope of better terms, I suppose. Well, you are returning to Strio, and my advice to you is—stay there. Many years to you!"

"My Prince would soon want me back again. I make my bow to you, lord," said Petros smilingly, but when he found himself outside the room with Danaë, his assurance wavered. "I have the promise, but I wonder whether the Lord Romanos is to be trusted to keep it? What do you think, lady?"

"You are pardoned for killing Despina, not the Lady," said Danaë impatiently. "If I were you I would take the advice given me. If you return to Therma, the Lord Romanos may hold himself quit of his promise."

"Why, then, it will be a case of who strikes first," said Petros, his swagger returning. "On the whole, I think I have got off pretty lightly, considering you were foolish enough to let everything out, Eurynomé my girl. I don't quite know what I thought would be the end of it all, but I certainly never expected to be taking you back to Strio in this way, like damaged goods. And the message to the Despot! Well, you will bear me out that I was charged to deliver it."

Danaë made no answer as she followed him gloomily through the Palace gate. It seemed as though all the odium due to the other conspirators, who were so placed that they could not be touched, had heaped itself on her. In the softened state of mind which had been the result of her last conversation with Zoe, she had hoped her brother would allow her to attend, as a sort of expiation, the imposing religious ceremony of the translation of Donna Olimpia's remains from their temporary resting-place to the principal church in Therma. But no, whatever favour might perforce be shown to Petros, she was to receive none. Nothing proved this more clearly than the prohibition to say good-bye to Janni, who would now be wailing his little heart out for his Nono. And the cruel message to her father! What could be the outcome but such a marriage as would justify ten times the dread with which she had looked forward to her return home?

The sea was no kinder to Danaë than the land, and the unpleasant experiences of her voyage to Therma were even intensified on her return— the sole comfort being the greater deference which infused itself gradually into the manner of Petros. From Tortolana onwards he took his proper place as the confidential servant who had been entrusted with the duty of bringing his young mistress home from school, and Danaë's European luggage aroused much interest, though she disappointed all observers by not wearing Frank clothes. Reluctantly she set foot on the soil of Strio, and climbed the steep street between the white houses. To the islanders she seemed a stranger, and they seemed strangers to her. It was less than a year since she had left home, and yet most of the pretty girls who had roamed over the roofs with her seemed to be already transformed into blowzy matrons. The people looked after her curiously as she passed, noting the atmosphere of detachment which appeared to surround her, and wondering how the Despot would like the result of his experiment. It was the same when she reached the fortress, to find her mother, hastily awakened, regarding her with apprehensive, faintly hostile eyes, and Angeliké frankly of opinion that if she must come back at all, she need not have timed her arrival precisely at this juncture.

For the desire of Angeliké's heart was in sight, and her betrothal to Narkissos Smaragdopoulos, the son of the chief man of Tortolana, within measurable distance. The old woman who was the recognised intermediary in such affairs among the aristocratic families of the group had voyaged from Strio to Tortolana, and informed Kyrios Smaragdopoulos that Prince Christodoridi might be brought to look favourably upon his son as his daughter's bridegroom. The prudent father, after polite disparagement of the honour done him, made the regulation inquiry as to the amount of the bride's dowry, and since then old Aristomaché had travelled backwards and forwards, on haggling intent. Over the last thousand drachmæ in dispute the projected match nearly came to shipwreck, but the contending parties had consented to split the difference, and the stalwart Narkissos was now a recognised suitor. Under his father's wing, he had paid two or three state calls on Prince Christodoridi, in which the subject of the marriage was never mentioned, and Angeliké, demurely handing round the coffee, never addressed, but it was understood that everything was going on most propitiously.

"It really is very unfortunate that you should have come back just now," lamented Angeliké as she and her sister knelt at their window that evening, with their arms upon the broad stone sill.

"I shouldn't have come if I could have helped it," snapped Danaë.

"Well, I wish you had managed better. I have had such trouble with our father about settling the betrothal, and all because of you. First he said that he would be disgraced if his younger daughter was married first, and then when I said that our brother was sure to find a husband for you, or if he didn't, at any rate we could say he had, he said he had promised you not to let me be married before you. Of course I pointed out to him that we might be betrothed for ages before being married, and I do wish you could have kept away until the rings had been blessed. When we had exchanged them, I should have felt safe."

"I believe," said Danaë slowly, "that you are afraid of my stealing your dear Narkissos. You needn't be."

"I'm not," said Angeliké sharply. "I know what he thinks of you. Oh, not that time long ago, when you spilt the coffee over him. He saw you in Tortolana yesterday, and he thinks you look quite old."

"How do you know what he thinks? Does he write to you?"

"Do you imagine I'm going to tell you? Of course he doesn't write. What good would a letter be to me? But we have ways of knowing about each other, and a good thing too. So don't flatter yourself——"

"I tell you I don't want him. I wouldn't marry him if he would take me without a drachma. I don't want to marry anybody. I should like to die."

"That's because you have nobody to marry you," said Angeliké smartly. "I have felt like that myself towards the end of the Great Fast. But not now—any more than at Easter. Danaë, *what did you do?*"

"Do—at Easter?" Danaë was puzzled.

"No, at Therma. Petros told our father that there was an English lord who would have married you, but when he heard all about you he drew back."

"It is not true! There was never anything of the sort!" cried Danaë hotly. "How did you hear?"

"Oh, I listened," said Angeliké, as calmly as Danaë herself would have made the same confession a year ago. "You were to have a husband found for you soon, lest you should disgrace the family."

"It is the family that disgraces me!" cried Danaë furiously. "Since Milordo heard that I was of the Christodoridi, he has spoken no word to me."

"Then there was something in it?" asked Angeliké greedily. "Tell me about Milordo, and I will tell you what Petros said about him." For Petros had learnt from the comrade who had attended Prince Romanos to Klaustra some things that had happened, and a good many that had not, and had superimposed his own interpretation upon both. But Danaë knew the worth of Angeliké's sympathy of old, and was not to be drawn.

"Milordo is rich and great, and will marry some beautiful European lady of wealth and high birth," she said drearily. "He made a picture of me, that was all."

"In European dress?" asked Angeliké eagerly.

"No, just these old things. He did not know who I was."

Angeliké was puzzled. Danaë did not seem even to care to know how Petros had calumniated her to her father—a recital from which she had promised herself a pleasant excitement. Already her shrewd mind had discovered various discrepancies in the published accounts of her sister's sojourn on the mainland. Contrary to his declared intention, Prince Christodoridi had sent his elder daughter to school, but coaxing and questioning alike had failed to draw from him the name of the school or its teacher. She had continued to wear her native costume, when everyone knew that all schools that were worth anything insisted upon European dress, and she had in some way come into contact with the English impostors who called themselves Theophanis. Moreover, she had incurred the wrath of Prince Romanos, and had been sent home by him with a message that was positively insulting to his father, and she was spiritless and miserable, and seemed to shrink from all her old associations. Angeliké felt herself challenged to discover the truth, the means of learning which, so she decided, must be contained in the large trunk Danaë had brought back with her. She did not offer to unpack it, never went to it when anyone else was by, never left it unlocked, and produced nothing from it but such clothes as she had worn before she went away. For days Angeliké watched and pried, until she discovered that the key was concealed in her sister's hair, a tress of which secured the handle. That night the tress was dexterously snipped off, and the key removed.

When Danaë woke in the morning, and discovered her loss, her anxious misery would have moved any heart less hard than her sister's. She said little, after Angeliké had, with a brazen face, disclaimed all knowledge of the key, for she durst not show the importance she attached to her box and its contents, but she went about searching unavailingly. Angeliké's favourite hiding-places, known of old, were all visited, for Danaë had not the slightest faith in her denial, but it was clear that the key could only be wrested from her by a personal struggle, such as Danaë had learnt to detest. It was indeed the irony of fate that had transformed the unruly barbarian of Klaustra into the unappreciated reformer of Strio, but the surroundings of her present life had taken on quite a new appearance to her. She experienced now something of the same despair that her own untruthfulness had caused in Zoe; she could trust no one, there was not a creature whose word could be accepted.

Wearily Danaë mounted the stairs to the room she shared with her sister, and stood transfixed as she opened the door. There was Angeliké peacocking about in Zoe's myrtle-green gown. The skirt was put on back in front, and the coat cruelly strained to make it meet over her plump chest, but she was trailing hither and thither and admiring herself just as Danaë had done in Linton's clothes. The recollection did not occur at the moment, however, nor would the effect have been a softening one if it had. Training and recent sorrowful musings were alike forgotten, and Danaë rushed at her sister and fairly tore the green gown from her. Her face was so white with rage, and she seemed endued with such irresistible strength, that Angeliké, not usually a coward, made no attempt to protest, and only whimpered feebly when a final push sent her violently against the wall. Half-awed, half-angry, she watched while Danaë gathered up tenderly the desecrated garment, and laying it on the bed, began to smooth it out and fold it as Linton had taught her. A hot tear dropped on the cloth, and she wiped it carefully away, then fetched a needle and cotton, and in the same furious silence sewed on a button or two which had been loosened by Angeliké's rough handling.

Angeliké's versatile mind did not retain impressions very long, and her anger was soon succeeded by an overpowering curiosity. Approaching her sister meekly, with a wary eye open for possibilities of danger, she addressed her in a conciliatory voice.

"When do you mean to wear the Frank dress, Danaë?"

There was no answer, but Danaë's brows were drawn together in a more pronounced frown. Angeliké tried again, becoming bolder.

"It is good thick cloth, like a man's coat, but not so fine as our silks. Are you going to put it on now?"

"No!" burst explosively from Danaë.

"On Sunday, then? Not? But when?"

"Never!"

"But what a waste! If you are afraid of what our father will say, let us each put on half of it. You can choose whether you will wear the coat or the skirt, and I will have the other."

"Are you mad? If any Europeans saw us they would die of laughing. The whole thing must be worn together."

"But why don't you wear it, then? Or if you won't, you might let me. Oh, sister mine, do! You would show me how to put it on properly, and our father might beat me black and blue afterwards, if only I got to church in it first."

"I would sooner tear it to pieces!" cried Danaë wrathfully. "No one shall wear it. It belongs to the Lady Zoe, to my Princess, and she herself helped me to put it on. Then I had to take it off, and I vowed that neither I nor anyone else should wear it until I saw her again. As for you—why, I would let one of the girls from the kitchen wear it rather than you."

"Oh, very well, my lady! I'll pay you out for that!" said Angeliké venomously, and slipped out of the room. A moment later, a wild tumult of shrieks and screams proclaimed to Danaë that her sister was in one of her fits of passion—which were credibly supposed in the household to be due to temporary demoniacal possession. In them Angeliké would tear her clothes, knock herself vehemently against the wall, and otherwise do as much damage as was compatible with avoiding obvious disfigurement. Danaë herself had been subject to similar attacks, of a somewhat less violent character, in the past, but now she went on calmly with her work of straightening the contents of her box, which Angeliké had disarranged, and laying the green gown carefully at the top. Suddenly the door burst open, and two stalwart women-servants paused rather sheepishly on the threshold. A stentorian shout pursued them up the stairs, however, "Hurry, children!" and ended their hesitation, and they marched across the room, banged down the lid of the box, and seizing it by the handles, carried it off.

"What are you doing with my box?" demanded Danaë angrily.

"The Despot's orders, my lady!" was the reply, and the two together bumped and banged the box down the stairs, at the foot of which stood Prince Christodoridi. When he saw his daughter, he shouted to her to come down too, in a voice that rose triumphant above Angeliké's wails and screams. In the courtyard two of the men who hung about the place were arranging armfuls of withered olive-branches, and another came up with a jar of oil. Angeliké's shrieks were growing fainter. It almost seemed as though the course of events had not fallen out precisely as she intended. As Danaë came down the stairs, her father seized her wrist in an iron grip. She made no attempt at resistance, but he held her fast while, with set face, she watched her treasures, Zoe's gown, the photographs of the Klaustra party, books, writing and sewing materials—all the relics of her life on the mainland—ruthlessly saturated with oil and piled into a bonfire. Angeliké was weeping now, unrestrainedly, but Danaë did not utter a sound. When the flames died down, her father suddenly pulled her round to face him.

"Now, Lady Danaë, I have a word to say to you. You bring back a European dress, intending to wear it at the next *panegyris* [Saint's day rejoicings] and steal your sister's bridegroom from her, do you? Well, you see the end of that. We will have no vile Frankish clothes or any other evil inventions in Strio, and any that are brought here will be treated as yours have been—" the voice was raised to reach the listening servants. "What you want, Lady Danaë, is a strict husband, and you shall have one, sooner than you expect. As for you, weeper!" he cast a scathing glance at the cowering Angeliké—"it will do you no harm to wait a little. You are in too great a hurry."

Danaë, released with two black bruises on her wrist where he had gripped her, walked upstairs again with admirable steadiness, and was seen no more until the evening. What brought her out then was the voice of Angeliké, a frightened and miserable voice, at the door.

"Danaë, come down. Come down at once—to our mother. Something terrible—oh, I cannot utter it——"

The tone seemed genuine, and after a decent pause, for the sake of her own dignity, Danaë pulled back the bed with which she had blocked the door, and came out, following Angeliké down to their mother's room. At first she thought that the obvious disturbance afflicting Princess Christodoridi was due to the destruction of the box and its contents, which she had promised herself much entertainment in examining, but she soon saw that it must be something worse. Her mother was sitting upright, and was clearly much excited.

"I cannot bear these sudden changes. They are so upsetting!" lamented the poor lady. "Why you should have chosen to come home just now, Danaë——"

"But what has happened?" asked Danaë breathlessly.

"I always said evil would come of sending you to be educated," her mother went on. "Your father had always declared he would never hear of such a thing, and I agreed with him. Then he changes his mind suddenly, and expects mine to be changed even before I knew that he had changed his. But I never changed. 'You will do what you like, of course,' I said; 'but mark my words, no good will come of it.'"

"Then I am sure you said it to yourself, and not to the Despot, my mother," said Angeliké impatiently. "No one would have minded Danaë's going away, if only she had not come back."

"But what is it?" urged Danaë, in despair.

"Oh, it is your fault too, Angeliké," said Princess Christodoridi, almost with energy. "What I have done to have two such daughters I don't know. And when everything was so nicely settled, and even the rings ordered—I am sure your finger is thinner than your sister's, Danaë. Oh yes, of course, that is what your father has done. He says it is you who are to marry Kyrios Narkissos, not Angeliké."

"I won't!" cried Danaë furiously.

"You shan't!" muttered Angeliké, with determination.

"Now, what is the good of talking like that?" inquired their mother plaintively. "It is what the Despot says that is done, not what you or I say."

"But Narkissos himself—and his father—" gasped Danaë.

"Kyrios Smaragdopoulos will be very pleased, for your father will give you the extra five hundred drachmæ they quarrelled about, because you are his elder daughter. And the young man will do as his father tells him, of course. And you will do as you are told, though really it is very awkward, with Angeliké's dress nearly finished embroidering for the betrothal——"

"I will never marry him!" cried Danaë.

"Oh, don't be foolish," said her mother wearily. "If you had not come back just now, we should not have had all this trouble. Once they were betrothed, nothing could have been altered. And you too, Angeliké; if you had not been so jealous about your sister's things, making your father destroy all that beautiful cloth and those pretty pictures, you would not have lost your bridegroom——"

And so on, and so on. Princess Christodoridi's Christian name was a rank libel on her, for she could not scold. But she could complain, in a feeble but persistent stream of lamentation, calculated to wear down the hardest rock if uninterrupted, and at present both her daughters were too much crushed to attempt a diversion.

CHAPTER XX.
GREEK AND GREEK.

IT was Angeliké who at last broke desperately into the flood of complaint. "Lady, are you on my father's side, or ours?"

"How can you be so foolish, daughter mine?" was the querulous reply. "Have I ever been on any side but your father's? How could I be anything else?"

"But you don't agree with him, my mother? You don't think it fair that Danaë, who has missed all her own chances, should come back and steal my bridegroom?"

"I'm not stealing him! I don't want him!" cried Danaë.

"It is no use asking me to oppose your father," said Princess Christodoridi, and this was obviously true.

"No, but if we can manage to get things right, you won't prevent us? It's all very well for Danaë to stand there and say she won't marry Narkissos, but our father will force the ring on her finger and the crown on her head. But I have a plan. My mother, I will not tell you what it is, lest my father should suspect, but you will do what I ask?"

"If you are sure your father will not find out," said her mother nervously.

"You will have done nothing for him to find out. His anger will be terrible, of course, but we are used to that, and it is worth it this time. Once the blessed rings are exchanged, no one can break the betrothal. My mother, Danaë and I must be dressed exactly alike. Leave the embroidered robe for the Sunday after the wedding, and let Danaë have a long coat like mine. And you were going to lend me your own veil."

"Yes, but your father said it was too large—like a Roumi woman's. I told him it was what everyone wore in my island, and he said we were ignorant heathen. I dare not let you wear it, child. He would pull it off you and tear it to pieces."

"Ah, but we will cut it in two, my mother. Then it will be quite small, and we shall be alike."

"But what waste! It is good muslin, real English. And when your father sees two brides——"

"He will not have time to think about it. And you will sacrifice your veil to save your daughter, mother mine? Ah, I knew it!" She kissed the Princess's hand. "Danaë, can you faint?"

"I don't know. Yes, I fainted once, not long ago."

"Well, you must be able to do it properly. You had better practise. When is the betrothal to be, my mother?"

"Your father said it was no use wasting more time. He has sent word to Kyrios Smaragdopoulos and his son, and Danaë's godfather, to be here in three days."

"I must let Narkissos know at once," mused Angeliké, under her breath. "He must be sullen, but not refuse to accept the change. And you, my mother, you will tell the Despot that Danaë is obstinate and swears she will not marry Narkissos, but girls are often like that, and very likely she will be all right on the day. And we will both offer gifts to the Fates, that all may be well. Let us go and make honey cakes at once."

"At Klaustra, they said that there were no such things as the Fates," said Danaë hesitatingly. Her mother sat up.

"Never let me hear you say such a thing again, Danaë," she said, with unusual decision. "Wretched girl, are you not afraid what will happen to you? No Fates, indeed? One would think you had been born in a house where the proper ceremonies were not observed. Did not your father himself tie up the dogs on the third night after you were born, that the august ladies might not be disturbed while they partook of the banquet prepared for them, and decided upon your future? Those unbelievers at Klaustra, whoever they may be, will say there is no such thing as witches next."

As this was exactly what Zoe had said, Danaë held her peace. Angeliké laughed.

"Even if we were not sure of the Fates, it would be prudent to propitiate them in case they existed," she said. "So I shall give them honey cakes, and if things go wrong with you and right with me, Danaë, we shall know why. And I shall also weep. My father calls me the weeper. Holy Marina! he shall see quite as many tears as he expects!"

And in truth, during the next two days, red eyes and perpetual weeping met Prince Christodoridi's gaze whenever he glanced towards his younger daughter. They made him impatient, but he did not really object to them nearly as much as to Danaë's set, tearless face. He was vaguely conscious of a conflict of wills between his elder daughter and himself, and he was determined that this should be the decisive battle. Once Danaë was betrothed, there was no help for her, and the greater her objection to the proposed bridegroom, the more signal her father's triumph. It was no business of his to forecast the course of a loveless marriage between an unwilling couple. Its working-out might safely be left to Narkissos and his parents.

As for Danaë, the fact of her dependence upon Angeliké galled her almost as much as her father's summary disposal of her hand. But for the assurance that Angeliké's heart was firmly set upon Narkissos, she would have feared being left in the lurch at the last moment. It was a consolation to feel that Angeliké was working solely in her own interests, since that ensured a certain amount of loyalty on her part, but it was not pleasant to be so deeply indebted to her, while to Angeliké the bitterest drop in her cup was undoubtedly the reflection that in securing her own happiness she was working temporary deliverance for Danaë. How to counteract this involuntary boon was a problem at which her busy brain was hard at work whenever it was not perfecting the details of the original scheme.

* * * * * * * *

"Danaë, wake up! There is a ship lying off the shore—a *pamporaki*!" [steamer] It was the morning of the betrothal day, and Danaë, who had lain awake the night before, was still plunged in heavy sleep when her sister's voice summoned her to the window. Out at sea, beyond the network of rocks and shoals which had formed an important part of the Striotes' stock-in-trade in their palmy days as pirates and wreckers, lay a trim vessel, very unlike usual visitors to the island.

"I have only seen a *pamporaki* twice—no, three times—before, when we went to Tortolana," mused Angeliké. "Certainly none has ever come so near Strio. Do you think it is the English lord's ship, Danaë?"

"Certainly not—why should it be? How can I tell? I have never seen Milordo's ship," replied Danaë, in such confusion that Angeliké was emboldened to make a further attempt.

"Oh, sister mine, tell me about Milordo! Why did he break off the marriage?"

"There was no talk of a marriage, therefore no breaking-off," said Danaë harshly. "I have told you before that Milordo never dreamed of marrying me."

This ought to have been decisive, but to Angeliké the blush and the sudden eager look called up by her suggestion as to the vessel's ownership were far more eloquent than words. Still, it was evidently hopeless to get anything more out of Danaë, so she turned to another informant. This was

Petros, who was still hanging about, though not at all by his own wish. By way of accounting at once plausibly and concisely for the various events that had occurred at Therma—a large proportion of which were quite unintelligible to himself—he had told Prince Christodoridi that it had been discovered too late that the Lady was Orthodox by religion and royal by descent, and that she was now openly acknowledged to have been the wife of Prince Romanos. Thereupon the Despot turned upon him furiously, and charging him with having brought a false report at first, drove him from his presence, ordering him to leave the island. But his master had ordered him to stay in Strio, and he felt it highly inadvisable to return to Therma without a protector of some kind, so that his position was most unenviable. Angeliké had first come upon him—in sufficient secrecy—two days before, and by the sacrifice of the least conspicuous coin from her cap had drawn from him a statement to the effect that the marriage-broker had certainly been busy, at the instance of Prince Romanos, in arranging a marriage between Milordo and Lady Danaë, but that the English lord had suddenly and insultingly broken off the negociations. Pressed as to the reason, he replied—with a lumping together of cause and effect, and a confusion of times, that were truly magnificent—that the Lady Danaë had chosen to masquerade for a while as a servant in the household at Klaustra, and it was the discovery of this that had made her suitor alter his mind. To-day Angeliké managed to get hold of Petros again. He answered her question almost before it was asked.

"Yes, lady, that is Milordo's ship. I have seen it in Therma harbour."

"But why does he come here? Does he wish to renew the treaty of marriage?" demanded Angeliké.

"How can I tell, lady?" Petros assumed a deep air of wisdom. "At any rate, it can hardly be very agreeable for the Lady Danaë to meet him after what happened."

"But did it happen?" flashed forth Angeliké.

Petros looked grieved. "Lady, you have asked, and I have answered. You know best whether the Lady Danaë desired to return to Strio. To me in my humility it appeared that she did not. If Milordo thought so too, may he not be visiting the island to show her what she has lost?"

"But that is insulting to us!" cried Angeliké.

"The English are like that, lady. They will take infinite pains to insult those they dislike. Nay, I have seen them show atrocious rudeness for mere wantonness."

Angeliké went slowly away, a new plan beginning to shape itself in her mind. As a preliminary step, she took the precaution of a whispered warning to Princess Christodoridi. "Keep Danaë with you in the kitchen all the morning, my mother. If my father sees her, he will know that she does not intend to submit, and we don't want him to be angry beforehand."

Her mother agreed with nervous readiness, and as a result Danaë was kept hard at work making cakes and sweetmeats, with no opportunity of stealing upstairs to look at the distant ship. For herself Angeliké had reserved the task of preparing the pillared loggia, which served as an open-air sitting-room, for the afternoon's ceremony. Sweeping and dusting, erecting a temporary altar for the blessing of the rings, and overseeing the servants as they beat up and arranged the cushions on the divan for the expected guests, she was elaborately busy, and constantly in her father's sight. Her cheerful aspect forced itself upon his attention at last, and was no doubt welcome, since even Prince Christodoridi could scarcely deny that Angeliké had been hardly treated. He caught one of her plaits as she hurried past him, and pulled it with something like approval.

"What, weeper! are the tears dried?"

"Quite dried up, lord!" showing a saucy and absolutely tearless face. "Are there not plenty of bridegrooms to be had besides Narkissos Smaragdopoulos?"

"Oh, that's what makes you so cheerful, is it? And you don't even mind your sister's getting him?"

She laughed, with gleeful appreciation of an absurdity. "Why, lord, it is Danaë who minds! She declares she won't marry him, and my mother is keeping her under her own eye lest she should try to run away. There is that ship, you know———"

"And what of that ship, girl?" His tone was thunderous, but Angeliké smiled innocently into his face.

"Why, lord, they say it belongs to a great and rich English lord, who is a friend of my brother. Now what I think is that this lord has been drawn to Strio by the report of the beauty of your second daughter. So there will be a marriage for me after all!"

"You are an impudent little minx!" said Prince Christodoridi, but without any show of anger. "But suppose it is Danaë he comes after?"

"Lord, you would not let her rob me of two bridegrooms?" The pretty face was so innocently grieved, the eyes so near tears, that Prince Christodoridi laughed and pinched Angeliké's ear encouragingly.

"One bridegroom will be quite enough for her, I warrant, and once betrothed she is out of your way. But suppose the English lord doesn't think you come up to the report he has heard?"

"Oh, do you think he will be disappointed, lord?" breathed Angeliké, with such anxious misery that her father's heart was melted.

"Suppose we let him see you, girl? Shall I ask him to the betrothal? It is well to be courteous to strangers."

"Ah, lord, if you would! And then nothing need be said unless—unless you should feel that you would like an English son-in-law. All the English are very rich, I have heard Danaë or some one say."

"What does Danaë know about the English?" suspiciously.

"I don't know, lord. She has never seen any of them, has she? I daresay," meekly, "that it was not Danaë who told me. But why should he come to Strio at all, if he did not desire to present himself for your approval?"

Curiously enough, Armitage was asking himself much the same question—what was he doing off Strio? He had been restless at Klaustra, and had gravely given utterance to the opinion that the sea was calling him. A short cruise in the Egean, and he would return to see what he had long promised himself as a rare delight—the unfolding of spring in the great beech-woods on the mountain slopes. His hosts acquiesced in the most understanding way, and Zoe begged him, if he found himself anywhere in the neighbourhood of Strio, to make a point of visiting the island and seeing how poor Kalliopé was getting on. At Therma it was only polite to pay his respects to Prince Romanos, and ask if he could do anything for him in the islands, and as the Prince wished to send an important parcel to his sister, it was only natural that Armitage, not guessing that it contained the various little clothes and toys which Danaë had made for Janni at different times during her career as his nurse, and was designed to emphasize the completeness of her separation from him for the future, should volunteer to carry it. Thus there was really no choice about the yacht's destination, but all the same, Armitage had a lurking fear that he was making a fool of himself when his boat took him ashore, and he noticed the critical way in which the inhabitants regarded him. Emancipation had not been by any means wholly a boon to the inhabitants of Strio—rather it had brought about a distinct diminution both of their liberties and their prosperity, owing to the restraints imposed by their union with the mainland kingdom. Therefore the friendliness for England and individual Englishmen, so noticeable in most Greek communities, was conspicuous by its absence, and the truculent looks of the swarthy loafers on the quay made Armitage feel as if he was venturing into a pirates' lair.

But after all, this was the environment in which his island princess—as he always called Danaë in his thoughts—had grown up, and in which it ought to be possible to see her free and happy, untrammelled by the conventions which had suited her so ill, and he rambled through the tortuous lanes of the little town with great contentment, noting endless subjects for sketches. Then he came suddenly on Prince Christodoridi, on his way to the harbour to visit him on board, and they renewed the acquaintance begun years ago at Bashi Konak, and fraternised cordially. The Despot would hear of nothing but the Englishman's accompanying him home at once to spend the day, preparatory to coming on shore for a regular visit. He should sketch as much as he liked, examine the Venetian work still extant in the fortress, and there was a little family ceremony that afternoon which he might find it interesting to attend—the betrothal of Prince Christodoridi's daughter. Armitage was conscious of a distinct shock at first, but he recollected that there were two daughters, and reasoned that it was not likely they would be marrying Danaë off so soon after her return home. Therefore he sent his boat, which was to fetch him off at a certain time, back to the yacht, and returned up the hill to the fortress with his host.

Everything was now ready for the betrothal, and presently the guests began to drop in. Kyrios Smaragdopoulos had rather the appearance of a policeman haling an unwilling prisoner, so sullen was the handsome face of his son, and so unsuited his bearing to his festal attire, which included the widest and whitest and stiffest kilt Armitage had ever seen, and a jacket rich with gold embroidery. Narkissos sat apart and brooded, his father taking no notice of him except to see that he did not run away, and it was a relief when a burly jovial man swaggered in, who was introduced to Armitage as Parthenios Chalkiadi. He had been Prince Christodoridi's best man and his elder daughter's godfather, it seemed, and not only took an important part in to-day's proceedings, but was also to be best man at his goddaughter's wedding. It was natural he should be in the family secrets, and he whispered loudly behind his hand to Armitage, with a nod towards the gloomy bridegroom, "Wanted the other one!" which caused the guest to regard Narkissos with more interest, as a rejected suitor of Danaë's. Meanwhile a priest, with flowing hair and beard and a frayed purple robe, had made his appearance with a youthful assistant, and there was a great sound of whispering and giggling through a doorway across which female forms sometimes flitted. Then an old woman looked out and called in an agitated voice for Kyrios Parthenios, and the godfather rolled across the room with great pomp. Above the whisperings of the women his rich voice was clearly audible somewhere in the back regions.

"Well, little one, back just in time to keep your sister from getting married first! She has plenty of time before her. But mercy on us! she's as tall as you are. Two brides instead of one! We must take care the wrong one doesn't get betrothed."

Then it was Danaë! Armitage was conscious of a feeling—not of disappointment; he assured himself it was not disappointment—but of flatness, as if a promising romance had come to an unexpectedly sudden end. But Kyrios Smaragdopoulos had marched his reluctant son to the extemporised altar, on which two gold rings were placed, and a procession was entering the doorway—Parthenios Chalkiadi leading a veiled figure by the hand, another veiled figure supporting the first one closely, and an indeterminate throng of girls and women behind. It was Danaë! Armitage must have started or made a movement of some kind, for her eyes met his with a look which made him turn away as if he had seen something he had no business to see. Shame, misery, reproach, unavailing protest—he read them all in that one glance and the movement of recoil which accompanied it, and he half rose, with a wild impulse to save the girl somehow, though how he had no idea. But attention was diverted from his action by a shriek from the bridesmaid.

"She is fainting! Help, quick! Carry her back!"

Armitage had seen no sign of fainting, but Danaë was undoubtedly lying limp in her sister's arms, and Kyrios Chalkiadi was looking down at the two in amazement. The women closed round them and hustled them back, and presently the godfather reappeared grumbling.

"The Pappas had better cut things as short as possible," he said, the radiance of his face eclipsed. "The girl is overwrought—joyful occasion—too much excitement—— But in our young days who ever heard of a bride fainting at her betrothal?"

"Girls are poor creatures nowadays," growled Prince Christodoridi. "Leave out the exhortation, Pappa," he added to the priest, who had prepared a flowery one, and was naturally reluctant to omit it. While he and his patron argued together in low tones, Kyrios Chalkiadi sat down again by Armitage.

"I verily believe the bride dislikes the match as much as the bridegroom," he said, in his roaring whisper, with a glance of contempt at the stolid Narkissos. "A nasty, sulky fellow—I don't wonder she doesn't want him."

"Can nothing be done?" asked Armitage involuntarily.

His neighbour looked at him in astonishment, then laughed. "You show yourself indeed a perfect stranger here, lord. What could be done, when the parents have arranged matters? You may be sure that in a case like this the young people would rebel, if they thought it would be any use. But they'll settle down. And let me advise you to exhibit less interest, friend Englishman," he added warningly. "We know that you English have a taste for interfering in other people's affairs, but it will do no good to the girl. Ah, I am wanted again!"

The warning he had received held Armitage fast in his place, but it seemed to him like a horrible dream as the veiled figure was brought in once more, supported by the strong arm of Kyrios Parthenios on one side, and by her sister on the other, Princess Christodoridi following anxiously close behind, and keeping back the other women, who were inclined to press unduly close. Narkissos was brought into position again, the rings were blessed, and a reluctant hand was disinterred from under the bride's draperies. Parthenios Chalkiadi was clearly resolved to do his duty to the utmost. He put the rings on, took them off, and exchanged them, with strict attention to the words the priest was gabbling, and callous disregard of the attitude of the betrothal pair, while his left arm held the bride in a grip which suggested constraint at least as much as support. When the brief ceremony was over, he gave a laugh of relief.

"Sorry to have done you out of your sermon, Pappa. Better keep it for the wedding. Lady Danaë will have got used to the thought of her bridegroom by that time—— Why, what's this? All-Holy Mother of God! we have betrothed the wrong one after all!"

For the shrinking form on his left had suddenly recovered strength, and stepped forward with extreme confidence to join the bridegroom, from whose countenance the clouds had instantaneously disappeared. Princess Christodoridi, running forward in obvious horror to lift the veil, disclosed the features of Angeliké, and dropped it with a shriek.

"Holy Nicholas! what is this?" roared Prince Christodoridi, charging at the triumphant pair like a wild bull. Angeliké sheltered herself immediately behind the stalwart form of her betrothed, with a trustfulness very pretty to see, and left him to answer, which he did with admirable courage.

"I engaged myself to marry the Lady Angeliké, lord, and I am now betrothed to her."

"Oh, are you?" cried his prospective father-in-law. "Take off those rings! Here, Pappa!" to the retreating priest, "come back and do the service over again. My stick shall make acquaintance with your shoulders for this foolishness, you hussy! Take off that ring!" he shouted to his daughter.

But Angeliké kept her hand behind her, and remained coyly in the shadow, and Narkissos rose magnificently to the occasion.

"You may take the Lady Angeliké's ring from my dead hand, lord, but while I live it does not leave me."

"Come out, girl!" roared Prince Christodoridi, making a dash at his daughter. "I will have that ring off if I have to cut off your finger to get it," but the priest, still sore on account of his wasted eloquence, interposed.

"That would be sacrilege, lord. Once the handfasting has taken place, the *symphonia* [contract] is as binding as marriage itself. None can break it. Carry the case to the Bishop—to the Œcumenical Patriarch himself, and he will tell you the same."

"I will go to the Patriarch, dog, and you shall see!" cried the irate father, and ceased perforce, foaming with rage. While he was still muttering inarticulately, Parthenios Chalkiadi, with considerable courage, stepped forward as peacemaker.

"I was as much taken aback as you, friend Agesilaos," he said frankly, laying his hand on the Prince's shoulder, "but I can't say that I am altogether sorry for what has happened. It seems to me that these two young people are a good deal happier than they were half an hour ago. The only one who seems to have been badly treated is my goddaughter. What says the Lady Danaë? Does she wish the betrothal broken, if it can be done?"

"Nothing less so, lord," cried Danaë eagerly. "I had no desire to marry the Lord Narkissos."

"Then it looks as if everyone was satisfied," said Kyrios Parthenios gravely. "Let us have the coffee, Danaë," in the most audible of whispers. "Come, friend Agesilaos," to Prince Christodoridi, "let the young folks kiss your hand. I'm sure I never saw a handsomer couple since the day I was best man to yourself and my friend Kyria Xantippe there. Ah, that's right!"

CHAPTER XXI.
MARRIAGE BY CAPTURE.

PRINCE CHRISTODORIDI sat alone on the terrace, in the most unamiable of tempers. Evening was drawing on, and the guests had departed, after doing full justice to the coffee and syrup, the preserves of roses and quinces, handed round by the girls. They were provided with a subject of conversation that would crop up for many a long day, and Prince Christodoridi writhed under the knowledge of it. He had been over-reached and publicly flouted, and what was worse, Loukas Smaragdopoulos held fast to the extra five hundred drachmæ. He had intended his son to marry the Despot's elder daughter, he said, and had prepared apartments for them on a suitable scale, and if he was to be put off with the younger, at least he would not be done out of his money as well. It had required all the diplomacy of Parthenios Chalkiadi, and the restraint imposed by the presence of the English stranger, to keep the wrangle within due bounds, but Kyrios Loukas had gone away without consenting to forgo his claim, which meant that it would have to be acknowledged. And this was not the worst. If Prince Christodoridi carried his grievance to the Patriarchal tribunal, and asked for the annulment of the betrothal, it was ten to one that he would merely waste more money without obtaining satisfaction. But if Angeliké were married before her elder sister, he would be eternally disgraced in the opinion of all his acquaintances, yet to find a husband for Danaë as well meant the provision of two dowries at once—a prospect which was enough to wring tears of blood from the hapless father. It was little wonder that when Angeliké made an unobtrusive appearance, and began to clear away the coffee-cups, he swore at her angrily and bade her bring him his stick. But it seemed indeed as if the very foundations of the earth were out of course, since this hitherto submissive slave made no attempt to obey. Instead, she stood before him meekly with clasped hands.

"Why would you beat me, lord?" she asked softly.

"You know very well. Fetch that stick!" vociferated her father.

"Nay, lord; listen a moment. You robbed me of the bridegroom you had promised. Did I rebel? I wept, but even my tears were put away in obedience to your will. But when the opportunity offered—ah, lord, I was resigned, as I thought, but a voice in my heart bade me seize my chance, and I listened. Beat me if you will, but had you been in my place, would you have suffered your sister to steal your bridegroom?"

"It was not your sister's doing; it was mine—and you have made your father a laughing-stock, girl."

"Ah, lord, not so—never! Surely no one could ever laugh at you!"

The tone was so serious, so reverential, that Prince Christodoridi found his wrath melting away in a most unwonted manner. The thought was a gratifying one—and Angeliké was nestling close to his knees, and gazing up with admiring eyes into his face. Quite without warning she gave a little laugh. "I wonder why Danaë fainted!" she said.

"Because she is a fool, and you are another," growled her father.

"I wonder—" Angeliké edged away a little—"I wonder why the English lord came here."

"Not to behold your beauty, at any rate."

"Oh!" with breathless interest; "was it to behold Danaë's, lord?"

"Nonsense! The thoughts of you girls run on nothing but bridegrooms. Milordo was passing by, and came like a well-mannered man to salute me on his way."

"Oh!" this time the tone breathed intense disappointment. "I did hope it might be on account of Danaë."

"What do you mean by that?" Prince Christodoridi gripped her shoulder as she made a movement to rise. "What should he know about Danaë?"

"I don't know, lord," gazing at him with wide eyes of terror. "I have never spoken to him, nor seen him."

"Of course not," impatiently. "Do you mean that your sister has?"

"I—I don't know. Perhaps—I don't think so. It may not have been the same man. Don't ask me, lord; ask Petros. I know no more than you do; how should I?"

"What has Petros been saying to you? What is this about your sister? Can this be the man——? Tell me at once, girl."

"Petros said—" whimpered Angeliké—"at least, I mean he told Aristomaché, and she told me (but he said you knew),—that all the talk at Klaustra was that Milordo would marry Danaë. And one night she was dressed up in Frank clothes—all in cloth of gold like an empress—and they made a great feast, and Milordo and she sat side by side. She—she even put her arm in his, lord," breathed modest Angeliké in horror, turning away her eyes. But Prince Christodoridi had been a scandalized participant in European dinner-parties, and had even, under pressure from his son, consented to offer his arm to a lady, so that he bore up under the shock better than she had hoped.

"But this cannot be the same man. How could he have the effrontery——? And yet he said—— Well, what of all this?"

"Why, lord, they all thought the betrothal would take place the next day, when my brother arrived suddenly, but instead of that, there was much talk at the house of Prince Theophanis, to which Danaë was summoned, and she came away looking like one dead, and the next day my brother brought her away to Therma. So everyone said that Milordo had refused to marry her, and they supposed it was because she had pretended to be a servant."

"But he knew all about that!" said Prince Christodoridi, thoroughly puzzled.

"Did you know of it, then, lord? Oh, why was it?" Curiosity had led Angeliké beyond the bounds of prudence, and her father frowned.

"That is no concern of yours, girl. If he saw her at Klaustra, it was when she was passing as a servant."

This was a bad blow to Angeliké's theory, but a happy idea struck her. "But perhaps his parents interfered, lord. They may have thought she would have no dowry."

"Your brother would have referred the matter to me. He knows that I should not grudge a—a reasonable sum to establish you both suitably."

"Of course, lord, he must know. And yet—the match was broken off, and Milordo is here."

"True. He is here," her father repeated mechanically.

"And his parents are not here, lord."

Prince Christodoridi looked at her sharply. "What do you mean by that, girl?"

"It looks almost," said Angeliké, with an innocent little giggle, "as if he wanted to marry her after all." This was going much farther than she had intended, but Armitage's arrival had fitted in so miraculously with her plans that she could not allow it to be wasted.

"After all? What do you mean?"

"As if he might be willing even to marry her without a dowry, lord."

The siren-voice was sweet, and Angeliké was crouching very confidingly close to her father. He shook her off with an oath.

"All-Holy Mother! He has said nothing about it."

"But perhaps he will, lord; or you might notice something that would enable you to speak."

"The fellow is not going to refuse my daughter twice!"

"No, lord; but since he has come here, surely he has no wish to refuse? And how could he say anything? Every civilised man knows that it falls to the maiden's father to speak first. And—and he might not be sorry—just to satisfy his parents——"

"Yes? Plague take the girl, why won't she speak out?"

"He might not be sorry if you insisted on the marriage, lord."

The idea appealed to Prince Christodoridi, since it savoured of the methods of his ancestors, and he welcomed it with a pleased smile. But none the less, he put it aside valiantly.

"No, no; he is my guest, and we can't force a wife upon him. But if I see anything to make me believe he has really come after Danaë, and that good manners are keeping him back—— But mind, not a word to your sister!"

"Oh no, lord!" said Angeliké heartily, with the full intention of disobeying at the earliest possible opportunity. When she went up to bed, creeping stealthily into their room, she found Danaë, as she expected, kneeling at the window with her eyes fixed on the distant lights of the yacht. With great tact, Angeliké took no notice of her immediate change of position, but yawned softly as she lighted the lamp.

"It has been a great day!" she said. "And to-morrow come the gifts. Oh, how I hope Narkissos will have chosen my dress the right colour! I told him blue and citron most carefully, but I know his father would get any other stripe that was a little cheaper, no matter how ugly it was."

"Well, you have got Narkissos, at any rate," said Danaë sharply. Angeliké's claws were out in an instant.

"I believe you wanted him after all! You didn't faint."

"You know I don't want him. I—I forgot."

"You wouldn't have done it at all if I had not cried out. If anyone had been looking they must have noticed. I know why you forgot," with awful directness. "It was because of Milordo."

"It wasn't!" cried Danaë. But Angeliké's distrustful eyes warned her that there was only one possible alternative, and she temporised. "Well, I was surprised to see him, of course."

"Of course! If you mean glad, why don't you say so?"

"Because I was not glad!" cried Danaë vehemently. "I was bowed down with shame—I could have died——"

"Oh, you are always talking about dying!" said Angeliké, altering her tactics skilfully to meet this surprise. "He is rich, and pleasant to look upon—though he has the face of a boy; I prefer men—and our father favours him."

"What are you talking about?" demanded Danaë.

"Promise not to tell—never to let out a word about it. Our father has chosen him for your bridegroom."

Danaë flung up her arms wildly, then dropped them in despair. "Has he—has he spoken to him?" she asked.

"I don't know. I think not; but perhaps he has." It was necessary to walk warily in dealing with such explosive material.

"Then he must not. Oh, Angeliké, sister mine, he must not! It is not the custom of the English. With them the man speaks first."

"But he might be refused!" cried Angeliké, aghast at the idea of subjecting the nobler sex to such an indignity. "Are you sure? Who told you?"

"Sofia, the Lady Zoe's maid. And she said that with them a woman whose parents spoke for her would be eternally despised. Nor would the man consent to marry her."

"Well, of all the barbarous customs! But fear not, my sister. No man refuses what the Despot of Strio offers."

"Do you think I want him to marry me against his will?"

"But why should it be against his will? Kyrios Loukas was glad enough for Narkissos to marry one of us, though he had to make a fuss about the dowry——" She stopped abruptly. The crowning shame, her suggestion that Armitage might be induced to marry Danaë without a dowry, must be discreetly concealed, for by immemorial custom, a Striote girl whose father refused without due cause to provide for her had the right of appeal to the people in public assembly against the insult put upon her, and such an exposure would not suit Prince Christodoridi.

"It's not a question of dowry!" cried Danaë. "Would you have cared to marry Narkissos if you knew he didn't want you?"

"Of course, if I wanted him," said the practical Angeliké. "And you want the English lord; you know you do."

"I don't! I don't! I don't want to marry anyone."

"But that's silly. You have got to be married. What else could become of you?"

"In Europe women do all sorts of things now. There are female teachers, and scribes."

"As if we should ever be allowed to do anything of the kind! Of course, if one had a chance like that of getting away from here, and living where there was something going on, one would not care about getting married. But as it is, we may be thankful that there are bridegrooms to be found for us."

"I am not! I won't marry him! I don't want to."

"You talk so foolishly," said Angeliké patiently. "If our father means you to marry Milordo, he will have to take you, and you will have to go to him. And once you are his wife——"

"Angeliké," said Danaë quickly, "how is it that you have managed to send messages to Narkissos when you wished? I never heard of anyone's doing it before."

Then the seed so casually dropped had borne fruit! Angeliké smiled to herself as she replied, "That's all you know about it! All the girls send messages if they wish. Why not make use of friend Petros?"

"I would not trust Petros if there was no one else in the world."

"Well, what I do," reluctantly, "is to get hold of Aristomaché. She is always going about, looking for suitable brides and bridegrooms, and she is to be trusted. She is sleeping here to-night, so as to see the gifts to-morrow."

And the next morning Angeliké smiled again, when she found Danaë missing when she woke, and saw her shortly afterwards returning breathless from a hurried visit to the women-servants' quarters. She could picture, as well as if she had heard the request uttered, the old woman despatching her grandson to waylay Armitage as he landed, and to tell him that some one wished to speak to him at a certain place. That would be the form of the message, since the matter was too delicate to be confided to the go-between, and the important thing now was to discover the place, and to contrive to direct Prince Christodoridi's steps thither at the right time. But the Angeliké of the last two days was such an ingratiating creature, and the ruse to discover the date of her wedding so prettily transparent, that her father was rather pleased than otherwise to be dragged off to examine her own particular myrtle, and decide whether it would flower in time to provide her wreath, or whether some bush growing on lower ground must be laid under contribution.

Armitage received his message duly, and with mixed feelings. He was to turn aside to examine a built-up archway some little distance to the left of the fortress gate, and some one—nods and winks and meaning gestures—would come to speak to him there. He hoped in one way that it might be Danaë, for it seemed that etiquette would otherwise prevent him from speaking to her at all, and he had Zoe's inquiries to make. But Parthenios Chalkiadi's warning rang in his ears, and he had caught certain looks passing among the women the day before which seemed to indicate that he was somehow connected with Danaë in their minds. This was the more undesirable in that he had no very definite idea what his wishes or intentions were, and only a vague notion that perhaps he had better not have come to the island. But this was forgotten when he saw Danaë standing in the shelter of the archway, and sprang forward to meet her. She allowed him no time for conventional greeting.

"You will wonder how I got here, lord. I climbed down the wall." She held out her hands, all bruised and scratched, and looked down at her torn and dusty skirt. "You will guess I should not have done that for nothing. Lord, turn back. There is a plot to kidnap you."

On this version of the facts she had decided, after much mental wrestling. But Armitage was incredulous.

"But who would do such a thing, Lady Danaë? I am more than sorry that you should have taken so much trouble——"

She interrupted him hastily. "Don't think of me, lord; but believe what I tell you. Do not enter the fortress. You would not have me betray my own people?" with the ghost of a smile. "But we are all pirates, you know, and you are rich, and can pay ransom. Go back while you can."

"But I have messages for you from the Lady Zoe. Are you happy here?"

The glance she turned on him thrilled him with the remembrance of that other glance of yesterday. But she recollected herself quickly. "At least I am happier than yesterday morning I expected to be," she said. "Yes, lord, tell the Lady Zoe that all is well. I am here in my own place, in the life to which I belong. It must be the best for me. Why should I not be happy?"

"Look me in the face and tell me that you are, Danaë."

He spoke very gently, but Danaë could not meet his kind eyes. "No, that is unfair. You have no right to ask me that!" she said incoherently, with both hands pressed to her breast. "Go, lord, go, and tell my Princess that I tried to remember what I had learnt from her, but it would be happier for me if I could forget it. Ah, lord, if you have any kindness for the poor girl whom you once called beautiful, go, and let me forget!"

She avoided his attempt to detain her, and fled. Armitage would have followed her, but started to find himself suddenly confronted by Petros, who might have sprung from the earth, but more probably from the recess formed by the side of the gateway and the wall.

"My lord the Despot awaits Milordo," he said with a bow.

Had he heard all that had passed? It was impossible to say; his face told nothing, and after one quick glance at him, Armitage turned again towards the great gate, very much perturbed in his mind. Should he ask Danaë to marry him? Pity, admiration, romance, urged him to do so; reason, prudence, a kind of shame that the man who had loved Zoe Theophanis should think of linking himself with a mere beautiful savage, held him back. In his mental struggle the warning Danaë had given him was slighted. These were not the days when British peers could be held to ransom in the islands of the Egean, nor would Prince Christodoridi be foolish enough to dream of such a thing.

"You have something to say to me, friend Milordo?" The words, uttered with extreme coldness, roused him from his reverie. Prince Christodoridi stood before him, but did not hold out his hand or offer any other sign of welcome. "I understand that such is the custom of your country," he added impatiently, as Armitage stared at him.

"You must pardon me, lord, but I have not the slightest idea——"

The truth never occurred to Armitage, for Petros was still behind him, and it was impossible he should have told his master yet of the meeting under the wall. The Despot waved his hand magnificently.

"From the rampart just now, Milordo, I saw you in close converse with my elder daughter. Perhaps that also is one of your national customs?"

"It is certainly not the custom for a man to turn his back when he happens to meet a lady whose acquaintance he enjoys," said Armitage with spirit. Prince Christodoridi smiled grimly.

"With us, when a man is found talking with an unmarried girl, he marries her—without a dowry."

"And that is a grave deterrent?" with an answering smile.

"If he refuses, he is found the next dark night with a dagger in his heart." Armitage's eyes followed his host's hand, by a kind of fascination, to the longest of the long curved daggers in his belt, but like most Englishmen, he had a rooted objection to being driven into any course. Five minutes ago he had been seriously contemplating the possibility of marrying Danaë, now it was absolutely out of the question.

"I can only recommend you to change your customs, lord. They are unduly old-fashioned," he replied deliberately.

"You have cast a slur upon my daughter's name, and you refuse to take the only step that can remove it. I suppose you are thinking of the dowry?" with a sneer.

"The dowry makes no difference whatever, but I refuse to be coerced into marrying any woman on earth—even the Lady Danaë. But nothing is farther from my wishes than to cast any slur upon her. In fact—— But we are neither of us cool enough to discuss such a question at this moment, Prince. With your permission, I will return on board, and you shall hear from me."

"Have I your promise that you will send a formal request for my daughter's hand?"

"Certainly not," replied Armitage, in the gentle, reasonable tone of voice which always led his opponents astray. "You are still trying to force a promise out of me, which is preposterous."

"You shall not go until you give it!" Prince Christodoridi had been coming nearer and nearer, and now he made a spring at his guest. Stepping back instinctively, Armitage set his back to the wall, but the wall gave way behind him, and the floor failed beneath his feet. Staggering helplessly, he had a momentary vision of the appalled face of Angeliké in the distance, before the wall which had opened to receive him closed again with a crash, leaving him in utter darkness on a steep smooth slope. Stumbling, sliding, clutching blindly at the walls, he descended swiftly, until he was brought up violently against masonry of some sort. To his left was a faint glimmer of light, and he groped his way towards it, to find himself in a chamber apparently hewn out of the living rock, with a small hole admitting light high above his head. The slope down which he had come was too steep and smooth to climb, and there was no means of reaching the window. Opposite the doorway of the dungeon, to the right of the slope, was a wooden door, which he shook in vain, and at the keyhole of which he shouted till he was tired. Most undoubtedly he was in a place from which it would be very difficult to get out, and he confessed to himself that he had walked neatly into a trap. For one moment he experienced a sinking of the heart as he wondered whether Danaë could be in the plot, but he drove away the doubt with a determination that surprised himself. No, she was not to blame, except for the attempt to save him which had led to this. Of course she could not tell him the exact nature of the demand to be made on him, and she had unwittingly precipitated the very danger she had tried to avert. Would they ill-treat her? he wondered, remembering her godfather's warning. It was horrible to think of. If that absurd old father would only let him see her for a moment! It would be ridiculous to marry her without knowing that she wished it. At present she was scarcely likely to wish it, since the terrified sister had probably rushed with all speed to tell her that the English lord had chosen a dungeon rather than marriage with her. It was a horrible tangle, and he saw no way out of it.

CHAPTER XXII.
IN FORMÂ PAUPERIS.

PARTHENIOS CHALKIADI and the two Smaragdopouloi were sitting in the loggia with Prince Christodoridi in the dusk. Kyrios Loukas and his son had come over from Tortolana to bring the silk gown and other presents to the bride that were demanded by custom from the father of the bridegroom, but Kyrios Parthenios had puffed up the hill uninvited, in a state of much perturbation. He had received a secret visit from Petros, who confided to him that he believed the Despot had seized the English lord, and was keeping him confined in one of his dungeons. As to the reason for this treatment, Petros professed ignorance so discreetly that his hearer was at no loss to divine the real cause; all he knew was that he had heard a voice, which he felt certain was Milordo's, issuing from the very foundations of the fortress, and gathered that the owner was imprisoned underground. With a view to making repentance on his friend's part as easy as possible, Kyrios Parthenios sent Petros off at once to the yacht, to request the captain to send a boat on shore for his owner at nine o'clock that evening, while he himself trudged up to the fortress, and breaking in on Prince Christodoridi and his friends, demanded boldly where the English lord was. In reply the Despot recounted his wrongs, which seemed to affect his hearers less deeply than the method he had taken to right them. Narkissos displayed little interest in either, for he was watching for Angeliké, with whom he hoped for a word or two in the shadows. Once he thought he saw her steal in and take down something from the wall, but she waved him back imperiously when he half-rose to follow her, and he sat gloomy, with his eyes fixed on the shadowy door. But his father took the news very much amiss.

"Holy Vasili! you can't do that sort of thing nowadays, lord," he observed sourly. "We shall be having a warship sent here."

"It won't interfere with you," snapped Prince Christodoridi. "But if you prefer to be out of the business altogether, you have only to pay back that dowry."

This was the last thing that Kyrios Smaragdopoulos wished to do, and he subsided grumbling. "I suppose a man may feel a little interest in the fate of a family about to be connected with his own, not to speak of the unpleasantness of such reports as will get about."

"Yes, friend Agesilaos," urged Parthenios Chalkiadi. "Think what will be said when it is known that the young man preferred imprisonment to marrying my goddaughter."

"He won't!" cried Prince Christodoridi furiously. "He will soon give in; you will see."

"Don't count upon it," said his friend sadly. "There is such obstinacy in these English that they will die rather than yield. And after all, if he has erred in following here the barbarous customs of his own place, we should pity rather than hold him guilty."

"Then is it such a deadly punishment to marry him to my daughter? You are too flattering, friend Parthenios! But it is more than a mere case of bad manners. My daughter Angeliké says——"

"The Lady Angeliké is anxious for her marriage, and knows that her sister must be married first," said Parthenios shrewdly. "Friend, give me leave to visit the young man on your behalf. He has a pleasing face, and the English always tell the truth. If he is not already betrothed to some maiden of his own nation—" Prince Christodoridi's face fell at the suggestion of this possibility—"let me see if we cannot find some way of getting out of the difficulty with honour to both of you and happiness to my goddaughter."

"You will let him escape, thick-headed one," growled Prince Christodoridi; "or at least he will knock you down and run away while you are rubbing your head and picking yourself up. Plague take you, girl! What are you standing there staring about for?" Narkissos had again made a motion to rise as Angeliké appeared in the doorway, but she waved him back and stood looking keenly round, trying to pierce the shadows with her eyes.

"Forgive me, lord," she answered meekly. "My mother was asking for Danaë, and sent me to seek her. I have looked for her everywhere, and I thought she must be here."

"Well, she is not here," said Parthenios hastily, rising with unwonted agility. "You will let me speak with the youth, friend Agesilaos? A boat from his ship is to fetch him at nine o'clock, so there is no time to lose."

"Give Kyrios Parthenios the key of the rock dungeon, Angeliké," said the Prince, and Angeliké went to where the keys hung on the wall. A frightened exclamation came from her, and the whole bunch fell to the floor. She picked it up and brought it to her father.

"I—I am not sure which is the key, lord," she faltered.

"Why, it is not here!" cried Prince Christodoridi. "What have you done with it, girl?"

"I, lord? I have not left my mother all the evening. Why should I take the key?" sobbed Angeliké, with ready tears.

"The Lady Danaë came in and took it away about a quarter of an hour ago," said Narkissos with conviction, coming to the help of his betrothed. Prince Christodoridi rose, and put back Parthenios Chalkiadi with a powerful hand.

"Come all of you, friends, if you will—or rather, I request it as a favour. You will justify me, if such a thing is needed, for the girl must be shameless. If the man still refuses to marry her, she has brought her death upon herself."

Angeliké's whole frame tingled with delicious excitement. Her lover thought she was shivering with fear, and since the elder members of the party were too much occupied to heed the breach of etiquette, he drew close to her and they followed hand in hand, through a rough door which had been left ajar, and down a rude flight of stone steps, the disturbed dust on which showed that some one in trailing clothes had passed down them not long before. Poor Danaë, feeling her way fearfully in the dark, with a bundle of clothes under her arm and the huge purloined key in her hand!

Armitage had spent many hours, so he believed, in his dungeon, before the prospect of escape offered itself. Very soon after his incarceration, while he was still trying to attract by shouting the notice of possible passers-by, a distant voice coming through the airhole informed him that Petros had heard him, and was going for help at once. Thereupon the prisoner ceased his efforts and sat down, lest if he made any more noise he should be transferred to some even less accessible prison before the arrival of the armed party which he confidently expected his captain to send off at once to rescue him. He was in a towering rage—a very unusual frame of mind for him—and felt positive pleasure in the thought of fighting his way down to the harbour at the head of his men; but the hours went by, and the opportunity was not afforded him. No one came near him. It was evident that his obstinacy was to be subdued by hunger, and also by cold, for as it grew darker the chill of the dungeon became extreme. No sounds penetrated to him, and now that no light came through the airhole, he felt as if he was buried alive. Very early he decided to make a fight for it if anyone came to bring him food. He would leap upon him and knock him down, and he only hoped it might be Prince Christodoridi himself!

At last, when he had fallen into an uneasy sleep, with his back against the rough rock wall, he was roused by the sound of a key in the lock. There was a good deal of groping for the keyhole first, and then the key turned slowly, as though held by hands not strong enough to deal with it properly, and Armitage renounced his murderous intention in haste. Whoever this visitor might be, it was certainly not Prince Christodoridi, and he rather thought he knew who it was.

"Lord?" said a faltering voice, when the door creaked slowly open at last.

"I am here, Lady Danaë," said an answering voice, so unexpectedly close to her that she gave a little shriek. But there was urgent need for haste, and she spoke rapidly.

"Here, lord, here are some garments. Put on the kilt over your own clothes, and the coat instead of yours, and pull the cap down well over your face. Then you will be able to pass through the servants without being perceived."

"Sotīri's clothes?" asked Armitage, taking the bundle from her hands, and she answered with a little laugh of shy pleasure.

"Yes, lord, Sotīri's clothes. He is a useful boy."

"Most useful. You must forgive me for slighting your warning, Lady Danaë. I did not know how completely you were still in the Middle Ages here."

"Ah, lord, be thankful that you don't live here! But hasten, for they may find out that the key is gone."

Armitage wrestled vigorously with the jacket, which refused to accommodate itself to his broad shoulders. Happily it was not needful to fasten it, and he pulled on the cap, and announced himself as ready.

"I thought I would lock the door, and slip back and hang up the key again in its place," said Danaë, pulling at it.

"Allow me," said Armitage, and their hands met on the great rusty key as they both tugged at the door. As they pulled, he felt Danaë's hands grow suddenly cold beneath his.

"Some one is coming! They have found out!" she gasped.

A distant light was glimmering round the turn of the passage by which she had come. There was no time to be lost. Armitage tore off the kilt and jacket and hurried into his own coat, flung the clothes into the cell, and dragged Danaë behind the door.

"I will go forward and meet them, and you must try to slip past when they are talking to me," he said. "Don't get locked up here, in any case. I'll get you through if I can, but if not you must trust to me to do the best for you. Do you understand? Promise."

"I promise," she whispered, and crouched behind the door, at the foot of the slope, while Armitage went forward to the turn of the passage, calculating possibilities. There were three or four people coming down the steps, so that a general scrimmage, in which they would all join to thrust him back into the dungeon, would offer the best chance for Danaë to slip out from her hiding-place and run up the stairs. But they paused upon the steps and looked at him, the reproachful face of Kyrios Parthenios peering over Prince Christodoridi's shoulder, and Angeliké's wide eyes glaring above him.

"Who let you out, Milordo?" demanded Prince Christodoridi.

Armitage laughed. "If you are kind enough to leave my door open, friend Despot, you can hardly wonder if I walk out."

"Who brought you the key, lord?" asked Kyrios Loukas curiously.

"If you don't accept my explanation, I can only invite you to come down and look for yourselves," replied the prisoner, with a shrug of his shoulders. Too late he remembered the Greek clothes he had thrown on the floor of the cell, but the lamp did not shed a very clear light, and he might be able to stand in front of them while Danaë escaped. His visitors followed him down through the doorway, and Prince Christodoridi swept the lamp round the place.

"We know some one must have——" he said angrily. "What are you making such faces for, girl?" for Angeliké was raising her eyebrows and pursing her lips with intense meaning.

"Oh, nothing, lord, nothing!" she stammered. "Do go; now; quick!" the words were a quite audible whisper. Armitage knew what was coming. From where her sister stood, Danaë was quite visible, penned into her hiding-place in all unconsciousness by Kyrios Smaragdopoulos.

"No escape for her or me!" he said to himself. "Well, let us do the only possible thing with the best grace at our command." He stepped across to the door, just as Prince Christodoridi swept the light savagely in that direction, and led Danaë forward. "Lord and friends, I have the honour to ask the hand of the Lady Danaë in marriage. It was contrary to our customs to make the request of her father this morning, since I was not assured of her consent, but since I have had the happiness of seeing her again, I need hesitate no longer."

"Such doings!" came in highly scandalised tones from Kyrios Loukas, while Narkissos giggled nervously in the background.

"I won't——" burst from Danaë, but Armitage pressed her hand sharply, and her father turned on her in a fury.

"Go back to your mother, girl, this instant! And you too, Angelikè; what are you doing here?" The two girls vanished up the steps. "Friends, you are witnesses that the English lord has asked my elder daughter in marriage?"

"And I could ask nothing better for her!" said Kyrios Chalkiadi heartily. "And when am I to have the pleasure of bringing your bride to you, friend Milordo?"

"The sooner the better," said Armitage gaily. "I must return to Therma next week. Why not take my bride with me?"

Narkissos was nudging his father, and Kyrios Loukas spoke. "Let us make a double wedding of it," he said, with a vain attempt to emulate the joviality of the other two. "The Lady Danaë and her bridegroom can be betrothed and married first, and the contract between my son and her sister completed afterwards."

"There is the dowry to settle," interposed Parthenios.

"The girl gets no dowry from me," said Prince Christodoridi laconically.

"Quite so," said Armitage. "I marry the Lady Danaë without dowry. That is decided. I absolutely refuse to accept anything with her."

"But why? There is no reason for it, lord, and among us such a thing——"

"Milordo has said that he is willing to take her without a dowry," said Danaë's father roughly.

"Certainly no one could expect you to force a dowry upon the bridegroom, lord," said Kyrios Loukas. "Here we are all poor men, but we know how rich the English are, and if he does not require it, why, let us commend his moderation."

"I refuse to take even a lepta," said Armitage. "May I walk down the hill with you, friend godfather?" he asked of Parthenios. "You will have to instruct me in all my duties."

"Yes, come, lord," said the old man hastily. "Your boat will be at the quay at nine o'clock, but you will take a little supper with me first."

"My daughter's bridegroom will sup here," said Prince Christodoridi, but Armitage shook his head.

"I take no food under this roof until my wedding-feast, lord," he replied, and for once Prince Christodoridi's fierce eyes sank abashed. His hospitality had been slighted, and he could not resent it. Armitage bade good-night to him and to his friends with marked formality, and took the arm of Kyrios Parthenios as they went out of the gate. "There are some things that are too much for flesh and blood," he said. "The Despot has treated that poor girl and me infamously, and I won't break bread in his house until I can do it with her."

"You have indeed been hardly used, friend, yet for my goddaughter's sake I could wish you had taken the cue I gave you. I would most heartily have supported you in standing out for a dowry, for when it is known that she was married without one, it will give grievous occasion to evil tongues to——"

"But it mustn't become known!" cried Armitage. "Oh, hang it! this will never do. You must put me up to every possible mark of honour I can show her, so that no one may ever guess."

The peacemaker's brow cleared. "Indeed, friend Milordo, I should have known that your heart was as noble as your name. If the usual presents are given——"

"Yes, of course. There is a silk gown for the wedding, isn't there?"

"That is very important. And if you were disposed to be munificent, I know of a piece of silk the like of which I have rarely seen in all my voyages. The man who owns it fears to offer it for sale, lest the Despot should force him to accept a price lower than what he gave for it, but I can settle the matter with him in secret."

"Secure it for me to-night if you can. And the bride's mother ought to have something handsome, I believe?"

"Ah, lord, Kyria Xantippe would kiss your feet if you gave her a gold watch! The young man Narkissos brought her a chain, but she has nothing to wear at the end of it."

"She shall have the best that can be got at such short notice. And if there is anything else you think of—presents for Danaë's nurse, or the servants, or anyone—get it, and send the bill to me. Now, in return, will you find me a chance of seeing my bride alone?"

"Before the wedding? It is impossible, lord!"

"It may be, theoretically, but I am certain that the other sister and her betrothed don't find it so in practice."

"Oh, one knows that the rules are not always strictly kept," confessed Parthenios unwillingly. "But you and Lady Danaë are not even betrothed, lord! For the sake of the unfortunate girl herself, make no further attempt to see her at present. Have you not done harm enough yet—though I trust we may manage to avert a scandal?"

This appeal put things in a new light to Armitage, but it must be confessed that it did not keep him from trying to effect his object by enlisting Narkissos on his side. Influenced by fellow-feeling, Narkissos accepted the office of sounding Angeliké as to the possibility of bringing Danaë to speak to her suitor for five minutes, and did his part faithfully. Angeliké received the suggestion dubiously, but promised to lay it before her sister, and returned to announce with great severity of manner that Danaë was shocked by the request, and could not dream of acceding to it. Armitage was perplexed at first, but the scene in the dungeon had implanted a certain doubt of Angeliké in his mind, and he reflected sagely that it was quite possible his entreaty had never gone beyond her.

Great was the excitement in Strio on the wedding-day of the Despot's two daughters. It detracted a little from the interest of the occasion that both the bridegrooms should be foreigners, for to the stern local patriotism of the islanders Tortolana seemed little nearer than England, but the alliances were so infinitely superior to any the island itself could have offered that regret was stifled. Narkissos, sniffing delicately at a bunch of basil, followed by his train of gaily dressed friends, would naturally have been the favourite, but Armitage, determined to do all possible honour to his bride, brought with him an escort of armed sailors from the yacht, whose smart appearance worked havoc with the hearts of the female population. So, too, Danaë easily carried off the honours as the better behaved of the brides. Custom demanded that she should appear absolutely miserable in the prospect of leaving her childhood's home, and she embodied the ideal so faithfully that Armitage started when he saw her.

"At this rate I shall never need to hire a model for Tragedy," he said dolefully to himself, having caught Princess Christodoridi's proud whisper to a newly arrived matron that Danaë had eaten nothing either that day or the day before. Her hand was cold and listless when the rings were exchanged in the betrothal ceremony, and when she retired to put on the gown he had sent her in preparation for the actual marriage service, there was not a sign of triumph in her face, though she returned wearing a silk which turned every woman in the room pale with envy. Angeliké was wearing the coveted blue and citron stripes, but Danaë's gown was crimson shot with gold, with fleeting glimpses of blue and straw-colour, green and purple, as she moved. It was the richest silk that had ever been seen in Strio, and Angeliké's looked poor and colourless beside it. But Angeliké and her bridegroom took their part in the service with the utmost zest, going through the crowning and the feeding with bread dipped in wine, the running round the altar and the pelting with sweets, as if it was a highly enjoyable game, which was entirely contrary to etiquette, but awoke a sympathetic chord in the bystanders. While she and Narkissos were being kissed, generally on the artificial flowers of their wreaths, by as many friends as could get near them, and the younger members of the congregation were scrambling for the sweets, Danaë, finding herself and her bridegroom for the moment unobserved, turned to him and addressed him in a tragic whisper.

"Lord, you know I would not have married you if I could have helped it?"

"I was afraid I couldn't flatter myself it was otherwise," he replied drily. "I hope I don't look as if I disliked it quite as much as you do?"

To his delight Danaë lifted her eyes from the floor for the first time, and looked up at him wonderingly. "Is it possible to appear happy when the heart is oppressed with misery, lord?"

"I can't see myself, you know. Don't you think I am doing it rather well? entirely for your sake, of course."

"Will you do something else for me, lord?" She declined to respond to his opening, and he wondered uneasily whether she thought he had spoken in earnest.

"To the half of my kingdom, lady."

"Well, then, let us leave Strio this evening, as soon as they have brought us to your ship."

"That's exactly what I was hoping to do, but I have not been able to get at you to find out whether you would like it or not," he replied, rather puzzled.

"Whatever pleases you, lord, must now please me," replied Danaë with great meekness, as Parthenios Chalkiadi came up and seized a hand of each to conduct them to the bridal feast. It was his duty also to remain and watch over them, to prevent their feeling shy, as he kindly explained to Armitage, and also to add to the hilarity of the occasion by exchanging jokes with Angelikè's godfather, who was chaperoning her and Narkissos on the next divan. Inexorable custom demanded that the brides should eat nothing on this, the only public occasion at which they would sit at meat with their husbands instead of serving them and the men generally, and they were also forbidden to utter a word, or even to answer if they were addressed. A demeanour indicative of extreme woe, and gestures expressing crushed subservience to the dominion of man, were the correct thing. Having once transgressed, Danaë refused to do so again by paying the slightest heed to any remark of Armitage's, but Kyrios Parthenios was happily able to act as his mouthpiece, conveying to her not only his commands, but such viands as she could decorously conceal under her veil, and eat when no one was looking.

After the feast came the procession down to the harbour, attended by music and singing, and youths and maidens waving boughs of myrtle. For the purposes of this wedding the houses of the bridegrooms, to which their brides ought to have been escorted, were represented by their respective boats. Danaë, as the elder sister, must of course start first, and Angeliké, who had eyed her sourly through her veil at the feast, embraced her affectionately in farewell.

"Your gown is lovely," she whispered. "With a silk like that, I should think you hardly mind being married without a dowry, do you?"

CHAPTER XXIII.
GUESTS OF HONOUR.

THE music and the shouting had died away, and the lights of Strio were growing dim across the water as the yacht headed for Therma. Armitage, released at last from the duty of making elaborate and grateful bows to his parents-in-law, which had claimed him as long as he was within sight of the shore, heard a meek miserable voice at his elbow.

"Lord, may I speak to you?"

"I hope you don't think it necessary to ask me that?" he said, turning round quickly. "Let us sit down here."

There were two chairs comfortably placed in a sheltered nook, and he pulled one forward for her, and arranged the cushions. Danaë took a precarious seat at the very edge of the chair, and evidently found it shaky.

"Do you mind if I sit on the ground, lord?" she asked, slipping easily to the deck. Armitage did mind very much, but took the cushions from the rejected chair.

"You must let me put these for you, then. I knew it!" to himself, as she settled herself at his feet, where she could see his face distinctly, while hers was in shadow. "Now what has my lady to ask of her servant?" as she clasped her hands together and hesitated.

"Your forgiveness, lord," was the prompt and unexpected answer. "And it is not kind to jest with me. Is it not yours to command? Here I am at your feet, ready to obey, but if your goodness will permit me to speak——?"

Unreasonably irritated, as he himself felt, Armitage leaned forward and took her hands. She made an instinctive effort to withdraw them, but left them passive in his. "My dear Lady Danaë—" he knew it was absurd to address her thus, but could not for the life of him resolve to shock her by calling her by name—"please understand once for all that you have a perfect right to speak to me on any subject you choose, and that I shall be delighted to hear what you have to say, and to do what you wish if it is in my power."

"You are very good, lord." Danaë's tone implied that his assurance was mere politeness, such as she would have expected from him in the circumstances. "You forgive me, then, for yielding to my father and mother? Truly, lord, I intended to refuse, knowing that you did not in truth desire to marry me, but had spoken only to shield me from my father's wrath. But my sister said to me, 'You are always talking about dying, and now if you don't marry Milordo you will die, and he will die too;' and I knew it was true, and I did not want to die. And you had said 'Trust me,' and I thought you had some plan————"

"So I had," said Armitage quickly, "but I could not get hold of you to find out your wishes. I sent you a message————"

"I received none, lord."

"So I imagined. Well, I thought if you did not desire the marriage, I would ask Kyrios Chalkiadi to bring you on board and come with us to Therma, where he could place you under your brother's protection."

"He would not have received me. It would have been no use," she said, and he read in her tones that she thought the proposal scandalous. "But ah, lord, it was good of you to think of it!" and to his utter horror she kissed his hand. He snatched the hand away and rubbed it involuntarily on his coat, as though to rub the kiss off.

"Forgive me, lord. I did not mean to offend you," she said, and he felt as though he had struck a child.

"It's not that!" he cried incoherently. "My dear girl, you mustn't think I don't like it—I like it very much. But it isn't the thing—for a woman to kiss a man's hand, I mean. It ought to be the other way about."

"Not among us, lord," she replied, gently but firmly. "But I will try to learn the ways of your people. And this, my offending you when I desire so much to please you, makes it easier for me to say what I wished to ask. Since I am now your wife, and it would grieve me to disgrace you before the great ones of your land, will you grant me a time in which I may study the things of Europe, and learn to talk about them?"

"It sounds a good idea," said Armitage, irresistibly amused by the businesslike way in which she spoke. "But what exactly would you wish to study?"

"Lord, I am very ignorant. I can spin and weave and sew and embroider, and cook—I made all the sweetmeats for the feast to-day—*loukoumi* and almond-milk and all————" she paused.

"And very good they were," said the bridegroom heartily.

"But I know nothing of the things European ladies do. I cannot write, nor read—save a very little—I can speak neither French nor English. Ah, lord!" she clasped her hands entreatingly, "take me to the Lady Zoe, and let her teach me. Indeed I will do my best to learn from her, to learn to be like her. And when you come back in two or three years——"

"That is quite out of the question," said Armitage, with great firmness. "A year at the very outside."

"As you will, lord. I must learn all the harder. But truly you need not fear that the Lady Zoe's kindness will be wasted, as when I was with her before."

"That certainly makes the plan more promising," said Armitage gravely. "Then when I come back, you promise that you will be exactly like the Lady Zoe?"

"Yes, lord, as far as I can," very meekly.

"And you won't then mind having married me?"

"Mind, lord!" The words and their tone stirred Armitage with a most unwonted thrill. He caught Danaë's hand again.

"Danaë, why should we trouble the Lady Zoe? Come on a long cruise with me, and let me teach you."

But Danaë knew her own practical mind far too well to encourage such foolishness. "How could you teach me, lord? I want to become a European lady for your sake."

"It's quite true that I can't offer to set you the example of that," he said, discomfited. "What is it exactly you want to do, then?"

Danaë bent forward, and rested her clasped hands on his knee. "Ah, lord, as soon as ever we land let me go to Klaustra! The sooner I begin, the sooner the year will be over," she added, with an evident effort at sympathy which would have sounded coquettish in anyone more sophisticated.

But Armitage replied seriously. "I'm afraid we can't quite manage that. We must pay our respects to your brother in passing through Therma. He would have reason to be very much displeased if we did not, and he will probably wish us to spend a few days with him." There was another reason for delay which he did not care to mention to Danaë. Experience of the complications which had beset the wedding of Prince and Princess Theophanis long before warned him that the Greek ceremony in Strio was almost certainly insufficient to make their own marriage legal, and he was anxious to consult Prince Romanos and the British Consul-General on the subject. Prince Christodoridi, to whom he had endeavoured to broach the question, persisted in regarding his efforts as an attempt either to back out of his engagement, or to cast a slur on the ministry of the Orthodox Church, so that he had abandoned them in despair.

Danaë hung her head. "But, lord—you will pardon me if I speak of it—there are European ladies at Therma, and I have only Striote clothes."

"And I like you best in them, as you know. But don't be afraid. You shall get just what you like in the way of clothes. We shall find some one who will advise you."

"Ah, lord, you are too good! Do I not know that it is shameful I should have to ask you for clothes on the very day of our wedding? But I could not bear that the European ladies should laugh at your wife, or I would have held my tongue, knowing—knowing——" her voice failed.

"Now who has been talking to you?" cried Armitage angrily. "No one was to know anything about it."

"Lord, it is better I should know. Otherwise how could I have understood the depth of your goodness to me?"

"Now you really mustn't," he expostulated. "It really is not what you think. I—I am sure your father would gladly have given you a dowry. It was I who refused it."

Danaë withdrew her hands from his knee. "I am sorry you thought I deserved this of you, lord."

"Oh, you won't understand!" cried Armitage desperately. "Our customs are different from yours. With us it is the highest compliment to be willing to marry a girl without a dowry."

Danaë's aggrieved attitude was slightly modified, though her silence showed that she considered the custom, however honourable to the lady, likely to be inconvenient in practice. But Armitage was evidently waiting anxiously for some remark. "I am glad you have told me this, lord," she said, in a repressed voice. "But I am also glad that my sister told me the truth. I might—I might have asked you for money."

"I hope you would not have had to do that in any case. Of course you will have your own allowance, which you will spend exactly as you like."

She lifted brimming eyes to his face for a moment then, mindful of her lesson, raised the corner of his coat and pressed it to her lips. Armitage rose abruptly.

"My dear girl, you mustn't make so much of the most ordinary things. I—I hope we shall be very happy together, I'm sure. But I don't know that I shall be able to spare you a year at Klaustra; six months or—or three—is more likely. I shall come now and then to see how you are getting on, and if I find that the improvement in you justifies it, don't you know—— Oh,

- 210 -

hang it! why will you make me talk like a prig?—well, I shall take you away."

"Yes, lord," was the meek and sorrowful reply, and Armitage realised that he was in danger of presenting himself to his bride as a tyrant depriving her little by little of what she was looking forward to as the most absolutely blissful period of her life. He spoke hurriedly.

"You must be tired, I am sure. I hope you will find your cabin comfortable. If there is anything you want, send your maid to row the steward. If he doesn't understand, be sure you call to me. Understand that everything and everyone on board is here entirely for your convenience."

For once Danaë was speechless. She seemed to have offended him in some way, and yet he only loaded her with fresh courtesies. Her impulse was to cover his hand with kisses, and entreat his forgiveness afresh, but happily she restrained herself in time. Passing the lighted deckhouse, she saw something that distracted her attention.

"Surely that was Petros, leaning against the door and talking to your officer?" she asked, turning on her husband eyes full of dismay.

"Why, yes," he answered, surprised by her agitation. "It was he who told Kyrios Chalkiadi where I was, and brought him up to get me out of the dungeon, you know, and it seems it has made the island too hot to hold him. So I could hardly refuse him a passage to Therma when he asked for it, and he wants me to intercede for him with your brother and get him to take him back."

"No doubt my brother will listen to you, lord, but I think friend Petros would be wise if he remained in his own place as he was told," said Danaë drily, and Armitage wondered what she meant, and reflected that he had almost everything to learn about her still.

Prince Romanos justified his brother-in-law's expectations by insisting on the bridal pair's paying him a visit of some weeks when they reached Therma. It is true that it proved necessary for them to be married over again at the British Consulate, but it was also true that they arrived just in the nick of time to afford at once a much-needed distraction for the inhabitants of Therma, and an opportunity of showing civility to the foreign representatives. The arrangements outlined at Klaustra by Professor Panagiotis for getting the Prince out of his difficulties had not met with all the success that their ingenuity deserved. Pannonia and Scythia were intensely dissatisfied with the respective shares assigned to them in the railway project, and particularly with the fact that the most important portion of the proposed line, that from Klaustra to Therma, carrying with it the control of the historic harbour, was withheld from their hands, though had it been entrusted to either, the sky would have been rent by the protests of the other. Now they presented Notes almost daily, sometimes separately and sometimes together, drawing attention to the totally inadequate fulfilment of the Prince's promises, while at the same time the popular orators in the Assembly were thundering against the surrender of so large a share in Emathian commerce and communication to the alien and the enemy. Nor was the dynastic question so easy of settlement as it had appeared. When Prince Romanos boldly announced at one and the same time his marriage with the heiress of Maxim Psicha, and the fact that she had been foully murdered some months before, no amount of splendour lavished upon her tomb, or of ostentatious provision for Janni as heir to the throne, could check the torrent of talk and scandal that arose. The general belief was that, for purposes of his own, the Prince had had his wife put out of the way—a slander which was not discouraged by the agents of the aggrieved Powers. Moreover, at the same time that the people tolerated the marriage because it promised at some future date to include Illyria within the Emathian boundaries, the Powers demanded assurances from Prince Romanos that he had no intention of taking any steps in that direction, so that he was hard put to it to satisfy their pressing inquiries without fettering himself with pledges that might prove inconvenient. Therma itself was also in a disturbed state. A certain low quarter of the city had become notorious for a series of mysterious murders, the perpetrators of which invariably escaped. The victims were chiefly foreigners, of such a class that their respective countries might have been imagined to be well rid of them, but their fate afforded the means of planting one more thorn in the pillow of the unhappy ruler of Emathia.

Thus, though it would have been Armitage's last thought to allow himself to be used to bolster up the tottering throne of Prince Romanos, this was the purpose that he and his wife served. Much against his will, he was obliged to allow himself to be appointed—in virtue of his yacht and his relationship to the Prince—an honorary Admiral of the Emathian fleet, which consisted of two or three steam-launches, intended to prevent smuggling, which they failed most signally to do. In return, wearing the uniform of his new dignity, he entertained severally the members of the Assembly, the Consular body, the heads of the army, and selected burghers of the city, on board the yacht, and delighted the populace with illuminations and a firework display. Meanwhile Danaë wore European clothes all day long, had Janni with her whenever she was not out of doors, and found herself and her husband the cynosure of every eye and the attraction at every social gathering they could manage to attend. Armitage's boyish face and grey hair made such a piquant contrast with the splendid beauty of his wife that it only needed the discovery that Lady Armitage was a child of nature from the islands to send Therma wild about them. The wife of the new British Consul-General who had succeeded Sir Frank Francis was herself newly married, and had a soul attuned to romance. The bride and bridegroom awoke in her a reminiscence of the Saracen maiden and Gilbert à Becket, and this in turn stirred vague memories of Pocahontas and the London locality supposed to be named after her. "*La belle sauvage*—" could anything be more appropriate? Mrs Wildsmith appreciated her discovery too well to keep it a secret. One whisper to her dearest friend, the wife of the Pannonian representative, and the nickname was public property throughout the foreign colony in Therma. As "la belle sauvage" Danaë was fêted to her heart's content, and never dreamed of the truth.

It was no wonder that her head was a little turned, and that the quiet and hard work of Klaustra began to look less attractive. Prince Romanos had sent urgent invitations to his Theophanis rivals to be present at the series of festivities which were to celebrate at once his sister's marriage and the anniversary of his own election, and it would have been natural enough for the Armitages to return with the Wylies when they went back. But Princess Theophanis was ill, and her husband would not leave her, so that the visit was postponed for the present, and Danaë took full advantage of her respite. She learned to drive quite contentedly in a carriage, which had frightened her horribly at first, and to endure with equanimity the scandalous spectacle of men and women dancing together. She never tried to sit at her husband's feet or kiss his hand nowadays; instead, she claimed little services from him, and treated him occasionally with a parade of indifference which seemed delightfully wicked to herself and secretly amused him. She ran riot in the matter of clothes. At first she was content to ask Mrs Wildsmith's help in selecting the least startling of the terrible ready-made German monstrosities which filled the "European" shops of Therma, and to let Armitage design her evening gowns. But beautiful as these last might be to the artistic eye, they were not conspicuously *chic* or "smart," and these two qualities, as she was now aware, comprised the whole duty of woman with regard to dress. At last fortune placed it in her power to gratify her supremest aspirations after these elusive qualities. Just before a great ball at the British Consulate, the wife of the Pannonian Consul-General was obliged to go into slight mourning, and could not wear the gown she had ordered from Vindobona for the purpose. She showed Danaë the gown and lamented its cost, and Danaë, too unsophisticated to feel any delicacy in the matter, promptly offered to buy it. The sum asked staggered her, accustomed as she was to regard her allowance as boundless wealth, and in fact it allowed Mme. Melchthal a comfortable commission, but she paid it, and the coveted garment passed into her possession.

To say that she created a sensation when she appeared at the ball would be a mild term. The gown was of vivid emerald-green satin, with a cuirass of glittering sequins of the same colour. It had long hanging sleeves of gold gauze, and a fringed golden sash about the hips. On a plump, fair-haired woman like Mme. Melchthal it would have looked striking; on Danaë it was melodramatic, almost sinister. She saw the look of dismay in her husband's eyes as she took off her cloak, and it spurred her to shock him still further. For the first time she tried to dance, which she did as badly as might have been expected, and having found a partner who spoke Greek, she talked and laughed—and both her voice and her laugh were louder than conventional custom prescribes. Prince Romanos, who held strongly to the opinion that a young dynasty could not be too careful of the strictness of its etiquette, watched her gloomily, and at length broke up the gathering at an unprecedentedly early hour by offering her his arm and leaving the ballroom, followed by Armitage and the suite. On the way home Danaë sulked undisguisedly. Her magnificent gown, the wonderful coiffure devised by the new Vindobonese maid who had superseded the old woman she had brought from Strio—with the strip of golden gauze twisted in and out of the blue-black locks—was all this to be wasted on a bare hour's enjoyment? Arrived at the Palace, her brother escorted her punctiliously to the suite of rooms allotted to her and Armitage, and entered for a moment. Pure bravado impelled Danaë to throw off her cloak and display the offending gown again. To her intense astonishment, her husband quietly replaced it. Prince Romanos laughed, not pleasantly.

"You are beginning to see what comes of marrying a beauty of the harem!" he said. "Well, I did my best to warn you. But I do not propose to have my family made the laughing-stock of Europe. If you had been remaining here, Lady Danaë, I should have recommended your husband to engage for you some elderly lady who would have taught you to behave with the propriety in which you are totally deficient, but happily it is not necessary."

"I wonder you don't recommend him to beat me," said Danaë insolently.

"If I thought there was the slightest likelihood of his doing it, you may be sure I would. But remember, however foolishly indulgent your husband may be, you owe a debt to me. You have yet to earn your life. I have the right to claim your services, and if you continue to repay me by such displays as this——"

"I don't understand you, Prince," said Armitage.

"One would think I was Petros," said Danaë.

"After all, you are not so very different from Petros," said Prince Romanos meaningly. "I hope your wife will be in a better mind in the morning, Lord Armitage. Good-night."

Armitage escorted him to the door, and came back to find Danaë sitting with her arms upon the table. "What did he mean?" she asked, without looking at him.

"I don't know. Your brother has been rather strange of late. Perhaps it is just as well that you will not have much opportunity of irritating him further at present, Danaë."

"What have you and he been plotting together?" she asked.

He took no notice of the tone. "You will be glad to hear that Glafko and Princess Zoe will be here in a day or two. They were to leave Klaustra to-day, and Theophanis will follow them when the Princess is stronger."

"You have asked them to come at once!" cried Danaë.

"You have no objection, have you? Purely as a matter of taste, wouldn't you yourself rather be like Princess Zoe than Madame Melchthal?"

"You want to shut me up where I shall see nobody!"

"But surely going to Klaustra was your own idea? I wrote to Princess Zoe by your request, but if you would rather not pay the visit just at present I am sure you will be able to arrange things with her, and we will go for a cruise first."

"But you have made this new arrangement without letting me know. You are determined to take me away from Therma and all my friends—do you think I don't see that? Why didn't you tell me what you meant to do? Have I ever disobeyed you?"

"I have never requested you to do anything that you have refused." Armitage evaded the point politely. "But as to my wishes——"

"Oh, you are like all husbands!" Danaë caught a twinkle in her husband's eye at the suggestion of her vast experience of matrimony, and qualified her words hastily. "Dearest Koralie says they are all alike—grumbling if one gets a single good gown. Now if this"—she flung out her train—"had cost only a few drachmæ, you would have been charmed with it."

"I can't imagine that I could have disliked it in that case more than I do now, but I assure you I should have objected to it quite as much."

"Yes, and I know why. Husbands are all like that—sweetest Koralie says—they are angry and make a fuss at once if anyone even looks at you."

"Then I think I have shown remarkable self-control this evening," said Armitage imperturbably.

"I suppose you will tell me next that you don't want to see me smart and *chic* and European?" There were tears in Danaë's voice as she sprang up and displayed her stately figure in all its bravery, but her husband remained irresponsive.

"You can hardly expect me to prefer you as you are now to the girl who sat on deck with me on the night of our wedding?"

This was the climax. She could not succeed in making him angry, but such a proof of irremediable bad taste destroyed the last remnants of Danaë's temper. She snatched up a large pair of scissors from the table— she had been cutting pictures from a Vindobona fashion-paper before going to dress for the ball—and deliberately slashed a long jagged rent in the front of the green satin skirt.

"Now I hope you are pleased!" she cried. "I can never wear it again!" and bursting into stormy sobs she rushed away and into her own room. Ordering her maid out in a voice which made the insulted menial vow mutely to give notice at the first moment when her mistress looked less capable of stabbing her on the spot, she slammed and locked the door, and throwing herself on the bed, sobbed and raged half the night.

CHAPTER XXIV.
THE TALLY.

PASSING in the morning through the room which had been the scene of the quarrel of the night before, Armitage saw what looked like a heap of many-coloured silk on one of the lounges. Coming closer, he found that it was Danaë, fast asleep, and as he paused near her she woke.

"I was waiting for you, and I fell asleep," she said, looking at him in a dazed way. Then she recollected herself, and slipped suddenly from the sofa. "Lord, grant me your forgiveness." She was on her knees before him, trying to raise his foot and put it on her head, but he was happily able to prevent this.

"My dear girl, do get up!" he said anxiously. "I am not angry with you."

"Then you ought to be," replied Danaë's muffled voice. "I shall stay here until you have forgiven me."

"I forgive you fully and freely. Let me help you up." But Danaë had sprung up without the help of the offered hand, and stood before him, evidently awaiting comment on her appearance. She was in her Striote dress again, the long close coat and plain skirt made of the silk he had sent her for the wedding, the gauze vest above and the embroidered apron below united by the voluminous girdle, and her hair, no longer waved and puffed, had returned to its two thick plaits, one unfortunately still a good deal shorter than the other.

"Lord," she said softly, "it is the girl who sat at your feet that night on deck."

"So I see, and I can't tell you how glad I am."

Danaë's eyes shone. "I gave the Vindobona gown to Toni, and told her to burn it," she said proudly.

"She will hardly do that, but I think you may be sure you will never see it again," was the dry reply. "And now, what about breakfast? You know I like you better in that dress than anything, but shall you have time to change? As we start so early for the review——"

"I am going to wear it all day," said Danaë decidedly.

"That's all right for me, but will your brother like it?"

"It is no concern of his. I wear it to punish myself. Unless you would rather I cut off my hair?"

"I forbid you to lay a finger on it." He forbore to suggest that it was not very flattering to him to wear his gift as a punishment. "Come along, then."

Danaë tucked her arm in his—an action not at all in keeping with her dress—and they went merrily to breakfast, Armitage bemoaning his day's fate.

"I wish I could have driven with you," he said, "instead of making a guy of myself on horseback. I shall look a regular horse-marine—worse even than Wylie in yachting-clothes. And you will be all alone."

"I shall take my Jannaki. Think how he will enjoy the soldiers and the horses! I meant to invite Koralie Melchthal into the carriage with me, but now I shall have no more to do with her. She gives bad advice."

"Well, don't drop her too suddenly, and hurt her feelings," said Armitage, amused by the thoroughness of this reformation. "Her husband may make an international affair of it if you do."

Breakfast had to be cut short that morning, for a servant came to say that the Prince was preparing to start. Danaë went with her husband to the portico to see him mount, and her brother smiled grimly when he perceived her costume.

"Your husband has known how to punish you after all, I see!" he said.

"Yes, it is my punishment," said Danaë, looking at him with guileless eyes. If Armitage would not uphold his own marital dignity, his wife would do it for him. They rode away, with aides-de-camp and guards, and Danaë's carriage, with her own particular escort, drew up. She was to be attended also by Petros, who had been allowed without much difficulty to slip back into his old post of confidential servant to Prince Romanos, and Janni and his nurse would go in the carriage with her. But here disappointment was awaiting her, for the nurse, an autocrat whom Danaë, greatly to her disgust, was forced to conciliate at every turn, sent down a message to say that Prince John had a bad cold this morning, and it would not be safe for him to drive in an open carriage. A little earlier Danaë would have gone straight to the nursery and fetched away her nephew by force, but she was beginning to understand now the relative importance of herself and the nurse in the household, and submitted to the fiat. Petros came forward to help her into the carriage, and as he did so, muttered a few words.

"There was another of those murders in the city last night, my lady."

Danaë paused with her foot on the step. "But what has that to do with me?" she asked.

"How can I tell, lady? Only, when the news was brought to the Lord Romanos this morning, he unlocked his private desk and took out a paper, and crossed out something that was written upon it. I had seen him do the same the last time, so to-day I placed myself where I could see the paper. There were a number of short lines of writing upon it, all crossed out but two, and one of these was at the foot of the paper, away from the rest."

"Well?" said Danaë impatiently.

"Lady mine, those who have died in this way were all members of the band whose help I hired in the matter of the death of the Lady. He who died last night was the last of them save myself."

"I can't imagine what you are driving at, friend Petraki!" said Danaë.

"So be it, lady. But what if the two names still on the paper are yours and mine? And why should yours be written separately from mine and placed by itself?"

"I really have not the slightest idea," said Danaë, her patience at an end. "You were never satisfied until the Lord Romanos took you back into his service, though he warned you not to return, and now I suppose you mean that he is trying to murder you. If he intended your death, would he leave himself in your power night and day?"

Petros retired muttering, and climbed to his seat on the box of the carriage. For the moment Danaë was fully occupied with kissing her hand to the forsaken Janni at his nursery window, but when he was out of sight the hints of Petros returned to her mind with unpleasant significance, fitting in as they did with her brother's words of the night before. Had she earned her life, or not? and if she had not, what further service might Prince Romanos demand of her as its price in the future? But her carriage and escort swept gallantly into the great parade-ground, bright with colours and uniforms, and all dark forebodings were put to flight for the moment. Her station was just behind the saluting-point, at which her husband and brother had already taken their places, and to right and left of her extended a long crescent of other carriages, containing on the one side the foreign representatives, and on the other the Emathian Government officials and their wives. Nearest of the latter was an unpretentious victoria conveying Professor and Madame Panagiotis. Though the Professor held no office in the ministry, yet his long efforts to achieve the independence of Emathia, and the varied diplomatic experience they had entailed, made him unofficial adviser-in-chief to every Emathian government, and mainstay of the throne. On the other side Koralie Melchthal's carriage was the nearest. It was clear that she interpreted the meaning of Danaë's costume as Prince Romanos had done, for she bent forward with her eyebrows raised and her lips pursed in an expression of intensest sympathy with a fellow-sufferer under the tyranny of unreasonable man. It afforded her ungrateful friend considerable pleasure to repay her with the coolest bow at her command.

The review was a splendid sight to Danaë, though the representatives of the great military Powers regarded it as of little more importance than a battle of toy soldiers. Emathia was in process of educating her own officers, but at present she was obliged to rely on foreigners and on Emathians who had served in other armies. A body of Wylie's police from Klaustra were received with much approval by the experts, and Danaë gathered that their workmanlike equipment was considered better value for the money spent than the more elaborate uniforms of the regular troops. But the latter made unquestionably the more showy figure on the parade-ground, and Prince Romanos himself was a gallant sight as he took the salute. Armitage, on horseback in his admiral's uniform, afforded an unpremeditated touch of comedy that caused the foreign representatives the keenest pleasure, and everyone was asking why he had not mounted the yacht's crew and brought them to add to the apparent strength of the Emathian forces.

Just recently Prince Romanos had devised an improvement in artillery transport, and the new method and the old were to be shown in juxtaposition, that the connoisseurs might give their opinion. Gun-carriages, limbers and waggons were careering about the parade-ground, apparently bent upon mutual destruction and evading it only by a series of miracles, when the Prince called up Petros, who was waiting close behind him, and entrusted him with a message to an officer at the opposite side of the ground. Petros measured the distance across with his eye, and hesitated.

"What!" cried his master loudly. "Afraid of being run over, most valiant Petros? Must I seek another messenger?"

The aides-de-camp pressed forward eagerly, but Prince Romanos waited, with his eyes fixed on Petros. "I really think you had better not take it, friend Petraki," he said, in a tone of good-humoured raillery. "You will fall through sheer fright, and blame me for your misfortunes." Petros gave him a glance of helpless hatred, like that of a savage animal in a trap, and fairly tore the paper from his hand, then started to run across the ground. The incident had attracted attention, and all eyes were fixed upon him as he ran. He held on until he was about halfway across, and then found himself the apparent goal of four separate teams, racing for him from as many different directions. He lost his head, turned, and ran back towards his master, pursued by one of the galloping guns, and welcomed by a shout of universal laughter. The sound seemed to madden him, and as, with eyes starting from his head, he reached the saluting-point and clutched the flagstaff for support, he flung defiance at Prince Romanos.

"That was your intention, then, my Prince—to kill me as you have killed those others! I know what orders you gave the drivers. There would have been an accident, and you would be rid of me. But if I go, you go too."

Before anyone realised what was in his mind, while all were craning forward to catch the shouted words, he loosed his hold of the flagstaff and flung himself at the Prince, his long dagger gleaming in his hand. There was a moment's wild confusion. Danaë, standing up in her carriage and gripping the rail convulsively, heard a pistol-shot, but did not realise that Petros had fired at her, and that Armitage had thrown himself between them, until she saw her husband fall. A fusillade from the revolvers of the aides-de-camp drowned the sound of a second shot, as the madman turned his pistol upon himself.

All was tumult, as people left their carriages and crowded to the spot where the aides-de-camp were keeping a space clear round the three fallen men. Professor Panagiotis was in the midst, and Danaë, seeing his fine white head towering above the throng, fairly fought her way through to him. He was giving orders rapidly, but paused to reassure her.

"Yes, lady, yes; look after your husband while the surgeons are busy with his Highness. Milordo is not much hurt, and one of the doctors will be at your service in a moment. Yes, the miscreant is dead."

An aide-de-camp moved aside, and Danaë was inside the ring. Two or three surgeons were kneeling round Prince Romanos, and a sailor, one of the yacht's crew, who had evidently been among the crowd of spectators, was supporting Armitage's head. He spoke little Greek, but Danaë gathered that he expected her to faint at the sight of blood, and was trying to assure her that her husband was not dead. But the daughter of the Christodoridi did not come of a fighting race for nothing. She examined the wound quite coolly, and to her intense relief found that though Armitage was unconscious, and had lost a good deal of blood, the bullet seemed to have grazed rather than penetrated the skull. With the sailor's help she tied up the wound roughly, and then became aware that the crowd was growing less dense. The aides-de-camp had mounted again, and were riding among the excited people. "His Highness was not dangerously hurt, but the doctors considered it advisable that he should return to the Palace at once. To his great regret, therefore, the review must conclude at this point." After this plain intimation the spectators could hardly refuse to disperse, the foreign representatives setting the example. One of the surgeons had been prevailed upon by this time to tear himself from the side of Prince

Romanos, and Danaë was helping him to strap up her husband's head, when she found herself addressed by the Professor.

"Lady, the doctors think it best to take his Highness to the Palace in your carriage, rather than wait while another is fetched. It shall return for you immediately."

"But let it take Milordo as well!" she cried indignantly.

"It is impossible, lady. Two of the surgeons and I myself must accompany the Prince. My wife, with her admirable common-sense, has already driven off to see that everything is prepared for his Highness's arrival, or I would have ventured to offer you her carriage. But you shall be sent for at once."

The Professor seemed anxious and perturbed, though not unduly so, and Danaë could not wonder at his preoccupation when she saw her brother carried past, evidently only half conscious, his white lips murmuring something about a paper, and his hands wandering on the folds of the cloak that was thrown over him. But her present concern was entirely with Armitage, and until his wound had been properly dressed she had no thought to spare for anyone else. When it was done she looked up to find the British Consul-General standing beside her. The other foreign representatives had departed long ago, Herr Melchthal, whose wife was in violent hysterics, leading the way as senior member of the diplomatic body, but Mrs Wildsmith was still standing beside her carriage in the distance.

"My wife asks me to take the liberty of offering you our carriage, Lady Armitage," said the Consul.

"She is very good," said Danaë, "but mine will return in a moment."

"Then will you permit us to remain with you till it comes?"

"But I am not frightened," she said, astonished. "The doctor is here, and the escort."

"Yes, the escort is here, certainly," said Mr Wildsmith, in a voice of so much significance that Danaë looked round. Men and officers were gathered in little groups, talking eagerly, with no appearance of being on duty. "I would not trust them overmuch," he added.

"But what has happened?" cried Danaë.

"Surely it is evident that there must have been a plot of some sort? The wretched man who attempted the Prince's life is bound to have had accomplices——"

"Oh no, there was nothing of that kind. I knew him well. It was a private grudge. Please don't let me keep you here. Really I would rather be left."

"As you please. But remember that Lord Armitage and yourself, as British subjects, have a right to protection at the Consulate. If you find yourselves in danger, night or day, come or send to me at once."

"You are very kind," she repeated, in a bewildered voice, as he bowed and walked away. When the carriage had driven off, she became sensible of a great loneliness, for the surgeon departed also, to find a stretcher, as he said. The parade-ground seemed very large, the talking troopers incredibly distant, Armitage, still senseless at her feet, might have been in a different world. The sailor, who was still supporting him, growled something which she understood to be uncomplimentary to the escort, and the words seemed to clear her brain. Undoubtedly the cavalry were behaving scandalously, and must be recalled immediately to a sense of duty, and by her.

"Don't leave him!" she said to the sailor, and receiving his gruff assurance, walked across the ravaged grass towards the troopers. As she neared them, she became aware that there were many more present than the twenty-five men who had accompanied her from the Palace—two hundred at least. They must have remained on the ground without orders when the review abruptly ended, and two or three officers of superior rank were haranguing group after group. It was too late to retreat now, and she marched boldly up to the nearest group.

"Have the goodness to detail four of your men to carry my husband to the Palace at once, Colonel, and a sufficient escort for his protection," she said sharply.

The Colonel, a foreigner who in his day had served under many flags, looked at her with contemptuous amusement. "And who may the lady be who gives her orders so coolly?" he asked.

"The sister of your Prince," she answered, the sonorous Greek flowing clearly from her lips. The soldiers were crowding round them now, and she had a feeling that events of importance depended upon the duel of words.

"A fine hostage for us, then!" He swooped from the saddle with extended arm, in the evident intention of seizing her and carrying her off. But Danaë had been watching for just such a movement, with the intuition which had descended to her from many generations born and bred in the midst of alarms. She swerved swiftly and suddenly, and he overbalanced himself and came to the ground, to the accompaniment of a chorus of smothered laughter. The sound thrilled Danaë. These men were still to be held for her brother, if she could seize the moment. Before the Colonel could pick himself up, her foot was in his stirrup, and in some miraculous way she scrambled into the saddle.

"Retire to your quarters, sir, and consider yourself under arrest!" she gasped to her discomfited antagonist.

"And to whom am I to have the honour of surrendering my sword, lady?" he asked, with a wink to a colleague.

"To me, sir. The belt as well, if you please. Be good enough to hold my horse," to a young officer who chanced to be near her, and then and there she buckled on her foe's sword, with the utmost deliberation. The operation finished to her satisfaction, she looked round at the ring of curious faces. "Gentlemen, your late Colonel was a traitor. I will now lead you myself."

"Long live the lady colonel!" cried the youth who had held her horse, and who evidently found the new development interesting, and the men took up the cry with hearty amusement. The late Colonel, as was only to be expected, was less pleased.

"Oblige me by getting off my horse, lady. This farce has lasted long enough." Danaë's hand stole out behind her towards the helpful youth, and he grasped her meaning instinctively. The Colonel, with his hand outstretched to drag her from the saddle, recoiled from the revolver that almost touched his forehead.

"I should be sorry to end the farce for you on the spot, sir," said his supplanter; "but if I am forced—— Dismount one of your men, and place the late Colonel under guard," she said to her helper.

"If any man dares to lay a finger on me——!" blustered the Colonel.

"Place the late Colonel under guard," repeated Danaë inexorably, and during the undignified rough-and-tumble struggle that ensued she thought hard, sitting motionless on her horse, like Bellona presiding over a scene of carnage. When the fight was over, and her predecessor, in a very damaged condition, was safely secured, she advanced a step.

"Are all here faithful to Prince Romanos and their military oath?" she asked loudly.

"All of us, lady!" was the cry.

"It is well, for had there been any other traitor, I would have shot him with my own hand. Lieutenant, be good enough to go to the Arsenal, and desire the Director in my name to close the gates and not open them without orders from me. Then go to your own barracks, and bring me the keys of the magazine and armoury. Do the same at the other barracks. You will find me at the Palace."

"Am I to leave you alone, lady?" he asked in a low voice.

Danaë looked round proudly. "I have two hundred swords of my own regiment to guard me," she said, so that all could hear, and the swords leaped from their scabbards to the salute. A grey-haired sergeant close at hand plucked off his fur cap.

"The Colonel must wear our kalpak," he said, and Danaë put it on and fastened the chin-strap. The soldiers shouted with delight, but her messenger still lingered.

"Would not a written order be safer, my lady?"

"I have not time to write," said Danaë hastily, unwilling to confess the deficiencies of her education. "See, take this as a token." With a pang she took off her wedding-ring and handed it to him. It was all she had. With instinctive chivalry he kissed it.

"The regiment is at the feet of the Lady Danaë and her husband," he said, and rode away. Danaë surveyed her troops helplessly. They were all mixed up, and she did not know how to get them straight. With a sudden inspiration, she turned to the old sergeant. "Sergeant, I must take Milordo to the Palace at once, but I want the regiment to escort me—in proper order."

The expedient succeeded. Two or three hoarse shouts, and the mob resolved itself into ranks as if by magic. Four men dismounted, and unrolling their cloaks, made a rough-and-ready litter. Under the vigorous superintendence of the sailor, Armitage was lifted and placed on it, and the cavalcade started for the Palace. Before they could reach it, a carriage with a lady in it appeared, driving to meet them, and Danaë recognised Madame Panagiotis, who stopped the carriage and came to speak to her. The Professor's wife was a German lady of great propriety, and even at this crisis she managed to get in a glance of disapproval at Danaë on the Colonel's saddle before she spoke.

"Lady, you must pardon us for not sending the carriage before, but his Highness was seized with another violent effusion of blood, and all our thoughts were for him."

"But he is not dying?" cried Danaë.

Madame Panagiotis blinked violently. "No, lady, far from it. His Highness is doing very well. He asked for his son—" why should he want Janni now? Danaë asked herself stupidly—"and inquired after your husband. Then he called for a paper from his desk, and displayed so much excitement that it was thought better to humour him. When it was brought he seemed satisfied, and consented to rest."

Then Petros was right, and the paper contained his death-warrant—and possibly Danaë's.

CHAPTER XXV.
THE MASTER OF THE SITUATION.

THE cold eyes fixed upon her recalled Danaë to the present. If her own brother had doomed her to death for the wrong done in her days of ignorance, this foreign woman should see no fear in her. She summoned her innate courage and her acquired politeness to her aid.

"Welcome is the messenger who bears good news!" she said. "Truly, lady, it was good of you to bring the carriage yourself for my husband. Now we can take him to the Palace in more comfort."

She beckoned to the men who were carrying Armitage, but as they approached the carriage, before she could slip from her saddle, Madame Panagiotis stopped her.

"Lady, may I entreat you not to dismount? There is work to be done before you return to the Palace."

"What work could prevent me from taking care of my husband?" asked Danaë in astonishment. "You can't mean that I should keep him here?"

"My husband bade me ask you to leave Milordo to my care, lady, and save Emathia for your brother."

Danaë stared at her. "But Emathia is in no danger!"

"We thought it lost until you brought back the cavalry to their allegiance a few minutes ago, lady. Now it is for you to finish your work, if you will."

"I don't know what you mean," said Danaë mechanically, as she watched the soldiers making Armitage as comfortable as they could in the carriage. He was regaining a measure of consciousness, for he smiled faintly as his eyes met hers. Madame Panagiotis laid a firm hand upon the bridle.

"Lady, you must listen, and you must play the man to-day, since your husband and brother are both helpless. There is a rising in the city."

"Against my brother? But who——?"

"Not against your brother, but a report of his death has been spread, and the forces of disorder see their opportunity. They may be led by the agents of the Theophanis family; I do not know."

"That is absurd," said Danaë with decision. "No one who knows them could believe it for an instant. There must be foreign treachery at work."

"So my husband says, lady, for the danger lies in this, that any widespread rioting, involving danger to foreign property, will bring the Powers—and especially Pannonia—down on us at once. Your brother is prostrate with weakness, and the doctors dare not excite him by informing him of the rioting. Is he to rise from his sick-bed to find himself an exile, and his son without a future?"

"No!" cried Danaë. "But what is to be done? Let Professor Panagiotis come himself and take command. I know nothing of the proper measures."

"Lady, my husband does not dare leave the Palace. Besides the doctors, he is the only person admitted to the presence of his Highness. The mob which is making a demonstration in the Place de l'Europe Unie, and threatening the government offices, must be dispersed, and the streets patrolled, and every attempt at a gathering broken up. The duty would have fallen to Milordo had he been able to undertake it, but now you are your brother's representative."

"And the force at my command?" asked Danaë sharply.

"This regiment, which you have saved for his Highness, as I saw by means of the Palace telescope. The Klaustra police, since you vouch for their loyalty. And as a reserve the Guard, but that must be kept to garrison the Palace unless the necessity elsewhere is overwhelming."

"And what support is to be expected?"

"The Ministers and officials will rally round you when they learn that the news of the Prince's death is false. At present they are afraid of becoming marked men if they take any decisive steps. My husband is preparing two documents for his Highness's signature at the earliest possible moment, one constituting you colonel of the cavalry regiment, the other—to be used only in case of necessity—proclaiming martial law in the city."

"It is well. Let him telephone to the various Ministries that if the mob do not scatter, they will be dispersed by cavalry," said Danaë resolutely. Then her eyes fell on Armitage's white face, and her courage failed. "Lord," she said, riding close to the side of the carriage again, "you hear that they want me to fight for my brother and Janni, when I would fain be tending you? Must I go?" She spoke in a low voice.

"Yes—if it is to save Emathia," he answered feebly.

"I hate the wife of Panagiotis!" was the inconsequent reply. "Lord, if I must go, give me your wedding-ring. I had to use mine as a token. There was nothing else."

Armitage took off the ring, and put it upon the finger she held out. "If I could go with you I would, but I should only hamper you," he said. "But don't be rash, or I shall come and fetch you."

There were tears in Danaë's eyes, but perceiving that this was a joke, she smiled dutifully and unwillingly. Stooping from the saddle, she caught up her husband's hand and kissed it fiercely, then commended him by a gesture to the care of Madame Panagiotis, and turned back to her soldiers. The messenger whom she had despatched was just returning.

"Lady, it is done as you commanded, and here are the keys. But there is fighting in the city, and no orders have come to the troops or the police from the Palace."

"The police have not given way?" cried Danaë in disgust.

"No, lady, but the chief of police fears to act without orders, and is keeping his men in reserve. His Highness's hand has always been heavy on those who acted without his leave, and now it is said that he is dead."

"That is not true. He is alive and doing well, and has appointed me to represent him. What is the fighting about?"

"I know not, lady, and I doubt whether the mob know themselves. Some are crying one thing and some another, but those who are threatening the Police Bureau have a red flag, and are calling out for a revolution."

"Can you get to the Police Bureau from the back?"

"Yes, my lady; through by-lanes."

"Then go, and tell the chief of police to march his men into the thickest of the crowd when we enter from the two opposite corners of the square. That will separate them and force them down the side streets."

She looked round, and saw that her strategy was approved. Only one of the officers seemed to have something to suggest, and she glanced towards him.

"The machine-guns, lady?" he ventured.

"To be sure. We will fetch them," said Danaë, but her troops were evidently waiting for a word of command. In despair, she turned to the officer who had spoken, and made a shot—happily a successful one—at his rank. "Captain, I appoint you my aide-de-camp. You will ride beside me, if you please, and transmit my words, lest my voice should not reach the men."

A smile flitted across one or two faces, but the captain thus honoured was equal to the occasion. With a perfectly grave face he gave the necessary order, and they clattered across the parade-ground in the direction of the cavalry barracks. The machine-guns were secured, and the force increased by the addition of a number of men who had not listened to the disloyal suggestions of the former colonel, and who had been informed by the messenger of the change in the condition of affairs. The smallest possible guard was left at the barracks, for Danaë did not underrate the difficulty of the task before her. Above all things she was anxious to overawe and not to infuriate the mob. A rising put down by bloodshed would be only less disastrous, as giving an opening for foreign intervention, than a rising which was successful, and this was her reason for leaving the streets at the side of the square open.

From the barracks a messenger had been despatched to the Klaustra police ordering them to join her, and they came up now, a welcome reinforcement to her own four troops. A judicious reconnaissance through the garden of a house deserted by its panic-stricken inhabitants showed her that the time was ripe for action. The splendid square was turned into a perfect pandemonium. The new Therma had contrived to attract to itself an undue proportion of the dregs of Europe and the Levant, and these seemed to have ranged themselves with one accord under the banner of revolution. Red flags dotted the seething, shouting, gesticulating mass of people, and garden-seats and railings from the trampled flower-beds had been torn up to provide weapons, though the frequent popping of revolvers and gleam of daggers showed that the demonstrators had by no means come unarmed to the place of rendezvous. The lack of unity in the would-be revolutionists was remarkable. Each flag seemed to mark the position of a separate orator with a separate panacea for the popular woes, and such fighting as had yet taken place was merely between the advocates of opposing remedies. But while Danaë waited for the Klaustra police to come up, the mob had become more homogeneous, and there was a distinct movement towards the north end of the square, where the Legislative Chamber, the Ministry of Justice, and the Police Bureau were situated. Before rejoining her troops, Danaë cast a glance to either hand. The other Ministries at the sides of the square were all barricaded and the inmates of the few private houses had either followed their example or fled. This particular house had a broad piazza in the front, and here she took her stand, with one troop and the two machine-gun detachments as a reserve in the garden below her. The Klaustra police and another troop of her own men had been sent some little distance down the broad street which left the square at the two northern corners, with orders to prevent the mob's re-forming, and it was now time for the two remaining troops to enter at the south-east and south-west openings, and drive their respective wedges into the crowd. Just before they appeared, the two or three terrified functionaries who had been vainly endeavouring to pacify the people from the portico of the Ministry of Justice fled panic-stricken before a shower of stones, and a handkerchief waved from the roof of the Police Bureau showed Danaë that her orders had been received and understood. One change she made in her arrangements at the last moment, even while her squadrons were entering the square. The two front gates of the garden were thrown wide open, revealing a quick-firer ready for action posted in each, with a force of soldiers standing by their horses behind it.

The first effect of the entry of the cavalry upon the scene was ludicrous rather than impressive. The mob were making so much noise themselves that they never heard the approach of the soldiers till they were actually upon them, pressing steadily on, though using only the flat of their swords, towards the centre of the square. The cries of dismay from the back had no sooner penetrated to the front of the crowd than a strong body of mounted police rode out from the courtyard of the Police Bureau, and the demonstrators showed little desire to face them. The troops were not in large numbers, and there were three roads on each side of the square down which flight was possible—who knew how long it might be so? There were one or two struggles round the red flags, here and there a soldier was struck by a revolver-bullet better aimed than its fellows, and fell from his horse, but his comrades pressed on, and the mob was broken up. That portion of it which was farthest from the police, at the back of the square, did indeed, on discovering the smallness of the forces at the command of law and order, make an attempt at a rush, which would have overwhelmed the slender line of horsemen, but Danaë flung her reserve troop upon them boldly, and they also gave way. Riding into the square with the machine-guns, she accelerated their flight, and meeting the chief of police, promised him the assistance of troops in keeping the space clear. But her own duties were not yet over, for while she was considering how many men she could spare him, two messengers reached her. One, coming from the Palace by way of the rear of the Police Bureau, carried the edict proclaiming martial law, which was put aside for use if necessary, the other brought the news of a mutiny at the cadet-school. The commandant had succeeded in keeping his pupils from actually joining the rioters, but they were encouraging them from the windows and roof, and the mob dispersed from the square was re-forming before the school.

Danaë was now becoming quite expert in dealing with crowds, and leaving the square to the police for the present, she led her troops to the neighbourhood of the cadet-school. This time the mob were expecting interference. Their nerve was shaken, and the men on the outskirts were keeping an eye open for the appearance of the soldiers. When the horses' heads emerged from the street opposite, and the troops, in three bodies radiating fanwise, began to ride through the crowd, all the cheers and reproaches of the rebellious cadets could not induce them to face the onslaught, while the discharge of the two quick-firers, though the bullets were judiciously aimed skywards, drove the young gentlemen pell-mell from their points of vantage. Once forced from them, they had to face their commandant, but the numbers within the walls were so equally divided that when Danaë demanded admittance, the gates were not opened without a considerable scuffle. The commandant appeared alone, in great disarray, and without any formal greeting entreated her Highness to retire, and honour the school with a visit on a more propitious occasion. He could deal with his rebels himself if he was only let alone. But the situation was too serious for the risk to be run of supplying the revolutionaries with trained officers, and an idea had suggested itself to Danaë, based on the discomforts of her own first voyage from Strio. Reluctantly the commandant allowed her to enter the place, and proceeded to muster the cadets at her request. The presence of the cavalry and the quick-firers stimulated obedience, even on the part of the rebels, though some of them had to be dragged to the parade by main force, and others indulged in disloyal cries and insulting remarks. Commanded, through the aide-de-camp, to separate themselves into supporters and opponents of the existing *régime*, they complied with some surprise, and an appeal to the commandant disinterred from the ranks of the loyalists only one or two whose political opinions had undergone a quick change since the collapse of the demonstration. With the thirty or forty recalcitrants ranged before her, Danaë pronounced sentence. They would proceed at once upon a disciplinary cruise, under the charge of the deputy-commandant, and would be escorted on board forthwith by the Klaustra police. The first result of the announcement was that the commandant presented his resignation on the spot, indignant that affairs should be taken out of his hands, but he was induced to withdraw it on being assured that the culprits should be restored to his jurisdiction the moment the crisis was over. Then Danaë called up the sailor, who had attached himself to one of the gun-detachments, and impressed upon him, with endless repetition to make sure that he understood, a message for the captain of the yacht. He was to get up steam at once, and sail as soon as he had received his unwilling passengers on board, and was then to cruise up and down outside the mouth of the harbour, in the roughest water he could find within sight of signals from the shore. The sailor grinned broadly when he understood the significance of the message.

"And are they to be fed, lady?" he asked, in his halting Greek.

"Certainly—if they are hungry," replied Danaë, without a smile.

"I see, lady. Fat salt pork is what we usually recommend in these cases."

"The captain will know what to do better than I," said Danaë, and having seen her captives on their way to the quay, rode away, heartlessly rejoicing that they would think no more of revolution for the next few hours, at any rate. Her own task was far from being fulfilled as yet. The infantry barracks had to be visited, and the temper of the men ascertained, but the result of the inquiry was encouraging. What might have happened if the revolutionists had met with an initial success was doubtful, but the rank and file were now staunch in their loyalty. Here and there an officer was missing, and had evidently thought it prudent to disappear before inquiry was made, but the empty places were quickly filled up from the loyal cadets, and guards were provided for the public buildings and the Place de l'Europe Unie as if nothing had happened. Then came more riding through the streets, breaking up any semblance of a crowd, and receiving complaints and appeals for protection from Jews, Moslems, and other unpopular people, and a hurried journey to the scene of a violent explosion, in an obscure house on the outskirts of the city, which proved to be an anarchist bomb-factory. Then, leaving the chief of police in charge of the public peace, since it had not been necessary to make use of the martial law proclamation, Danaë retraced her steps to the Palace, so tired that she could hardly remain in the saddle. One further ordeal was awaiting her, in the shape of an interview with the foreign Consuls, who had come in a body to enforce the rather obvious truths that the riotous proceedings of the day were calculated to prejudice Emathia in the eyes of the Powers, and that steps ought to be taken to put a stop to them. Supported by Professor Panagiotis, Danaë had no difficulty in showing that the necessary steps had been taken, and that she had a reserve of force in hand if further riots occurred. This was so clear that the dreaded offer of outside help in coping with the situation could not well be made, and the diplomatists withdrew, congratulating Danaë on her own escape and her brother's progress towards recovery. Then at last she was free to find Armitage, who had defied all the doctors by refusing to go to bed, and was awaiting her eagerly.

"At last!" he said, as she slipped into her old place on the floor beside him, and rested her head against his arm.

"You ought to be in bed," she murmured reproachfully.

"Not a bit of it! You know I was coming to fetch you, if you did anything rash. Now tell me all about it."

She obeyed with immense delight, fighting the day's battles over again as if she had been reciting one of her island ballads, and ended with—

"And the chief of police said that I had saved everything by acting at once. The crisis was so sudden that the Anarchists had not got their bombs charged. They were charging them in a hurry when the explosion occurred.

But if they had had them in the square, the troops must have been driven back."

Armitage's hand came down and pressed hers tightly, and he asked, "Were you frightened?"

"I had no time to be—except when I wanted the soldiers to go on, and I did not know the words. Shall I have to command them for long, do you think?"

"Only till some time to-morrow. Panagiotis has telegraphed to Wylie to beg him to leave his wife where she is, and come on at once."

"I am glad. All will be well when the Lord Glafko comes. But I wonder whether I shall have earned my life by then?"

"What do you mean? That's what your brother said last night. Have you found out——?"

"He had a list of all who were concerned in the death of the Lady. Petros told me so this morning, when his own name was the last but one on the list. All the rest were dead, and now he is dead too. I am the only one left."

"If I had known this, you would have wasted no time in saving your brother's throne for him," said Armitage wrathfully. "We would have gone on board the yacht at once. Let us go now."

"Ah no, lord, not when things are so nearly safe! Besides, you forget that I am making use of the yacht already. And I am not afraid, with you."

"I should not be afraid for you, but that I think your brother must be a little mad on the subject. Danaë! to please me, will you ask if you may see him now? I will come with you if you prefer it. It is only natural that you should wish to see him, and he can hardly refuse. Then we can judge by what he says whether he has laid aside his grudge against you, or not."

"Are you really in earnest?" she asked, puzzled. "I will go if you wish it," and she rose stiffly, for she was aching in every limb. "No, do not come. I am not afraid he will hurt me. But if he has still not forgiven me, what should we do?"

"Keep watch all night, and go on board at daybreak," said Armitage decisively, and Danaë laughed in sympathy as she went out. She returned very soon.

"They won't let me see him. He is asleep, and the doctors forbid him to be disturbed. The wife of Panagiotis is in charge of the nursing. I was angry, and asked her husband why she took so much upon herself, and he said she had been trained under the best German surgeons."

"But did you want to nurse him?" asked Armitage, in surprise.

"No, indeed; she is welcome to him, though I did not see why she should be there. But if it had been you, I would have dragged her out of the room by her hair!"

"I believe you would. But meanwhile, we are still in the dark as to your brother's feelings."

"Oh no," said Danaë unconcernedly. "Panagiotis says that he was pleased to hear what I had done, and spoke of me as one who had deserved well at his hands."

"I hope that puts things all right," said Armitage, still anxious.

"Surely his gratitude ought to last while we are here," said Danaë, with an irrepressible yawn. "And when I am at Klaustra, he can't do anything to me there."

"Klaustra! I had forgotten all about it."

"But you spoke about it only last night. Besides, you promised!"

"I hadn't spent a whole day without you then. Oh, you shall go if you wish, but I shall go too. I can't spare you."

"I am so sleepy!" murmured Danaë irrelevantly. But her head nestled down against his shoulder, and she fell asleep crouching beside him.

CHAPTER XXVI.
THE FAIR PRIZE WON.

"HAIL, lady!" Wylie rode up to Danaë and saluted, as she sat on her horse, the picture of hopeless bewilderment, in the midst of a clamorous crowd.

"Oh, how glad I am that you have come, lord!" she cried. "These people say that certain Roumis dwelling among them are responsible for all yesterday's rioting, and they have broken into their houses and dragged them out. The police have no evidence against them, but I am afraid to send them home lest they should be killed."

"Case of police protection, evidently," said Wylie. "You want me to settle it?" Receiving an eager affirmative, he spoke in Roumi to the unfortunate Moslems, who were held by many hands, then scolded their assailants roundly, and remarked that it would be well for everything stolen from the looted houses to be back in its place when he arrived there in a few minutes to settle the lawful owners in their homes again under a police guard to protect them. Meeting Danaë's grateful eyes, he laughed.

"I didn't intend to take your work out of your hands in this way," he said; "but Panagiotis seemed to think you would be glad to be relieved at once. I have not seen your brother, but he sent polite messages, and an order putting me in charge of the city and the troops."

"Oh yes!" with infinite relief. "I can leave it all with you, and go back to my husband. But how is the Lady Zoe?"

"Very well, thank you, but she is not so very far off, you know. You will find her at the Palace. She refused to let me leave her behind."

"Oh, I must go to her!" cried Danaë. "You won't mind if I leave you? This gentleman, my aide-de-camp, will explain everything, and you will know what to do far better than I do."

Hardly waiting for his answer, she rode away, and on arriving at the Palace demanded eagerly where the Princess Zoe was, and ran upstairs to find her. Zoe, instructing the rough Emathian handmaid who had accompanied her in Linton's place in the art of unpacking, found her door suddenly burst open to admit a human whirlwind with flying plaits and draperies, which dropped at her feet.

"Oh, lady, lady mine!"

"Kalliopé, my dear child! Come, let me look at you. Why, you are taller than ever—and so much improved!"

"Really, lady? Not a savage any more?"

"I never called you a savage, I am sure."

"Artemisia did, and Princess Theophanis, and all of them. Tell me quickly, lady—am I different?"

Zoe turned her face to the light, and looked at her searchingly, while the girl knelt blushing and trembling. "Very different. You have found your soul, my little mermaid."

"A water-nymph, a Nereid—do you indeed call me that, lady?" To Danaë's ears this was the highest compliment that could be offered her. "But—" she hid her face in Zoe's gown—"you know how it is that a water-nymph obtains a soul?"

"I do, and it has come true in your case, hasn't it? He shares his soul with you, and you accept the gift."

"Even so, my lady, but if you only knew—! I was so wicked, so ungrateful—he ought to have taken it back."

"He won't do that, I am sure. He met us at the door when we arrived, and I could see that he did not repent. You had a very narrow escape of losing him, Kalliopé."

Danaë hung her head. "Yes, lady," very faintly.

"But, my dear child, it was not your fault!"

"But I had to leave him, my lady. I wanted to stay at his side, and he bade me go. I durst not even let myself think how nearly I had lost him, or I must have returned to the Palace at once. And it was only the night before that I found out how much—— Oh, lady, I think that my European clothes, and all the feasts and sights, and the kindness of the European ladies, made me mad at first. I forgot who I was, and that Milordo in his goodness had made me his wife; I even thought him unkind. But it came to me in the night that all these things were nothing to me if his face was turned away, and in the morning I humbled myself and set his foot on my head, and he forgave me, and I was content."

"My dear child!" said Zoe involuntarily, realising the acute discomfort this reconciliation must have caused to Armitage. Danaë misunderstood her.

"Not content with myself, lady mine—I don't mean that. You will teach me what I ought to be, and I will give myself up to learn from you. But you do think that he is willing I should be his wife?"

"More than willing, I should say."

"And—lady, tell me truly—you don't think my being his wife will do him any harm—that I shall disgrace him?"

"Not while you feel as you do now."

"And that will be always. It is well, then. Now I shall fight for my life. Otherwise I would have let my brother do his will."

"But what has your brother to do with it?"

"He has condemned me secretly to death, my lady, like all those who were concerned in the death of his wife. They are all dead but me now—Petros was the last."

She spoke with such evident sincerity that Zoe was impressed, though she would not show it. "My dear child, you must be dreaming. Your own brother! You mustn't let yourself get morbid. Let us go downstairs now. I see my husband coming back."

They went down to find Armitage, and presently Wylie joined them, with a somewhat perturbed face.

"When did you see your brother last, lady?" he asked of Danaë.

"When he was carried wounded from the parade-ground," she replied. "None of us have seen him since. He asked for Janni at first, but the poor little one was frightened and cried, and the doctors said he must not come in again."

"Haven't you seen the Prince, Graham?" asked Zoe.

"No, I was to have seen him now if he was well enough, but the doctors think it wiser not. He is to keep his strength in reserve ready for seeing Maurice."

"Maurice!" cried Zoe and Armitage together.

"Yes, Panagiotis has sent for him. He has some deep-laid plot on hand, but I don't see it at present."

"But what is the idea?"

"So far as I can see, it is to magnify the Prince's illness sufficiently to make it natural for him to appoint Maurice regent. That would be an important step gained in uniting our rival interests against the Powers, but I don't see that it justifies deception."

"But you can't be certain that there is deception," said Armitage.

"Not certain, but why should the Prince not see me for a minute, if he is well enough to send messages and sign documents? I should not disturb him, and it would be much more satisfactory. But one can't force one's way into a sick man's room against the will of his doctors."

"Who is his doctor?" asked Zoe.

"Terminoff, who was with us in Hagiamavra. That's one thing that makes me think there is something up. Anyhow Panagiotis intends to see Maurice established as regent as soon as he arrives, and apparently attaches immense importance to his arriving as soon as possible."

"Then he should have written to Eirene instead of Maurice, or at any rate to both of them," said Zoe.

"Since he knows the Princess by this time about as well as we do, I should think it is highly probable that he has," said Wylie, in his driest tone.

"Then we may expect them here to-morrow—he is sure to have wired—if Eirene is able to travel. She will send Maurice if she cannot come herself, but perhaps this will be just what the doctor said she needed to rouse her."

"I hope the Princess is better?" said Armitage.

"Oh, poor thing!" said Zoe. "It is her mind that is suffering more than her body. You remember how delighted she was when you gave her back the Girdle of Isidora, Kalliopé?—Danaë, I mean—and how she seemed quite different? Well, I think she must have felt, somehow, that this baby was sure to be a boy. When she found it was a girl, it seemed to take from her all desire to live. She just said, 'Call it Isidora,' and turned her face to the wall."

"But she is not dead?" asked Danaë, awestruck.

"No, poor Eirene can't even die dramatically. Her schemes never come off," said Zoe, with a touch of her old flippancy. "Don't look at me so reproachfully, Graham. You know that poor baby would have died if I hadn't gone and fetched it and given it into Linton's charge. And poor Maurice so fond of it, and creeping in by stealth to see it for fear of hurting Eirene's feelings! I have no patience with her. She might be fond of it for his sake, if not for its own."

"And how does the Lord Harold like the baby?" asked Danaë.

"Not at all. He objects most strongly to Linton's attentions being diverted from himself."

"Ah, you will want me in the nursery again," murmured Danaë ecstatically; but Zoe caught a look from Armitage which implied that he would have a word to say as to the way in which his wife disposed of her time.

With Wylie's arrival, quiet seemed to settle upon Therma. Troops and police and populace all welcomed him, or found it politic to seem to do so, and the European Consuls abandoned concerted action for the moment in favour of drawing up separate claims for compensation for damage done in the riot. Whether Professor Panagiotis had planned it or not, the publicity which attended Wylie's assumption of the command of affairs served to distract attention from the movements of his brother-in-law, and on the next evening the Consuls were astonished by the intelligence that Prince and Princess Theophanis had arrived in the city, and were staying at the Palace. They had been received at the station by Colonel Wylie and the troops, the Ministers and the municipality, and the guard of honour appointed to attend them during their stay was composed exclusively of veterans who had fought in Hagiamavra. Addresses of welcome had been presented to them, and on the morrow they would visit the Legislative Chamber, and receive the welcome of the Assembly. It was all very proper, and the explanation that this was the state visit planned some time before, but postponed on account of the lack of health of the Princess, appeared quite satisfactory; but the Consuls were not satisfied. Why had they not been invited to the station to take part in the arrival ceremony? they asked, only to receive the obvious reply that Prince Theophanis was not welcomed as a sovereign prince, but as one of the liberators of Emathia, allied by close ties with the throne.

While the Consuls were busy taking counsel with one another, and Professor Panagiotis was employing every means in his power to ensure a full attendance of the members of the Assembly on the morrow, the party at the Palace was the same as that which had met at Klaustra on the night of Danaë's short-lived social triumph. Many changes had taken place since then, but the most surprising was the transformation in Princess Theophanis. It was difficult to believe that she was the woman who but a short time ago had turned her face to the wall in bitterness of soul and longed for death, or the weary chatelaine of Klaustra, haunted by the knowledge that the battle she was fighting had already been decided against her. Now she moved regally about the stately rooms, almost as if she felt she had a rightful place there. She showed marked kindness to Danaë, and Danaë and Zoe commented on the fact to one another.

"What a change to have been brought about by the mere prospect of a temporary regency!" said Zoe. "I suppose she feels that it establishes Maurice's position, but really she is no nearer her ambition than ever."

"The Lord Theophanis is pleased to see the change," said Danaë.

"Yes, isn't it pathetic to see his eyes following her about? She is like what she was when he married her, before her ambition had come between them. There really was a time when she seemed to think love was enough, but it didn't last."

"I wonder," said Danaë slowly, "whether she would speak to me so kindly if she knew that, were the choice mine, the regents would be the Lord Glafko and you, lady?"

"I really don't think it would affect her. She knows that nothing would induce us to take Maurice's place, and I'm afraid she wouldn't care much what your wishes were, Danaë. What are you going to wear to-morrow?"

"Not kalpak and dolman, at any rate," said Danaë, with a sigh of relief, for her two days of command were like a nightmare to look back upon. It was an immense comfort to feel, when she rose on the morrow, that all the military arrangements were in Wylie's capable hands, and that Armitage and she could resign themselves to take a purely decorative part in the day's proceedings. There was an unusual sense of stir about the city, for the country-people, with whom the story of the hard-fought and apparently hopeless fight in Hagiamavra was rapidly assuming the character of a national epic, were pouring in to see Prince Theophanis and his brother-in-law. The Palace square was crowded long before the carriages were ready to start, and the Place de l'Europe Unie so closely packed with a friendly, good-humoured throng that it was difficult to make a way for them. The elements of disorder were not in evidence to-day, at any rate, and the soldiers received cordial welcome, while Maurice and Eirene were greeted with tremendous cheering. The triumph lasted until they had actually reached the threshold of the Chamber, but here came a disagreeable interruption. The foreign Consuls had learnt or divined the cause of the visit, and were assembled to protest against it in the name of Europe. That Prince Theophanis should be proclaimed regent during the illness of Prince Romanos was not to be thought of. Since there was no question of a hereditary dynasty, Janni had no rights that needed protection, and if it was simply a matter of appointing a guardian for him, it would be most incorrect to choose a person who had made himself so prominent in politics. As for the maintenance of government and tranquillity in Emathia, that might safely be left to the Powers. If Prince Romanos felt himself unequal to his duties, he had only to resign them into the hands of Europe, and Europe would proceed to agree upon his successor, as it would have done if he had held office for the full five years of his appointment.

The protest was read in the name of his brethren by the Pannonian Consul-General, who succeeded in restraining a smile even when he spoke of the agreement of Europe, and it evoked loud murmurs among the members of the Assembly who heard it. The language in which it was couched was distinctly unfortunate from the point of view of its promoters, for the Emathians had been learning for nearly four years to regard themselves as a free people electing their own sovereign, and now they were abruptly reminded that their country was still technically dependent on Roum, and that their liberties existed at the mercy of the Powers. The news filtered through the crowd in the portico to the greater crowd in the square, and cries of anger began to rise. But Professor Panagiotis kept his head. Requesting Maurice's permission to reply, he inquired deferentially what exactly it was that the representatives of Europe desired. Since the natural anxiety of Prince Romanos, in view of the events of the past week, for the safety of his family and the stability of his government was not to be allayed, would he be permitted simply to appoint a guardian for his child? There was much murmuring among the nearer Emathians at the Professor's conciliatory tone, especially when Herr Melchthal replied, with scarcely veiled contempt, that Europe had no desire to interfere with the guardianship of a mere private individual such as Prince Joannes Christodoridi. The Professor countered swiftly. Yet it seemed that his Highness was not allowed to appoint his honoured brother-in-arms, Prince Theophanis, to the charge of his child; might he, then, appoint the Cavaliere Pazzi, the father of his deceased wife? There was some demur at this, for was not the Cavaliere the heir of Maxim Psicha? But the discontent of the deputies and the people was growing so highly pronounced that the Consuls yielded the lesser point, having gained the greater, and the Professor went down the steps to lay the news before the invalid at the Palace. But the square was now in a turmoil, and the crowd, unreasonable in their indignation, refused to let him pass. He had betrayed Emathia, and they would keep him until the Prince's answer arrived. Professor Panagiotis bowed to the storm, and a messenger was sent off. A time of tension followed, the Consuls, though masters of the field, looking decidedly uncomfortable in face of the sour looks cast upon them. The deputies glared askance at the Professor, who chatted with great unconcern to the party from the Palace. They were almost as uncomfortable as the Consuls, not knowing whether anything had gone wrong, or whether a preconceived plan was being worked out.

"If only the Consuls had made their protest before we started!" lamented the Professor, as the moments went by. "It is so thoughtless of them to keep the Princess standing like this! You would not care to wait inside the building, madame?" he asked solicitously of Eirene, who shook her head. "His Highness's answer must come soon, of course," he resumed. "Perhaps he will even telephone—" he was looking in the direction of the Palace, in spite of his words, and his jaw fell. "*Kyrie Eleēson!*" he cried violently, and crossed himself.

The rest followed with their eyes the direction of his shaking hand, and Consuls, deputies and crowd turned with them to look along the street which led to the Palace. The standard of Prince Romanos was flying at half-mast from the flagstaff.

"What is it? What has happened?" everyone was crying.

"The spoilt child of Europe has abdicated in a pet," said the Pannonian Consul-General confidently, but the snarl of hatred which rose from the deputies made him turn aside with a rather unsuccessful laugh.

"A messenger! a messenger!" came the cry from the square. In the strain of the moment, no one thought of the telephone. All stood gazing with white faces towards the man who was forcing his way through the crowd.

"Holy Peter! it is Terminoff!" cried the Professor, and as the surging throng washed up Dr Afanasi Terminoff, hatless and with torn coat, at the foot of the steps, he ran down to meet him. "Doctor, why have you left your patient?"

"Because he needed me no more!" shouted the doctor furiously. "His Highness is dead!"

"Dead! dead!" the word was echoed by a thousand throats, and the people in the square tore their clothes and cast dust upon their heads. Dr Terminoff was still facing the Professor.

"How did you dare send that message?" he cried. "You knew on how slender a thread his life hung. Here have we kept him alive from day to day, in the hope that this morning's ceremony would set his mind at rest, and give him opportunity to recover, and you destroy all the result of our care in a moment!"

"Don't blame me," said the Professor, pale with anger. "All-Holy Mother of God! the fault was not mine." His eagle-glance round called the deputies and the crowd to witness as well as the Panagia, and in one moment the air was rent with shrieks of "Down with Europe!" The life of a foreign Consul in the Balkans is not at any time a very peaceable one, but it is probable that the assembled diplomatists had never been in quite such imminent danger before. Mr Wildsmith leaned over the parapet by which he was standing.

"Colonel Wylie, we shall hold you responsible," he said. There was a stir of hoofs as the troopers under the wall moved forward a pace or two, pressing back the crowd from the immediate neighbourhood of the Consuls, but they were still in most unpleasant proximity to the deputies, whose full-dress array allowed of a considerable exhibition of weapons. Hands were on daggers and revolver-butts, when Professor Panagiotis spoke again, this time from the top of the steps.

"Free citizens of Emathia, our Prince is dead. The descendant of the Emperors, the hero who led us in battle, the statesman who has made Emathia what she is, is lost to us. Shall his work be destroyed? Is Europe to snatch away from us the liberties we wrested from Roum at the cost of untold suffering and bloodshed? You say she shall not. I take you at your word. Let us proceed at once to the election of another Prince, who shall carry on the work our lost hero had begun. Is there any doubt whom we should choose? Is not the friend, the comrade of Romanos with us, who submitted to waive his own claims and labour for the good of Emathia, to whom he whom we have lost desired to entrust the safety of the nation? Theophanis for Prince!"

From the deputies and the crowd in the square burst an overwhelming shout, "Theophanis for Prince!" Daggers were drawn and revolvers fired in the air, and the shouting went on unabated. Herr Melchthal retained his presence of mind through all the noise. He approached the Professor.

"In the name of Europe I protest against this farce," he said loudly. "No mandate has been given for an election."

"No mandate is needed," was the fiery reply, and the deputies cheered again. "Here are the representatives of free Emathia, responsible only to God and their country. They will now proceed, with all possible solemnity, to repeat by means of the ballot the election they have just made by acclamation. Mr President, will you be good enough to convene the Assembly?"

The crowd in the square were silent now, watching with eager eyes the deputies as they filed into the building. An attempt at further protest on Herr Melchthal's part was met with cries of "Privilege!" and he and his colleagues were forced to assert the dignity of Europe in no more effective way than by withdrawing in a body, lest by their presence they should be supposed to countenance what was going on. It was a bitter pill to be obliged to request safe-conduct from Wylie for their passage through the streets, but the choice lay between this and sneaking out at the back of the Chamber, and each diplomatist was duly guarded through the hostile throng by equally hostile soldiers, and seen safe to his own door.

The actual election occupied a very short time. The last of the Consuls had barely left the square when a deputation of members came to invite their Highnesses to enter the Chamber. Here there was a slight difficulty, for some of the deputies wished to impose a condition which Maurice declined to accept, but the rest prevailed upon them to withdraw their stipulation, and Maurice and Eirene Theophanis emerged under the great portico Prince and Princess of Emathia. Eirene had cast aside her cloak, and stood magnificent in a gown of Byzantine splendour, with the Girdle of Isidora about her waist. The jewel was recognised at once and another shout went up. "The talisman! the talisman! Hail to the Orthodox Empress!"

She stilled them with a motion of her hand. "The Princess of Emathia to-day, friends; and to-day is the proudest day of my life so far."

The underlying thought was so clearly implied that the people shouted again, and the hastily formed processions bringing bread and salt to offer to the new sovereigns could hardly pass. Everywhere in the crowd travelled persons who had visited Klaustra were lauding the administration of Maurice and Wylie and prophesying benefits to Emathia from their rule, and Zoe, Armitage and Danaë shared in the enthusiasm aroused. When they escaped at last from the many hands held out reverentially to touch their clothes, it was to be thankful for the refuge offered by their carriage, as it moved at a foot-pace across the square. Danaë sank into her place like one dazed. The events of the last two hours—her brother's death, the instant election of his rival—were not to be grasped as yet.

"What I should like to know," said Armitage suddenly to Zoe, "is when Prince Romanos really died."

"Oh, that has struck you too, has it?" said Zoe. "When do you think?"

"At first I thought last night, but now I am inclined to wonder if it may not have been as soon as he reached the Palace after Petros stabbed him."

"In that case Professor Panagiotis must have a good deal on his conscience—in the way of forgery and so on."

"I think we may safely say that his conscience will never trouble him to the point of making him confess," said Armitage.

"And therefore we shall never know, I suppose," said Zoe.

"Not unless Terminoff quarrels with the Professor, and splits."

"Or the Professor quarrels with us all, and writes his memoirs. But in that case one could hardly depend on what he said, so it would be as doubtful as ever."

"Whenever it was," said Armitage with conviction, "Princess Theophanis knew of it last night. She is in it with him." Zoe's eyes met his, and he saw that she agreed with him.

"Do you mean, lady," said Danaë, rousing herself from her trance of bewilderment, "that all the time they told me I was preserving the throne for my brother and Jannaki, I was keeping it for your brother instead?"

"I am afraid it looks like it, Danaë," said Zoe gently. "You would not have done it if you had known?"

"I would have done it for you, lady," was the doleful reply.

"But if it means that Princess Zoe will live here instead of at Klaustra?" suggested Armitage.

"Oh, that we shall all live together at the Palace?" said Danaë, with reviving cheerfulness. "Ah, lady mine, then I shall be able to be with you always!"

"In that case, I fear Lady Zoe would have to put up with a good deal of me," said Armitage. "Shall we say sometimes instead of always?"

* * * * * * * *

That evening, in response to the shouts of the people who filled the square, Prince and Princess Theophanis appeared upon the balcony over the principal entrance to the Palace, and exchanged greetings with their new subjects. As Maurice handed his wife back into the room after one of these appearances he pressed her hand.

"Happy at last, Eirene? I hope so, dear."

"Not quite," she said quickly. "Maurice, why did you refuse to betroth Isidora to Janni as the Greeks wished? It was such a natural and proper thing to do."

"What! to bind those two babies irretrievably to one another?"

"These people do it constantly, to end a feud. And there would be no hardship in it. I should bring up Isidora to regard the boy as her destined bridegroom, and she would never think of anyone else."

"But suppose she did? You were brought up to regard a Scythian Grand Duke as your destined bridegroom, but that didn't prevent you from thinking of me. Why should your daughter be different? Or suppose Janni preferred to marry some one else? No, we won't risk making the children unhappy."

"They are princes. It is the drawback of their position."

"Then we will save them from it as far as we can. And even for our own sakes—— Why, Eirene, think. Would the Powers tolerate our linking the claims of Maxim Psicha with our own at the present moment, even if they consent to acknowledge my election as valid?"

"It might have been managed secretly," she said, and walked away restlessly, to look out at the dark masses of people in the square. It was always like this; Maurice would thwart her to the end, not merely by means of obstinacy, but with some show of reason and equity. If the way to her goal involved a breach with his convictions, he would not follow it. And that day had brought her so much nearer! In this age of revolutions and counter-revolutions, of compromises and buffer states, the phantom glories of a revived Eastern Empire might not be so very unreal, after all. She saw them clearly enough, but it was through a mist of passionate tears. No son of hers would sit on the throne of the Cæsars, it was only too probable now that even her daughter would never be acclaimed in Hagion Pneuma as Orthodox Empress. She had gained the prize which was to be the stepping-stone to the greater glory, but to her husband it was a burden rather than a gain, and the child for whose sake she had first grasped at it lay buried in Hagiamavra. The coveted fruit was little but dust and ashes after all.

THE END.

Milton Keynes UK
Ingram Content Group UK Ltd.
UKHW030623061024
449204UK00004B/387